Kovels' Guide to Selling Your Antiques & Collectibles

Updated Edition

BOOKS BY
RALPH AND TERRY KOVEL

American Country Furniture 1780-1875

Dictionary of Marks — Pottery & Porcelain

Kovels' Advertising Collectibles Price List

Kovels' American Silver Marks

Kovels' Antiques & Collectibles Fix-It
  Source Book

Kovels' Antiques & Collectibles Price List

Kovels' Book of Antique Labels

Kovels' Bottles Price List

Kovels' Collector's Guide to American Art Pottery

Kovels' Collectors' Source Book

Kovels' Depression Glass & American Dinnerware Price List

Kovels' Guide to Selling Your Antiques & Collectibles, Updated Edition

Kovels' Illustrated Price Guide to Royal Doulton

Kovels' Know Your Antiques

Kovels' Know Your Collectibles

Kovels' New Dictionary of Marks — Pottery & Porcelain

Kovels' Organizer for Collectors

Kovels' Price Guide for Collector Plates, Figurines, Paperweights,
  and Other Limited Editions

Kovels' Guide to Selling Your Antiques & Collectibles

Updated Edition

by Ralph and Terry Kovel

CROWN PUBLISHERS, INC., NEW YORK

To our three special collectors who are far ahead of the crowd. May you find oxford, those special pitchers and glasses, and tacky tech at every sale, still so unwanted and at such low prices that they are not even listed in this book.

Library of Congress Cataloging-in-Publication Data
Kovel, Ralph M.
  [Guide to selling your antiques & collectibles]
  Kovels' Guide to selling your antiques & collectibles / by Ralph and Terry Kovel. —
    Updated ed.
    p.   cm.
  Includes index.
  1. Antiques — Marketing. I. Kovel, Terry H. II. Title. III. Title: Guide to selling your
    antiques & collectibles.
NK1125.K68   1990   745.1'068'8 — dc20
ISBN 0-517-58008-X   90–2164

10 9 8 7 6 5 4 3 2 1

This publication is designed to provide accurate and authoritative information in regard to the subject matter covered. It is sold with the understanding that the publisher is not engaged in rendering legal, accounting, or other professional service. If legal advice or other expert assistance is required, the services of a competent professional should be sought.

from a Declaration of Principles jointly adopted by a committee of the American Bar Association and a committee of publishers

Contents

Introduction

Everyone has something to sell. Maybe the table your mother gave you twenty years ago that she said was "very old and valuable," or maybe the baseball card or toy collection from your childhood that is taking up needed space and could be worth thousands of dollars. Newspapers are always reporting stories of unsuspected treasures that have been sold at auction. There is a story of a Chinese vase that was kept on a shelf in a playroom where the children played catch every day. Fortunately it was never broken and it sold for over $150,000. "Thunder Robot," a 1950s toy, brought $9,020 at a 1989 New York auction. A dish purchased at a tag sale for $2 was later sold for $60,000. It was identified as a very early piece of American porcelain.

This book will tell you where you can get the information about what, when, where, and how to sell. It is based on thirty-five years of reporting antiques prices and writing about the antiques and collectibles market. *Kovels' Antiques & Collectibles Price List* is a best seller found in almost every library and bookstore. Over 1.5 million copies have been sold. Our newspaper column, "Kovels: Antiques and Collecting," appears in hundreds of newspapers. We read thousands of letters each month, many of them filled with questions about what to sell, how to sell, and what is it worth. There have been so many questions that over sixteen years ago we started a monthly newsletter, *Kovels on Antiques and Collectibles*, a subscription publication for those who collect or actively buy and sell antiques. To fill the need for information about other collectibles, we have authored special price books about bottles, advertising collectibles, Depression glass, Royal Doulton, collector plates, and more. We have written reference books on art pottery, country furniture, pottery and porcelain marks, and silver marks. And we have written several books filled with information for beginning collectors. Our television shows about collecting, including prices, are seen on The Discovery Channel and public television channels in many cities.

Have you ever thought about your Barbie or Shirley Temple doll, your glass dishes from the 1930s, your silver candlesticks, or Great Grandmother's embroidered shawl? If you wanted to, could you sell them for the best possible price? Barbie doll dresses have sold for as much as $800 each, but her boyfriend's clothes are priced even higher. Wouldn't you like to get $1,000 for Ken's tuxedo? One sold for that price in 1989. Would you ever dream of asking $4,000 for a pink Mayfair Federal pattern Depression glass shaker when other shakers sell for under $50? If you ask the right questions and sell in the right places, you can get top dollar for your items.

"What is my antique worth?" "Where can I sell it?" "How do I know if I am being cheated?'' ''Should I sell my things to a collector or a dealer?'' All these questions arise when you decide to try to sell an antique or collectible that is no longer of interest to you. The dealers know the answers to these questions because they make money buying and selling antiques. You should know the answers before you lose money by selling foolishly. This book has been written to help you dispose of a few items or a houseful of treasures accumulated over the years. It will warn you about the legal and ethical pitfalls. (For example, it is illegal to sell any form of firearm, even a World War I souvenir, without a special license. It is bad form to sell an American flag; it should be given away.)

This book is divided into two parts. The first section is a general overview of how and where to sell. The second section lists antiques and collectibles by type and suggests how to price and who might buy them. Be sure to read through the general instructions, and then use the Index to find the special instructions for selling the type of collectible you own. An Appendix at the end of the book lists current price books, publications, clubs, research sources, auction houses, appraisal associations, matching services, and other important information on where to sell and how to price. We have written an entire book giving up-to-date prices, *Kovels' Antiques & Collectibles Price List*, so we have not listed many actual prices here. This is a set of directions on how to sell, where to sell for the best price, and how to discover the best price. Our price book helps, but there are many other sources, too. All these are included in the Appendix.

Usually an antique should be sold ''as is,'' with no restoration or repairs. But sometimes, to get the most money, you should have the antique repaired. *Kovels' Antiques & Collectibles Fix-It Source Book* is a companion book we have written to help you find parts and restorers.

Typical ''for sale'' ads from antiques publications. Notice that descriptions are short but have the needed information. The seller's name, address, phone number, time of day to call, and SASE are indicated. For a large ad it might be advisable to use a heavy line border. Don't use too many abbreviations.

RARE Boy Scout 1911 certificate $50; Victorian items-lg. walnut frame $50; Lg. ladies jewelry box $90; Sm. one $25; Toys-Orig. boxes-Coke Ping Pong set $50; Lg. harmonica $25; Child's tea cup, beater $30; Telephone booth bank $50; Flip Wilson music doll $15; Child's 10 pc. band set $40; Rare child's Cherry Blossom dinner set $250; 2 lg. Bubble Glass frames $80; Wolverine toy washer with ringer $45; Cast iron Fido Dog bank $60; Drinking Capt. battery toy $30; Rare 1925 Frantz Baseball Game $75; Wind-ups-Fuzzy Seal, dog, monkey $20 ea.; Early Japan child's 15 pc. tea set $50; Victorian banana boat with women $50; Paintings-3, Pharaoh horses, Statue of Liberty, U.S. Capitol $50 ea.; Rare German sampler $50; Milk Glass Sunkist juicer $20; 3 Cupid's Awake, sm. $10; Med. $15; Lg. $20; Austria Moose pitcher $40; Very old 10" tin cannon $60; Milk Glass barber bottle $15; 1899 ice skates $30. Many items not listed. M.O. only. UPS extra. Old Things Antiques, Box 5, Oldtown, Kans. 00000. SASE. Ph.(121)555-1111 eves. & weekend. Thank you.

NO FOOLIN', IT'S CHRISTMAS!! Alaska Mica Snow $10; Aluminum Foil wreath $7; "Brush-type" Christmas wreath $10; Crepe paper tree $7; Noma Kristal lights $11; "Brush-type" tree/Choir Boy $6; Red Santa papier mache boot $11; Vintage Christmas decorating seals $4 pkg.; Sm. Christmas ornaments, 3/5c $5.50; Religious picture "Jesus With Little Child" (Victorian frame) $66; Santa Claus planter $21; White Christmas wreath $10; Pennet Christmas lights $9; "Action Toy" (early 40s) 6 pc. Christmas set $17; Noma fancy figurine (light/angel) $6.50. OLD FRONTSTORE ANTIQUES, POB 000, Towne, Ind. 00000. (333) 555-2222. Please send LSASE for detailed list with more of the same. Thanks!!

Only an expert can tell the difference between Windsor chairs. One of these is worth $700, the other $4,000. If the furniture is too large to move, take a clear picture and show it to an auction gallery, appraiser, or dealer. Did you realize the chair on the left is the more valuable one?

HOW TO START

Don't throw away or dispose of anything before you check on values. Everything can be sold, from old magazines to half-filled bottles or broken toys. The biggest mistake you can make is to throw away items before you offer for sale. We once helped settle an estate of a recluse. The family cleaned the house before we were called. We noticed a shelf of stamp-collecting books and asked to see the collection. "The only stamps we saw were on some old letters and postcards. We threw them away." They also burned fifty years of old magazines (probably worth over $2 an issue) because the basement was too crowded. Another, wiser family had a well-advertised house sale after they found their elderly aunt had saved clothes. They found over 2,000 dresses (which were sold for $5 to $20 each), 500 hats ($4 each), 25 plastic purses ($12 each), and hundreds of scarves, bolts of fabric, belts, gloves, etc. The clothing stored in the closets and attic brought more money than the furniture, china, and silver.

If you plan to empty an entire house, you must first sort the merchandise. Empty every cupboard, trunk, drawer, and closet. Put the pottery and porcelain in one place and the clothes in another. You may have to borrow or rent tables. Try to sort everything into the separate categories used in this book. Your job is to decide on a fair price and the best place to sell the items. If you have kept records of purchase prices through the years, or if you have had insurance covering major items, try to look for these lists. Old antiquers quote

The man had collected for years, never spending much money on any item but always buying good pieces. When he developed Alzheimer's disease at the age of seventy, his relatives were concerned about how to pay for his care. The contents of his apartment were sold. His Steuben glass, Gouda pottery, Tiffany lamps, and folk art solved the problem. The income from the sale will keep him in a fine nursing home for many years.

When Wellesley College in Massachusetts sold the contents of its old science building, including several stuffed birds, federal game wardens arrived after the sale to arrest the person responsible for selling the stuffed birds, which was against the law according to the Migratory Bird Act of 1918. Fortunately, the college could prove that these birds had been killed, mounted, and stuffed before the law was enacted. Be careful when selling any item that might be protected by endangered species laws.

the ''Damn Fool Theory'': ''If I was damn fool enough to pay that much for this piece, there will be another damn fool who will pay more.''

If you are still buying antiques and plan to sell them someday, start keeping the proper records now. Buy a notebook, a card file, or an inventory book. Record each item with a description including size, color, marks, condition, price paid, where purchased, any history, and the date. You will need this for proof of loss in case of fire or theft, and it will help you set a selling price in later years. Keep all labels, stickers, auction catalogs, and original boxes. They all add to the selling price of the antique. A toy car from the 1940s with a box is worth 25 percent more than the toy without the box. If the antique belonged to a famous person, try to get a letter from the seller with any of the history. It will also add to the resale value. If you reframe, restore, or repair your antique, be sure to list all costs in your inventory. Proper restoration can often add to the value. Improper restoration will lower the value.

Assemble your tools: a ruler, magnet, magnifying glass, marking crayon (one that can be used on porcelains), paper tags (that can be pinned on clothing), small sheets of paper for notes to be placed with items, colored dot stickers, pencil, pen, loose-leaf notebook with lined paper, a price book (we suggest *Kovels' Antiques & Collectibles Price List*), and a flashlight.

Examine all the items, and make notes about any of the marks, labels, breaks, or family history. Measure all large pieces of furniture you want to sell. Check to see whether the metal pieces are bronze, brass, or iron (a magnet will stick to iron). See if the clocks, toys, and musical items work. If you decide you do not want to sell an object, try to move it to another area. Put your notes on the small pieces of paper, and put the paper in or on the object.

If you have friends who are collectors or even flea market and house sale buffs, you might ask for advice. This can be complicated because they may be your best customers later. Explain that you are in the investigative stages and will not sell anything yet. Put a colored dot on anything you might later want to give or sell to your advisers. Otherwise you might forget it, and you could possibly lose a friend.

If you have enough knowledge and information, use a price book to look up the retail prices of your antiques. Include these in your notes. There will be many pieces that you will not be able to identify or price at this time. Do not be discouraged. Remember, the more you

A — ARTHUR J. WILKINSON, Burslem, Staffordshire, England. Earthenware, ironstone. Printed. ca.1930 + (1885–1964 +)

B — KAISER PORCELAIN, Staffelstein, Bavaria, Germany (W. Germany). Porcelain, figurines. Blue underglaze. 1970–present (1872–present) (Kaiser Porcelain)

C — Alboth & Kaiser BAVARIA. ALKA-KUNST ALBOTH & KAISER, Staffelstein, Bavaria, Germany (W. Germany). Porcelain, figurines. ca.1953–1970 (1872–present) (Kaiser Porcelain)

D — ALFRED MEAKIN ROYAL SEMI-PORCELAIN ENGLAND. ALFRED MEAKIN (LTD.), Tunstall, Staffordshire, England. Earthenware. Printed. ca.1891–1930 (1873–present) (Myott-Meakin Ltd.)

E — alka. ALKA-KUNST ALBOTH & KAISER, Staffelstein, Bavaria, Germany (W. Germany). Porcelain, figurines. ca.1953–1970 (1872–present) (Kaiser Porcelain)

F — ALLERTONS LTD. ENGLAND SEMI-PORCELAIN. Longton, Staffordshire, England. Porcelain, earthenware, luster decoration. Printed. 1915–1929 (1859–1942)

G — ROTHEMUND & HAGER & CO. Altenkunstadt, Bavaria, Germany (W. Germany). Porcelain. 1919–1933 (1919–present) (Karl Nehmzow Porcelain Factory)

H — ARABIA. ARABIA PORCELAIN FACTORY, Helsingfors (Helsinki), Finland. Porcelain, stoneware. 1949–present (1874–present) (Upsala-Ekeby Group)

I — ASHWORTH BROS. G. L. ASHWORTH & BROS. Hanley, Staffordshire, England. Earthenware, ironstone. Printed. ca.1880 + (1784–present) (member of Wedgwood Group)

J — AYNSLEY ENGLAND Bone China. JOHN AYNSLEY & SONS, Longton, Staffordshire, England. Porcelain. Printed. 1891 + (1864–present) (Waterford Glass Ltd.)

K — Bareuther. WALDSASSEN PORCELAIN FACTORY, Waldsassen, Bavaria, Germany (W. Germany). Porcelain. Green. 1960–ca.1970 (1866–present)

L — Bareuther. WALDSASSEN PORCELAIN FACTORY, Waldsassen, Bavaria, Germany (W. Germany). Porcelain. Green. 1970–present (1866–present)

M — Bavaria Germany. OSCAR SCHALLER & CO. SUCCESSOR, Kirchenlamitz, Bavaria, Germany (W. Germany). Porcelain. 1921 + (1918–present) (Winterling group)

N — BAY W.GERMANY KERAMIK. EDWARD BAY, Ransbach, Rhineland, Germany (W. Germany). Stoneware, earthenware. 1970–present (1933–present)

O — BBB ENGLAND. BOOTHS, Tunstall, Staffordshire, England. Earthenware. 1930 + (1891–present) (Royal Doulton Tableware Ltd.)

P — Bloor Derby. DERBY PORCELAIN WORKS, Derby, England. Porcelain. 1811–1830 (ca.1750–present) (Royal Doulton Tableware Ltd.)

MILK GLASS, Toothpick   362   MINTON, Washstand Set

Toothpick, Hat Shape, White	13.00
Toothpick, Owl, Westmoreland	25.00
Toothpick, Sunset, Blue	65.00
Toothpick, Swans & Cattails, Gold Trim	15.00
Toothpick, Swirl & Leaf, Blue	40.00
Tray, Hand, 5 In.	15.00
Tumbler, Dewdrop	10.00
Urn, Lion Mouth Handles, Dancing Couple, Covered, Germany, 11 In.	75.00
Vase, Grape, Westmoreland, 12 In.	17.00
Vase, Grecian Figures In Circle, 11 In.	35.00
Vase, Horn-Of-Plenty, Pink, 6 In.	37.50
Vase, Indian, Brown Shades, 7 1/2 In.	22.50
Vase, Portrait, French Lady, Gold Trim, Signed, 20 In.	260.00
Vase, Stars & Stripes, 6 1/2 In.	22.50
Water Set, Netted Oak, 7 Piece	210.00

Millefiori means, literally, a thousand flowers. It is a type of glassware popular in paperweights. Many small flowerlike pieces of glass are grouped together to form a design.

MILLEFIORI, Bowl, Blue & White, Handles, 4 In.	85.00
Paperweight, 4 In.	75.00
Vase, Yellow, Twig Applied Handles, 3 1/4 X 5 1/2 In.	55.00

Minton china has been made in the Staffordshire region of England from 1793 to the present. The firm became part of the Royal Doulton Tableware Group in 1968, but the wares continued to be marked "Minton." Many marks have been used. The one shown dates from about 1873 to 1891, when the word "England" was added.

MINTON, Ashtray, Dutch Boy, Sitting On Leaves, 5 X 4 X 3 In.	48.00
Ashtray, Swan, Swimming On Rug, Coiled Snake, 5 X 4 X 3 In.	55.00
Bowl, Cereal, Garden Pinks	13.00
Bowl, Vegetable, Covered, Gold Rose Pattern	75.00
Bowl, Floral Design	15.00
Cup & Saucer, Roses, Turquoise Ribbons & Cornflowers, C.1860	125.00
Game Dish, Cover, Rabbits, Ducks, Piecrust Color, 1864	1500.00
Jardiniere, Nautilus Form, Turquoise Blue Glaze, 19th Century	300.00
Luncheon Set, Cobalt Blue & Gold, White Ground, 34 Piece	150.00
Pitcher, Milk, Hand Painted Fox Scene, Bulbous, 1870	52.00
Plate, 2 Molded Handles, Green Leaves, 8 In.	65.00
Plate, Maidens, Reticulated, Artist, 1883, 10 1/2 In., Set Of 8	1320.00
Plate, Mythological Beast Design, White Ground, 10 In., Set Of 8	130.00
Plate, Rose Wreath, 8 In.	32.00
Soup, Cream, Underplate, Enameled Hands, Latticework, Double Handles	16.00
Soup, Dish, Gilt Rim, Enameled Flowers, C.1900, 9 5/8 In., Set Of 12	125.00
Sugar & Creamer, Audley	25.00
Sugar Shaker, Floral Shape, Marked, 5 In.	48.00
Tea Caddy, Tile, Stylized Floral, Blue, Green, Pink, Yellow	75.00
Teapot, Salt Glaze, Twig Handle, Berry Design	45.00
Tile, Aesop's Fables Scene, Brown & White Glaze, 6 X 6 In., 3 Piece	95.00
Tile, Bonthron Accuses Rothsay, Marked, 8 X 8 In.	100.00
Tile, Fair Maid Of Perth, Marked, 8 X 8 In.	100.00
Tile, Heart Of Mid-Lothian, Marked, 8 X 8 In.	100.00
Tile, Stylized Floral, 6 X 6 In.	45.00
Trivet, Flying Turkey, Chinese Green	28.00
Trivet, House	22.00
Tureen, Soup, Underplate, Golden Fern	225.00
Vase, Secessionist, 7 In.	90.00 To 100.00
Washstand Set, Genevese, Blue, White, 4 Piece	465.00
MIRROR, see Furniture, Mirror	

Mochaware is an English-made product that was sold in America during the early 1800s. It is a heavy pottery with pale coffee-and-cream coloring. Designs of blue, brown, green, orange, black, or white were added to the pottery.

MOCHA, Bottle   363   MONMOUTH, Vase

MOCHA, Bands, Condiment, Metal Rim, Brown Marbleized, No Stopper, 3 1/4 In.	25.00
Bowl, Bands, Embossed Green Rim, Wavy Lines, 6 1/2 X 3 3/8 In.	200.00
Bowl, Earthworm & Circle Design, Blue, White, Yellow Ochre, 7 1/2 In.	230.00
Bowl, Embossed Stripes, Dots & Dashes, 5 1/2 X 2 3/4 In.	235.00
Bowl, Gray Band, Stripes, Embossed Green Rim, 4 5/8 X 2 3/4 In.	165.00
Bowl, Marbelized & Seaweed Design, Brown Bands, 3 3/4 X 2 7/8 In.	425.00
Bowl, Rust With Brown, Blue & White Earthworms, 4 3/4 X 2 3/4 In.	300.00
Bowl, Seaweed, 8 1/4 In.	48.00
Chamber Pot, Blue & White Seaweed, Miniature	125.00
Compote, Marbelized, Blue, Black, White, Brown, Footed, 3 1/2 In.	100.00
Creamer, Blue, White Dots, Red Centers, Yellow Interior	365.00
Cup Plate, Yellow, Black Seaweed, 3 1/2 In.	375.00
Mug, Band, Stripes, Seaweed Design, 6 In.	130.00
Mug, Bands, Black Stripes, Seaweed, Leaf Handle, Marked, 4 3/4 In.	195.00
Mug, Blue Design	245.00
Mug, Brown & White Marbelized, Black Stripe, 4 In.	55.00
Mug, Brown Stripes, Blue Seaweed, 2 3/4 In.	95.00
Mug, Embossed Geometric Design, 3 3/4 In.	45.00
Mug, Gray & Blue Bands, Seaweed & Seaweed, White Ironstone, 5 In.	55.00
Mug, Green Bands, Stripes, Dark Brown Zigzags, 5 5/8 In.	335.00
Mug, Orange Band, Brown Stripe, Seaweed, Leaf Handle, Ovoid, 2 7/8 In.	175.00
Mug, Porringer, Balloon Design, Tan, Brown Stripes, 4 1/4 X 2 3/4 In.	600.00
Mug, Seaweed Design On Stripes, 5 In., Set Of 4	165.00
Mug, Seaweed Design, Tan, Blue, Black Stripes, 5 In.	95.00
Mug, Stripes, Embossed Green Band, Leaf Handle, 6 In.	75.00
Mug, White, & Wide Blue Bands, Applied Acanthus Leaf Handle, 5 In.	175.00
Mustard Pot, Hinged Metal Lid, Brown Marbleized, 3 1/8 In.	85.00
Mustard, Band, Seaweed, 3 X 2 1/8 In.	45.00
Pitcher, Bands, Stripes, Earthworm Design, Leaf Handle, 6 1/8 In.	325.00
Pitcher, Blue & White Stripes, Sanded Finish, 5 1/4 In.	10.00
Pitcher, Blue, White & Gray Stripes, 6 1/8 In.	85.00
Pitcher, Brown & Gray Bands, Earthworm Design, Leaf Handle, 7 3/4 In.	450.00
Pitcher, Chocolate Brown Band, White Designs, Leaf Handle, 7 In.	350.00
Pitcher, Embossed Dots & Stripes, Seaweed, Leaf Handle, 5 3/4 In.	550.00
Pitcher, Green Band, Bordered By Stripes, 5 1/8 In.	85.00
Pitcher, Marbelized, Wide Band Top, 7 1/2 In.	85.00
Pitcher, Stripes, Blue Seaweed, 8 5/8 In.	275.00
Pitcher, White & Brown Stripes, Earthworm Design, 6 In.	250.00
Salt, Master, Blue Band, Stripes, Earthworm Design, 3 1/4 X 2 1/4 In.	200.00
Salt, White & Gray Bands, Earthworm Design, 3 X 2 1/8 In.	85.00
Saltshaker, Blue Bands, Earthworm & Cat's Eye, 4 5/8 In.	450.00
Sugar Shaker, Black & White Wavy Lines, Blue Dome Top, 4 1/4 In.	135.00
Sugar Shaker, Brown Stripes, Yellow Ochre Bands, Brown Dome Top	135.00
Sugar Shaker, Checkerboard, Orange & Green On White, 3 1/4 In.	425.00
Sugar Shaker, Cream Band, Orange Stripes, Seaweed, Dome Top, 4 In.	275.00
Sugar Shaker, Orange Band, Stripes, Seaweed	260.00
Sugar Shaker, Orange Bands, Black Stripes, Seaweed, White, 4 1/2 In.	270.00
Sugar Shaker, White Stripes, Earthworm Design, Covered, 4 In.	265.00
Tumbler, Brown Marbelized, 4 1/8 In.	85.00
Tumbler, Marbelized, Brown, White, Black, Yellow, 3 3/4 In.	350.00
Vase, Block Handles, Galloway, 12 In.	95.00

Monmouth Pottery Company started working in Monmouth, Illinois, in 1892. The pottery made a variety of utilitarian wares. They became part of Western Stoneware Company in 1906. The maple leaf mark was used until 1930. If the word "Co." appears as part of the mark, the piece was made before 1906.

Marks are easy to decode if you read the right books. A typical page from Kovels' New Dictionary of Marks (Crown) pictures each mark along with the name of the factory, the dates, and other information.

MARKS ON LONDON PLATE

Year	Date Letter		Year	Date Letter		Year	Date Letter
1816-7	a		1836-7 (VICT.)	A		1856-7	a
1817-8	b		1837-8	B		1857-8	b
1818-9	c		1838-9	C		1858-9	c
1819-20	d		1839-40	D		1859-60	d
1820-1 (GEO. IV)	e		1840-1	E		1860-1	e
1821-2	f		1841-2	F		1861-2	f
1822-3	g		1842-3	G		1862-3	g
1823-4	h		1843-4	H		*1863-4	h
1824-5	i		*1844-5	I		1864-5	i
1825-6	k		1845-6	K		1865-6	k
1826-7	l		1846-7	L		1866-7	l
1827-8	m		1847-8	M		1867-8	m
			1848-9	N		1868-9	n

This page is from The Book of Old Silver by Seymour B. Wyler. At first it seems difficult to identify silver marks, but a few minutes of study will show you how. The king's head and the letter tell the exact year the silver was made. The other marks indicate the maker and the town where it was made.

Prices and descriptions of antiques can be found in Kovels' Antiques & Collectibles Price List, shown here, and in other price books available at libraries and bookstores.

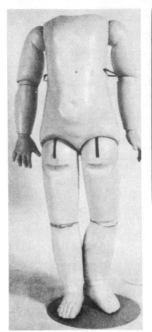

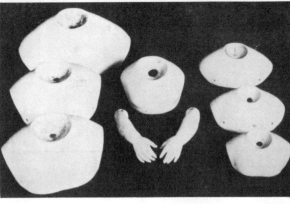

Even broken antiques can be sold. A clock peddler tin figure in mint condition would sell for $900. This bent, broken figure brought $300. The various doll parts and bodies sold for up to $1,500 in spite of their obviously dilapidated condition. (Richard A. Bourne Company)

know about an antique, the higher the price you can ask. We have a friend with a very rare prisoner-of-war ship model made about 1820. We have been trying to determine the price for months. Prices for these models range from $1,000 to $25,000. We now know an ivory model is more valuable than a wooden one, and the original glass case and straw mat almost double the value. The question is, should our friend ask $5,000 from a dealer and see what happens, or should he sell it at auction where it could fetch as little as $1,000, or possibly much more than $5,000? Of course at auction you can always protect the price with a reserve, but we will explain that later.

HOW TO SET PRICES

One of the most difficult aspects of selling an antique is determining the price. If you have a salable item, everyone wants it. Dealers will offer to buy, but they will almost always insist that *you* set the price. Friends and relatives may want the antique, but will either expect it as a gift or will tend to offer less than the top price you might get from a stranger.

Your old Christmas ornaments are worth more to a collector of ornaments than to anyone else. And you would probably think an ornament shaped like an angel is worth more than one that looks like a potato. It isn't. (The potato is very rare and is currently worth over $100.) The problem is that you must know what categories of collectibles are in demand and who wants them, and you must learn the requirements of the serious collector. For example, an out-of-production Cabbage Patch doll in used condition is worth about 20 percent of its original price. A Cabbage Patch doll in mint condition is worth about 80 percent of its original price. The same doll in mint condition with the original box in mint condition is worth about 30 percent more than the original price. This is true of most collectibles; the original finish, box, labels, and directions add to the value. Poor condition, flaked paint, chips, dents, or missing parts may make a collectible almost worthless. Repairs may add or detract. A good repair to an old, usable nineteeth-century country chair will add to the price you can ask. A new coat of paint on an old tin toy will *lower* the price by 80 percent. The toy would be worth more with the old, flaking paint.

**Exceptional Oak
Winged Griffin
Corner Chair**

ANN TEAQUE, OWNER
(999) 555-0000
P.O. Box 1917
Unknown, TX 00000

If you have only one large item to sell, the best ad may be a picture and your name and number.

A table of contents from The Antiques Trader, a typical antiques buy-sell publication. Your ad will be placed in the appropriate category.

Watch for these price-increasing features:

Original box.

Mint condition.

Provenance. Absolute proof that the item belonged to someone important, ranging from rock stars to Civil War generals. Proof must be a letter or photograph. Family gossip doesn't count.

Maker's label.

Direction book that might have come with the item.

Miniature size of a normally full-sized item.

Event-related objects such as souvenirs of World's Fairs, coronations, or political campaigns.

Brands or makers that are especially popular such as Avon, Hummel, Coca-Cola, or Royal Doulton.

Anything that pictures a railroad, streetcar, train, or sport.

Plates or figurines that are part of a popular series.

A pair is worth more than two singles; a full set is worth more than the sum of the parts.

Occupation-related objects like medical instruments.

Documents or objects related to local or national history.

Objects related to the history of the women's movement or to black history.

The "naughty factor." We first heard this term from an auctioneer with a prestigious New York City gallery. He said the rule was "The more erotic the piece, the higher the price." Col-

---

The advertising rates appear in each issue of the antiques papers and magazines. The smallest ads are priced by the word or by the column inch (one inch in a column of the paper). There is sometimes an extra charge for borders, pictures, or typesetting.

WHAT YOU SHOULD KNOW:

PAYMENT: Ads must be accompanied by payment. You may pay with a check, money order, or credit card.

CREDIT CARDS: We will accept the following credit cards: VISA, Mastercard, Mastercard II, Barclay Card, Access Card, Eurocard, Diamond Card, Union Card.

DEADLINE: For all advertising is noon, Thursday for the issue dated the Friday 22 days later.

FORMAT: The BUYER'S GUIDE uses the column inch format for advertising. Each page contains 80 column inches - 5 columns wide by 16" high. One column is 11 picas (1-13/16 inches) wide.

TYPESETTING, PICTURES, BORDERS, LOGOS are all available free along with custom layout of ads. Contact our advertising department for details.

PROOF OF PUBLICATION: Tear sheets of new display ads are mailed each week. We regret we cannot provide this service to classified advertisers.

CONTRACTS: Reduced rates are available for contract advertisers. See chart on this page.

CLASSIFIED ADVERTISING RATES

Subscriber Rates: 20c per word, $3.50 minimum per issue, 33c per word for ads set in 8 point bold type, 42c per word for ads set in 10 pt. bold type. Bold lines above & below ads $2.

Non-Subscriber Rates: 30c per word, $5.00 minimum per issue. 43c per word for ads set in 8 point bold type, 50c for ads in 10 point bold type. Bold lines above and below ads $2.50. All abbreviations are counted as one word. We reserve the right to abbreviate wherever possible. Each of the following groups would be counted as three words: (T.J. JONES), (100 BRYANT ST.), (DUBUQUE, IA 52001). Include the name and address in the word count. NOTE: When the name and address is withheld and our Box No. is to appear instead, add $4.00 extra per issue. We will forward the replies from our office. We cannot mix 8 pt. & 10 pt. type sizes in classified ads.

Display Advertising Rates: Write for rate card. All advertising must pertain to Antiques and/or Collector's Items. All merchandise is subject to prior sale and The Antique Trader assumes no responsibilities as to the description or condition of antiques and/or collector's items advertised. Efforts are made to insure correctness of advertisements and antiques but this publication makes no warranty as to either.

Color Display Ads: Black plus 1 color, regular rate plus $120.00. Four color process ads are $505.00 plus cost of space used for your ad. Also there is a charge for color separations if not supplied by the advertiser.

DISPLAY ADVERTISING RATES
(We print by offset - $2 per photo charged for processing)

No. Col. Inches	Cost Per Issue	No. Col. Inches	Cost Per Issue	No. Col. Inches	Cost Per Issue
1	$11.25	12½	136.00	44	368.00
1½	17.00	13	140.00	46	382.00
2	22.50	13½	145.00	48	396.00
2½	28.25	14 (1 col.)	150.00	50	410.00
3	33.75	15	159.00	52	424.00
3½	39.50	16	167.00	56	452.00
4	45.00	17	175.00	60	480.00
4½	50.75	18	183.00	64	508.00
5	56.50	19	191.00	68	536.00
5½	62.00	20	199.00	72	560.00
6	67.50	21 (¼ page)	207.00	76	580.00
6½	73.25	22	$215.00	80	600.00
7	79.00	24	229.00	84 (full pg.)	620.00
7½	84.50	26	242.00	1 Full Col.	$150.00
8	90.00	28	256.00	2 Full Col.	256.00
8½	95.75	30	270.00	3 Full Col.	354.00
9	101.25	32	284.00	4 Full Col.	452.00
10	112.25	34	298.00	5 Full Col.	550.00
10½	116.50	36	312.00	¼ Page	$207.00
11	122.25	38	326.00	½ Page	354.00
11½	126.50	40	340.00	Full Page	620.00
12	131.00	42 (½ page)	354.00	2 Full Pgs.	1,154.00

NOTE: Any ad falling between sizes listed will be charged for only space occupied (in ½" steps.)

lectors seem to pay higher prices for anything connected to tobacco, alcohol, gambling, drugs, or sex.

There is not always *one* correct price. You must decide if you want to set a low price in order to sell the item quickly. In general, the more work you do studying the antique and who might want to buy it, the higher the price you will get. This takes time, but it can also be fun, especially if you buy low and sell high.

These are the only five places to learn the correct price for an antique or collectible. There are advantages and disadvantages to each source.

1. A knowledgeable collector friend. Your friend's advice is free, but as the old saying goes, "You get what you pay for," and it could be wrong.

2. A price book. Price books come in all qualities. Bad ones are inaccurate and may misinform. Good ones tell prices, but often you must know a lot about the subject to be able to locate the price. This takes time. There is a current list of general price books in the Appendix at the back of this book. Specialized price books are listed for each category in Section 2.

3. The antiques publications (see Appendix) are filled with "for sale" ads with descriptions and sometimes pictures. Some items, like Depression glass or common toys, appear over and over in the ads. You can try to confirm your prices by reading these ads. Your sale price to a dealer will be a third to a half of the advertised price. If you decide to try selling through the mail yourself, you should ask the full price.

4. Visits to shops, shows, auctions, flea markets, and house sales. Your observations, although free, can be time-consuming, but they may help you to understand why one chair is worth more than another. Don't be obnoxious or demanding, but talk to the dealer. If the dealer isn't busy, you can get an abundance of information.

5. A formal appraisal. An appraisal is usually expensive. Appraisers are like doctors. They sell their expertise and training, and their time is valuable. The average big-city appraisal costs about $100 an hour or more. Never get an appraisal for a few inexpensive items. Jewelry, sterling silver, or large collections of coins, stamps, or other specialties probably should be appraised if you do not plan to sell at auction. There is no reason to have an appraisal if you sell at auction. The estimate placed on the item by the auction house is the appraised value. You may want to put a reserve on the piece at auction to ensure that, through bad weather or other factors, you do not risk your item being sold well below value.

Never hire an appraiser who sets charges based on a percentage of the value of the items. *Never* expect the person that appraises your antiques to buy them. If your appraiser offers to buy at the appraised value, beware! Do *not* expect a dealer to be a free appraiser. The

Watch the papers for ads that offer free appraisals.

There are many different types of antiques shows and sales. The ads will tell you what types of antiques and collectibles to expect at each event.

dealer is trying to buy at the lowest possible price and will not want to tell you what your antiques are worth unless you are paying for that information. A dealer will often ask to be permitted to buy (at the price you set) rather than take the job of appraising for a fee.

All of this "dancing around" by dealers is frustrating to those who know very little and wish to sell some antiques or collectibles, but that is how the market works. Dealers are selling antiques to make a living and not to make you happy. The better they buy, the more they make; but the more they buy, the more they have for sale.

There is a list of national appraisal associations in the Appendix. Other appraisers can usually be found in the Yellow Pages of your telephone book under "Appraisers." Most auction galleries will appraise. Many antiques dealers and household liquidators can appraise average items. Information about specialized appraisers is listed in the Appendix.

SNEAKY WAYS TO GET PRICES

There are a few tricks to learning prices that may help. Some types of antiques and collectibles are purchased because they are inexpensive, attractive substitutes for new department-store furniture and tableware. If you are trying to sell dishes, silver flatware, furniture, or even linens, you should always check on the price of comparable new ones at your local gift or department store. Your old furniture and dishes will sell quickly at a third to a half the price of the new, so that should be the lowest price you should ask. They could be worth more than the new. Old, used linens usually sell for 20-30 percent less than new ones, unless they have hand embroidery or lace, or are very unusual, hard-to-find sizes, like a five-yard tablecloth.

There are auction galleries in some cities that give free appraisals. They need merchandise to sell, and this is one of their forms of advertising. Check in the Yellow Pages of the phone book for auction houses. Watch the antiques section of want ads in your newspaper for special announcements of free appraisal days by out-of-town galleries.

It is possible to send a picture and description (include size, condition, history, and marks) of a seemingly valuable item to an out-of-town auction gallery and ask what it would bring at auction. Some galleries will write an answer to this type of inquiry. They are under no obligation to answer your inquiries, and you are under no obligation to sell your antique through the gallery, although you may later decide it is the best way to sell it. You should include a stamped, self-addressed envelope to encourage an answer and the return of your pictures.

All dealers and matching services buy as well as sell. A matching service buys old pieces of silver, glass, or china and resells them to customers who are trying to complete old sets. This solves the constant problem of what to do when you chip the twelfth cup or grind up Grandma's silver teaspoon in the garbage disposal. If you are trying to sell a standard item like Depression glass, silver flatware, or Haviland china, you can check the retail prices of these items at the shows or through the mail-order listings. You should be able to sell your pieces to these or other dealers for about a third to a half of the quoted prices.

HOW PRICES WORK IN THE ANTIQUES MARKET

If you sell it yourself. Once you have learned the correct *retail* price for an antique, you must still be concerned about how to price your item. No matter which method of selling you use, you are not selling from a retail store. An antiques dealer must at least double the cost of an item when selling it. This is considered a fair business practice because the dealer must pay rent, advance money to buy stock, pay expenses to move the item, and store it until it is sold. In addition, an item might have to be restored. The dealer must meet a payroll, pay taxes, advertise, and cover the other expenses of a small business. If you have your own garage or flea market sale, you will learn that dealers usually expect at least a 20 percent discount for buying more than one item. Collectors are often given this 20 percent "dealer discount" at shops, sales, and shows if they ask for it. There is also a quantity discount. Dealers and collectors expect a "lump sum" price for ten items to be less than the sum of the ten prices. Let's take some examples.

An antiques dealer buys a rare French paperweight for $1. It is offered for sale in the shop for $1,000, which might be the appropriate price for such a rarity. That markup would be based on knowledge and not on the cost.

A dealer buys a spindle-back oak chair at a flea market for $40. He does minor refinishing and prices it at $79, which is roughly a 100 percent markup. It would not be priced at $80, because the psychology of pricing for antiques is much like that at a grocery store. A $79 item sells much faster than an $80 one. He puts the chair in the shop. At the next sale he sees an identical chair for $60. He purchases it at dealer's discount and returns to the shop where he prices the pair of chairs at $225. A pair is usually worth more than two singles. His cost for the two chairs is $88, and now his markup for the two is about 155 percent. If another dealer comes to the shop to buy the chairs, the selling price might have to be $180 (that 20 percent "dealer's discount" has to be considered). That means the chairs only cost $88 and were sold for $180, a profit of $92 with a markup of about 105 percent. Usually the dealer who is buying is getting a large number of items or is a good customer, so a discount is a form of promotion for the shop.

A dealer has a customer for a large oak dining room table. While bidding at an auction, the dealer sees one that is just what the customer wants and bids $350. She moves it to the shop at a cost of $25, calls the customer, and offers the table for $500, which was the top price the customer seemed prepared to pay. The markup from a cost of $375 to a sale price of $500 is only 33 percent. A quick sale at a low price is sometimes a good idea.

A "picker" buys a tin toy for $5 at a church rummage sale. He sells it for $10 to a flea market dealer, who then sells it to a toy dealer for $18. The toy dealer goes to a toy show in Ohio and sells

Styles change and once ignored antiques become popular. This vase, made by Loetz, was evidently signed with the false signature "LCT" for Tiffany. Now Loetz glass is selling well. The vase was correctly identified for a 1978 Sotheby's New York auction and sold for $450 in spite of the forged name.

Even the White House restoration committee has been fooled. This églomisé Baltimore desk was once in the collection but has been removed because it was found to be a Victorian copy of the early nineteenth-century form.

Can you tell why one of these highboys is worth more than ten times the other? The valuable one is the curly maple Massachusetts highboy with the carved shell, made about 1760. The Queen Anne-style, pine and poplar highboy is a reproduction made about 1850.

the toy to another dealer for $35. It is sold again to another dealer from California for $70. A customer in California walks into the shop and eagerly buys the toy for $175. It sometimes happens this way. We always joke that if the dealers ever stopped buying from each other, there would be no antiques business. An item is often bought and sold four or five times before it reaches the ultimate collector. Each time there is an increase in price. This is not too different from the food business. A farmer sells peas to a processor who sells to a distributor who sells to a grocery store who sells to the consumer. Each time the price rises.

How does all of this affect the price of the collectible you are selling to a dealer? You should be warned that prices in the antiques business are based on supply and demand. The closer you can get to selling it to the ultimate collector, the higher the price you can ask. The general rule is that a dealer's gross profit margin should be 100 percent of the antique's cost. A dealer usually charges double what he pays you. This means that when you look in *Kovels' Antiques & Collectibles Price List* and see a doll worth $100, you should plan on selling yours to a dealer for half, or about $50. You must also remember that most of the prices listed in price books are those found in retail shops, not from small flea market dealers or yard sales. We often hear people complaining that they sold an antique to a dealer and later saw it in the shop at a much higher price. Of course! The dealer must make a profit! No one complains that a dress shop buys clothes for $10 and often sells them for $30, making a 200 percent markup. Many other shops sell this way. There are few that sell for less than a 100 percent markup, the typical pricing formula for the antiques dealer.

If you sell through an auction gallery. Auction galleries sell for a commission that usually ranges from 10 to 25 percent of the sale price, so you receive less than the announced sale price. If your dresser sells at auction for $150, you will get from $135 to $112.50, depending on the commission you contracted for. If the dresser sells for $300, you get from $240 to $225, depending on the commission rate. If you have given the auction gallery instructions not to sell the dresser for less than $150 and no one bids high enough, you will still owe the auctioneer a fee for trying to sell it, probably 5 percent ($7.50).

Sometimes it is far more profitable to donate your items to a charity than it is to sell them. The tax deduction for charitable contributions can be valuable if you are in a high tax bracket. There may be a fee to pay for an appraisal if the item is worth more than $5,000 (part of the tax law enacted in 1985). Some things are very valuable to a museum but very hard to sell because of limited interest. We once appraised a donation of annotated sheet music that was used in a landmark-status burlesque house. Not everyone wants a selection of the popular music of the day, but for historic reasons this collection was of great value to the music section of a large library. Architects' drawings, old photographs of local scenes, historical documents, and old maps are often worth much more as a donation. The tax laws seem to change each year, so if you are considering a large gift, consult your own accountant or the local Internal Revenue Service office.

WHERE TO SELL

There are only eight ways to sell your antiques and collectibles. Each of these methods requires some work. The more you work, the more money you will probably be able to keep after the sale. You get your cash immediately by some methods; others take months.

Each of these methods is successful only if you learn the rules and secrets of others who sell antiques and collectibles. Remember that the usual rules of credit apply. Get cash or assure yourself that the check offered will be good. You don't know the customer, and once in a while there are problems with checks or credit. Don't let anything leave your possession until you have cash, a check, or a written agreement about the sale.

A typical ad for an auction to sell the household belongings of a deceased collector. Notice the words "Estate auction."

Sell to an antiques dealer, friend, or acquaintance. The easiest way to sell an antique or collectible is to call a dealer and sell anything you can for whatever price is offered. This might be a good method if you are from out of town, have inherited a few large pieces, and must move them as soon as possible. The dealer will probably not set the price, so if your asking price isn't low enough, your item won't sell. The dealer's travel time counts. Try the closest dealers for quickest results. Find a list in the Yellow Pages of the phone book or in the antiques publications listed in the Appendix in the back of this book. Never let anyone in the house when you are not there. If possible, make sure at least two people are in the house when a potential buyer arrives. Be sure you get the money when the collectibles are taken. The antiques business is never run on credit. If you or your relative bought the antique from a dealer, try to sell it back to the same dealer. The dealer knows the piece, liked it before, and knows how it will sell, so usually the original dealer will offer the highest price.

Sometimes friends and relatives want to buy. Offer the antique to them first, at the price you plan to ask the dealer. Tell them that if the dealer refuses at that price, you will offer it to them again at a lower price. Would you give your friend a $100 bill? Then don't give away your antiques for lower-than-wholesale prices. If you want to *give* the antiques to your friends, don't charge anything. Sometimes it is best to avoid even offering to sell to friends and relatives. It can become a source of friction that can last for years.

If you have a few antiques and a lot of time, you can look up your items, determine the best price a dealer can offer, and take the items or a picture of the items to nearby dealers.

> We recently attended an auction advertised as an "untouched estate." At the start of the auction the bidders were informed that, as a stipulation in the will, the sons and daughters of the deceased would be bidding also. Not a bad idea if you are selling pieces to settle an estate for a family that cannot agree on who gets the favored items. You might also have your own sale with the help of an appraiser. Let the family members buy, then sell the rest at an open auction or house sale.

Sell at a garage or house sale. If you have a house full of goods, you can call one of the local house sale (tag sale) firms or auctioneers. Look in the Yellow Pages of the phone book under "Liquidators" or in your newspaper's weekly listing of sales. The entire sale (advertising, pricing, security, permits, staff, and special problems) can be handled by these people. You pay them a percentage on all items sold. Be very sure that you check references for the people you hire. They will be handling *your money,* and the money you receive is based on *their records.* Before anything is started, you must have a written contract which should list your responsibilities and the seller's responsibilities and fees. Be sure the seller is insured in case of serious damage or loss. Many of us are emotionally involved with our personal items. If you are, do *not* attend the sale. You may be upset and may even interfere with the sale and discourage a potential customer. If you are fond of some pieces, set a price and tell the staff not to sell below that price without your approval. It is always best to cut prices on the last day so that you can sell whatever is left. Arrange in advance (put it in the contract) that the unsold pieces should be sent to your favorite charity and the house should be left "broom clean." If you have only a few items to sell, the dealer might be able to place them in someone else's sale. This is illegal in many cities; but silver, jewelry, and furs are often sold in this way.

You can join a group of friends and arrange a big garage or house sale. Choose the most prestigious address. It helps if it is near parking and a main road. Go over the methods of bookkeeping and payment very carefully beforehand. There is often confusion about who owned the items sold. Price your own items, and be sure everyone knows all the rules about cutting prices. This works best if at least one of the group has had experience with other sales.

Anyone can run a garage or house sale. There are books about how to do it in many libraries. Before making any arrangements, check with the local police to learn about permits for sales, parking, signs, sales tax, and other problems. Some apartments and towns do not allow sales. It is illegal in some states to sell guns, whiskey, endangered animal parts, used mattresses, gambling devices, and other objects, so it is important to learn the law. Your local police can be of help. Go to some local sales and notice their setup for the sale, their security precautions, their tagging and pricing, and even their price reduction policy if it's possible. Your local newspaper may offer a free garage sale kit, including directions and signs. Advertising is always important. Place your ad in the weekly or daily paper for your neighborhood on the same day that all the garage sale ads appear.

Theft is the biggest problem for a novice running a house sale. Watch out for large open bags, pocketbooks, large unbuttoned raincoats, or any sort of box or bag that is brought into your sale. If possible, have shoppers check all large items and coats at the door. If you are having a garage sale, never let anyone in your house. If you are having a house sale, always have one salesperson in each open room, so they can watch and discuss prices. Be sure each sales slip is written by your salesperson in the room with that particular item. For example, have one sales helper in charge of all linens and clothes, and put all of their items in one room. Keep the small valuable items like jewelry in a special case near the cashier. All money should be paid in one place. It is best to use a table that faces the exit door. *Watch the money box.* If it is a very large sale, it might be advisable to hire an off-duty policeman. Be sure all other exit doors are locked. Tape shut all doors and cabinets that do not contain merchandise for sale. Before leaving at night, check all window and door locks. Burglars have been known to visit a sale, open a window, and return later that night for ''free'' antiques, knowing the house is unoccupied. Thieves might even take sinks, radiators, and copper plumbing. It is sensible to inform your local police of the sale, so they can put an extra watch on the house at night. After all, you did place an ad in the paper telling everyone that there is an empty house filled with merchandise.

Expect to have some losses. We have heard stories from professional house-sale staffs that are hard to believe. Price tags are often switched. Boxes are filled with unpaid-for items. A two-foot-high vase disappeared from a room that was guarded by a policeman. One saleslady even lost her lunch because she had brought it in a fancy department-store bag.

Take your items to a consignment shop. Most cities have consignment shops. These stores sell other people's merchandise and charge a commission. Some antiques shops will take merchandise on consignment for sale with their own antiques. Look in the Yellow Pages of the phone book for ''Consignment Shops.'' Visit the stores to see if your collectibles will fit in with the other items on sale. Ask antiques dealers if consignment is possible in their shops or at shows. Be sure to get a signed, written copy of the consignment agreement. It should include all charges, how long your money is held, and how the items are insured while in the shop. You, in turn, will probably have to sign an agreement with the shop and you should retain a copy. Write a full description of the objects on the consignment agreement. Include the words ''mint'' or ''flaked paint'' or any other indication of wear. If your item doesn't sell and you take it back, you want to be sure that it has not been damaged in the store. The shop or dealer is probably best able to set the price. Visit your consignment item after a few weeks to see if it has sold. If it has not, you should discuss reducing the price.

Sell through an auction gallery. Most major collections, important paintings, sculptures, and large antique furniture pieces are sold through auction galleries. These pieces require a special buyer who is either a professional antiques dealer or a knowledgeable collector. The gallery should mail announcements of the sale to these people, advertise in national antiques publications and local papers, and handle all the problems of the sale. *Everything is negotiable* at an auction gallery if you have enough items to consign. The printed rates usually say the consignor must pay 10-25 percent commission. Some auction galleries charge 10 percent to the buyer, a ''buyer's premium.'' They then charge only 10-15 percent to the seller. Always try to get the best rate. There are often extra charges for shipping, pictures in the catalog, etc. With negotiation, many of the extras

This tiger maple bureau was correctly cataloged for an auction by Richard A. Bourne Company of Hyannis, Massachusetts. The experts at the gallery knew that this was a ''marriage.'' The top of a tiger maple bureau, made about 1780, has been cut in back to permit the later addition of a secretary top. There were other alterations, including Victorian replacement hardware, a repaired leg, and a new top. In spite of all the alterations, the bureau sold for $1,600 in 1986.

Auction galleries often have special sales featuring dolls, Americana, paintings, clocks, toys, or other specialties. Watch for announcements which mention the ''wanted'' items for these shows.

CONSIGNMENT AGREEMENT

You agree with us that the property set forth on this receipt will be sold at public auction, in accordance with the terms set forth below

1. **Date of Sale.** The property described on the reverse side of this agreement ("Property") will be sold on _____ (subject to change without notice in our absolute discretion). We, however, may withdraw any Property before sale if we deem it unsuitable for auction for any reason whatsoever or if we believe that you have breached this agreement.

2. **Commission.** You agree to pay us, and we are authorized to retain from the proceeds of the sale as a commission an amount equal to 10 percent of the final hammer price on each lot sold over $1000, 15 percent of the final hammer price on each lot sold for $1000 or less and 25 percent of the final hammer price on each lot sold for $250 or less. In addition, it is understood and agreed that 10 percent of the successful hammer price of each lot sold is to be collected by us from the purchaser.

3. **Other Charges.** Packing and shipping charges of _____ will be deducted from the proceeds of the sale. Catalogue illustration charges of $50.00 per illustration will be deducted from the proceeds of the sale.

4. **Insurance.** Unless we have made previous arrangements with you, insurance costs of $1.00 per hundred dollars will be deducted from the proceeds of the sale. In the event of loss or damage to your property, settlement will be made based on the final median estimate. Our liability to you resulting from loss or damage to any property shall not exceed the above mentioned insurance coverage of such property. In no event, however, will we have any liability for damage to glass, frames, or lampshades, regardless of cause.

5. **Title.** You represent and warrant that the property consigned hereunder is your own unencumbered property and that you have the right to consign the property for sale and that it will be kept free of claims of others so that at the sale, good title and interest will pass to the purchaser. If you are consigning the merchandise as fiduciary, you warrant that you are fully authorized to consign the property, and agree to assume all of the obligations in this Agreement to the same extent if the undisclosed Seller was acting as principal, and will, if required by us, supply any additional documents which we may require.

6. **Estimates.** The estimates set forth in our catalogue are a statement of opinion only and are not to be deemed a representation by us in any way as to what the property will actually fetch at auction.

7. **Reserves.** All agreed reserves are set forth on the pre-sale advice which will be mailed to you prior to the auction. Reserve prices do not include premiums or taxes. You, or any representative designated by you, expressly agree not to bid on the Property, it being understood that all bids to protect this reserve will be made by us as your agent. We may sell any Property at a price below the reserve provided that we pay you on the settlement date the net amount you would have been entitled to receive had the property been sold for the reserve price. In the event that property does not reach the agreed reserve and is bought in by us for your account, you agree to pay us a commission of 5 percent of the reserve price and to reimburse us for all "out of pocket" costs incurred by us in connection with your Property.

8. **Withdrawal of Property.** You agree that no property may be withdrawn by you after the execution of this Agreement. In the event that you request withdrawal, of a lot, you agree to pay us 20 percent of the mean of our most recent pre-sale estimate and to reimburse us for all "out of pocket" costs incurred by us in connection with your property.

9. **Unsold Property.** All Property which is not sold at auction will be returned to you, at your expense, unless the Property is reconsigned

A sales agreement or sample contract from an auction gallery. Notice the commission is left blank, to be filled in, so it is not a set rate. The contract tells the date of payment and the approximate date of the sale. There is nothing in this contract about charges for catalog pictures, insurance, repairs, or rates for moving the antiques, or payment in case the antique is stolen or damaged before it is sold. You should discuss all these problems before you consign the antique.

could be free. You can ask for extra advertising, a catalog, even a preview party. No demand is unreasonable if your items are important enough to be a major sale for the gallery. Of course, a major sale in New York City is very different from a major sale in a small country town. If you permit the auctioneer to use your name in the advertising, it may mean higher prices at the sale. Collectors like to buy "fresh" antiques; these are pieces that have not been sold and resold in shops recently. Be sure to get a *written* contract from the auctioneer stating the terms, the approximate date the pieces will be sold, the time of payment to you, extra charges, and the advertising that is to be placed. Make sure the gallery has insurance. If you are unfamiliar with the auction house, ask for references.

Discuss the "reserve." Sometimes you decide you do not wish to sell below a certain price. This is the reserve price. If no bid is made above this reserve, you must usually pay a fee of approximately 5 percent of the agreed reserve price to the auctioneer. Do not place a high reserve on a piece. If you want too much, it will not sell, and you should not be auctioning it at all. Some major auction houses and many small auctioneers prefer only sales without reserves. If your antique does not sell above the reserve price, you can decide if you want to take your item back or have the auction gallery "sell it out the back door." If your antique fails to sell, the auctioneer can often sell it privately after the auction for a lower price. The usual commission rates apply for this kind of sale.

Check the credit rating of the auctioneer. Should the auctioneer go bankrupt, you have very little chance of getting your money for items that were sold. You may even have trouble proving that you own the unsold but consigned pieces. If you go to the auction, remember that it is not only in poor taste but also illegal in some states to bid on your items. If you bid the item up, you are a "shill." If you end up with the high bid, you would still owe the gallery the buyer's premium plus your charges.

At a country auction, which is very different from an auction gallery, the auctioneer usually goes to the house or farm and sells the items on the site. There is very limited advertising, no catalog, and often no chairs for the buyers. There are rarely reserves. The commission may be lower, and there is almost never a buyer's premium. This is a very successful method of emptying a small-town or rural house filled with the accumulation of a lifetime. If there are valuable pieces of antique furniture, the major dealers somehow seem to find out and pay good prices. If there are no major items, just typical seventy-five-year-old things, you will be pleased at the prices you can get for some items that an auction gallery would sell in box lots or not at all. The half sets of dishes, basement tools, old lawn mower, and even torn magazines and rolls of chicken wire will sell to someone.

Go to a flea market or show and offer to sell your items to the dealers. A slightly sneaky way to sell antiques and collectibles is to

sell to dealers or even customers at shows and flea markets. This is discouraged at most big shows. Take clear photographs of anything you want to sell. Record the size, marks, and any other interesting history on the back of the picture. You might also include a price, but do it in code so only you can read it. (The easiest code uses letters. Pick a special word or words of ten different letters. Try "my antiques." In that code, m = 1, y = 2, etc. The letters "aqm" are the code for $371.) Check in the local newspapers for dates and go to a major antiques show. Put the small antiques in your car and take the photographs. Find a dealer at the show who sells items similar to yours. *Wait until the booth is empty*, ask the dealer if he is interested in buying, then show your pictures. Dealers are usually interested because it is harder to buy than to sell. Never start a selling discussion when a dealer has a customer. Most dealers will ask *you* to set the price. Add 20 percent to the lowest price you will accept and negotiate from there. If you ask too much, the dealer will just say no. Remember, the dealer should be able to sell the piece for twice what you ask. Sometimes a dealer will not want your items but can suggest a customer, either another dealer or a collector who is attending the show. Be discreet. Don't bring big objects into the show. The dealer has paid for the exhibit space. If you are selling in competition with the dealers, you might be asked to leave. Don't expect a free appraisal. You must know the value of your antique to be able to sell it.

Take your items and set up your own booth at a flea market. If you have time, enjoy crowds, and don't mind packing and unpacking, you can set up your own booth at a flea market. Look in the local newspaper or an antiques paper in your area (see Appendix). Flea markets will be listed. Visit a few, talk to the dealers, get the information about how to rent space. Sometimes a table for the day is under $10. Notice how the tables are arranged and what you do in case of rain. It is also important to know whether you bring your lunch, or if a lunch stand is available. Always ask how early you can set up. Dress for all types of weather: bring umbrellas or sunshades, sweaters or heavy boots. Bring a chair. Bring a closed box to hold money, newspapers and bags for wrapping. Try to take an assistant. You may want to eat or go to the rest room or visit other booths, and you should never leave your booth unattended. You *must* stay for the full day, even if it rains. You must price the items, keep records, give receipts. It is almost the same as having your own garage sale. Learn the state sales tax regulations. You may need a resale license. Flea markets are often checked by state inspectors. Remember that in some states it is illegal to sell items like guns, slot machines, liquor, endangered species' pelts or parts, and a few other things. Watch out for theft.

Place an ad and sell by mail. Specialized collections of small items, like political campaign material, buttonhooks, or souvenir spoons, can be sold by mail. The best pieces to sell this way are well-known, easy-to-describe pieces like Royal Doulton figurines, carnival glass, beer cans, or Depression glass. Large items are difficult. Furniture is almost impossible unless it will be picked up by the buyer. Check the ads in the antiques papers. Anyone selling antiques may be buying antiques, so anyone offering to sell an item like yours is a prospective customer. There are also "antiques wanted" ads that can give you leads. Be sure to ask for a self-addressed stamped envelope (SASE) from anyone asking for more information. Otherwise you may find you have to spend about 25¢ a letter to answer queries, and that can add up. A U.S. resident should ask for a check payable on a U.S. bank, because a Canadian bank check will cost you a fee to deposit. International sales are easiest by credit card. If you are selling between the United States and Canada, be sure to specify the currency expected and the exchange rate.

You may want to send out a numbered list of the objects, with a full description of each, including size, marks, and condition. Include every defect, and set a price. If possible, take pictures or make photocopies and add these to the list. Make photocopies of the list and send it with a letter of explanation. Include your name and address, zip code, and phone number, including the area code. Enclose an SASE for the return of your list and pictures. Don't try to sell damaged items by mail unless they are very rare. The very rare Hungarian Hummels could be sold, but a more common out-of-production Hummel probably could not.

You will have to pack and ship the items. Wrap them carefully. Breakage is *your* problem. Always insure all packages. Ask for a check before you ship the antique and be sure the check is good. Offer the pieces with geography in mind. Some items sell for higher prices in the West than in the East. Get a return receipt to show that the package arrived. It should be understood that there are full return

privileges and that the antique may be returned to you for a refund. The buyer pays the return postage.

If you place an ad in the local paper or the antiques papers to sell your items, study the format of other ads for ideas in composing your own. Include a full description and either a phone number or address. Ask for an SASE for inquiries. Security may be a problem, so don't use your address if you live alone. Consider renting a post office box. Make appointments to show the antiques, but always have someone else with you for security. In the antiques papers it is best to include the price. In your local paper it is not necessary. A local ad is best for large items like a dining room set.

Find a customer by writing or calling. A few special pieces might be sold to a particular customer who is nationally known. For example, The Hoover Company has a collection of vacuum cleaners. They might want one that is not in their collection. Write to that customer or to a museum, enclosing a picture, description, price, your phone number, and an SASE. Museum collections are listed in *The Official Museum Directory*, the American Association of Museums, 1987 (National Register Publishing Co., Wilmette, IL 60091). The directory can be found in your local library or perhaps at your local historical society or art museum.

Information on reference books, price guides, and clubs of interest to the collector are listed in the Appendix.

Advertising &
Country Store Collectibles

The first serious advertising collectors began their buying in the 1950s. There are collector clubs for people who specialize in everything from bottle openers to tin containers. The nostalgia craze in restaurant decorating and the ''country look'' for homes have made unusual items with interesting graphics and company names into prize pieces. There are clubs for collectors interested in special brands like Planters Peanuts or Coca-Cola, for collectors of certain items like tin containers, sugar packets, or bottles, and for collectors fond of a general theme like fast-food restaurants. Publications for many of the clubs accept advertisements, and these are the best places to offer your items for sale. You can also write to dealers to advise them that you are selling items (they have to buy them from someone), or you can place your own ad. Ads in general-interest publications also sell items. A visit to dealers at mall shows, flea markets, or other antiques shows where advertising pieces are sold will help you locate a possible buyer. Highest prices are paid at the special advertising shows held during the year. These shows are announced in the general publications for the collector.

Tin containers with lithographed designs, signs, bottles, boxes, giveaways, cut-out magazine ads, or any advertisement can be sold. Neon signs, cash registers, calendars, lunch boxes with brand names or attractive graphics, and gas-pump globes or any other auto-related, brand-marked items sell quickly. If your advertising collectible pictures a train, automobile, airplane, flag, bottle, a black person, or partially clad female, it is worth a premium, up to 50 percent more. If it includes the name COCA-COLA, PLANTERS PEANUTS, MOXIE, CRACKER JACK, HEINZ, or JELL-O, it is worth two to ten times as much as a similar ad for a less popular brand. If it

55W Pens-Pencils Wanted

Cash for old fountain pens or parts. Frank Damante 123 Sysco Street San Town, CA 00000 626/555-0634 (55w-t51)

Buying Fountain Pens — pre-40's. Parkers, Waterman's, Wahl-Eversharp, Swans. Excellent to good condition. Bette Boote 1st Street Beach City, IA 00000 (55w-t62)

FOUNTAIN PEN LITERATURE wanted such as catalogs, repair manuals, sales literature, and magazine ads (1875-1960's). Edie Smrekar 999 The Ct. Nowhere, VA 00000

Baranger .mechanical display usually for diamonds, some clocks, etc. Used in jewelry stores to help sell their diamonds. Little scenes (40 different) all moving around or going back & forth. Came in a red cardboard box especially made for proper shipping. Paying $300 ea. & up for rare ones. Contact The Brandts 34 Beach Boulevard Cousinsville, PA 00000 535/555-3562 from 11-7 pst. (18w 4)

52W Advertising Wanted

Coffee Tins. 1 lb. tin litho, no key opens. $100 for Turkey, Foltz Maid, similar. Pete Harmon and Friends 999 Chickenright Our Town, UT 00000 744/555-2882 (52w-tf)

Borden Dairy Elsie the Cow neon, toys, clocks, Xmas cards, porc. signs, puzzles, lamps & comics. Dorothy Ackerman, 124 Way Road Our Town, MO 00000 449/555-7989 (45w-tf)

Mr. Peanut wanted. Seeking older, unusual Planter's Peanut items. John F. Hunter III 1234 Apple St. Nova, OK 00000 433/555-5011 (45w-67)

SPOOL CHESTS BRAINARD ARMSTRONG, corticel wanted. Write or call Bill Wel 666 Their Place Mytown, 00000 633/555-7902 (15w

COLLECTOR GLASSES from Fa Food rest. — Arby's, Burger Ch McDonalds, etc. Price, describ P.O. Box 000 Puffyville, O 00000 332/555-1919 (45w

is an ad for whiskey, beer, cigarettes, or a drug-related product, it will sell quickly. A tin sign is worth ten times as much as the same sign on paper. If you have a set of old roly-poly tins or a Coca-Cola item dating before 1900, it is worth extra research to determine the value. It could even be worth thousands of dollars. Beer can collectors have their own clubs, publications, and shows. They usually trade cans but rarely buy them. Only the very unusual or the old cone-top cans sell well. For more information, see the Beer section.

Even boxes can be worth selling. When the estate of movie actress Agnes Moorehead was auctioned in 1975, the storage boxes went for $11 each. Buyers liked the name "Beverly Hills Moving and Storage Co." on the boxes.

A Pennsylvania man, remodeling an old garage, found the ceiling seemed to be made of tin. When he tore it down, he discovered that the thrifty previous owner had indeed put tin on the ceiling to repair leaks, and the exposed tin was actually the backs of twenty-five colorful embossed signs showing a man and woman drinking Fort Pitt beer and giving thanks to the president and Congress for repealing Prohibition. He started to throw the signs away but decided instead to talk to a friend who collected beer cans. The friend suggested he take the signs to a local beer can show, where one of the dealers bought all twenty-five and later resold them to collectors at $100 each. Luckily, the man did not throw away his valuable find, but he also did not cash in on its full value.

Large items like the bar in a saloon, counters, floor-standing coffee grinders, and popcorn wagons are expensive. There are dealers who specialize in them. Look for ads in the special publications, or talk to the dealers at the shows. These items often sell well through an ad in the local newspaper.

You may think that you own a piece of advertising art, but an auction gallery may consider it folk art. Folk art brings higher prices. If you have a very large collection, a handmade wooden piece, a very large figure, or an unusual clock, it might bring the highest money through a large auction gallery that usually would not sell advertising collectibles. Advertising clocks sell to both the advertising collectors and the clock collectors, so check publications and shows for both groups.

ooo

Architectural Antiques

The tops of stone pillars, pieces of carved wooden fretwork, doors, windows, stair railings, exterior tiles, wooden flooring, paneling, and many other pieces of buildings are now bought and sold in the antiques market. Many of these items are large, heavy, and difficult to move; but there are specialists in every area who deal in "archi-

tectural antiques." Sometimes they are the salvage dealers who demolish buildings and remove any of the special or salable parts. If you have rights to a large building or an old house that is about to be destroyed, examine it carefully to be sure that any valuable collectibles are saved. Not only should the wood or stone carvings be saved, but many other parts of a building can be sold. Any sort of ornamental ironwork is in demand, including elevator doors, radiator covers, ventilator grills, locks, handles, or hinges. Light fixtures, church pews, carved marble benches, anything decorative is desirable. Even very special wall coverings or carpeting can be sold. Usually, the best way to sell architectural items is to place an ad in the paper and have the buyers come and take their pieces out of the building. Don't even be upset if they knock down the walls or floor to remove something. If you own doors, phone booths, or a wrought-iron fence, you can sell them through an ad or by contacting an auctioneer or a dealer who sells this type of collectible. Most dealers are not interested because architectural pieces are so large and heavy and sell slowly.

There is added value if the building or house was designed by a well-known architect. To price architectural pieces, think of them in terms of use. A used door should sell for less than a new door. A carving sells for its decorative value.

ooo

Autographs

Nineteenth-century autograph collectors wanted just the signatures of famous people. They often cut the names from the bottoms of letters or other documents and destroyed much of their value. Today's collector prefers the entire letter or document. Never cut out a signature! If you find old books, letters, deeds, or even scribbled notes signed by an author or famous person, keep them intact. Never cut, erase, or repair anything. Torn pages are preferred to taped pages. The glue from the tape can eventually destroy the paper. All correspondence can have a value. This includes letters from distant relatives describing

An Ohio man bought a folded, aged document at a flea market for $10. He took it to be examined and the experts decided it was an original copy of George Washington's orders for the Continental Army. The document was put into a New York auction and estimated to be worth over $500,000. The day of the auction another expert examined the paper and declared it to be a copy. The document was withdrawn from the sale. The experts are still arguing about it.

a war, an old Western town, the food eaten for dinner, or many other everyday events. Content, condition, date, place written, signature, postmarks, and other factors all affect the value. Very high prices are paid for letters or diaries about American life, especially if they describe disasters, the Gold Rush, Indians, whaling, the Revolutionary or Civil wars, or pioneer life. Hand-drawn maps, sketches by artists, and inscribed or annotated books are of value.

Very high prices are paid for letters and documents of presidents, signers of the Declaration of Independence, important political and military figures, composers, authors, or scientists. But many government documents were signed by secretaries or even by machines that reproduced a president's signature, and these are worth very little.

Land grants, army discharges, and many other legal papers were signed with the president's name and not always hand-signed by the president. There are many of these, and their value is very low. Slave-related documents have become more valuable because of their historic value, and they sell best at black collectibles shows.

There is little interest in documents written in foreign languages, so you may find that a letter written by a famous French statesman will sell for a high price in France but not in an English-speaking country. Some autograph dealers have international outlets and can get good prices for foreign material.

Supply and demand is the key to pricing an autograph. Button Gwinnett and Thomas Lynch, Jr., signed the Declaration of Independence and died soon after. Because there is such great demand for a complete set of signatures of the Declaration's signers, these two autographs have a very, very high value. Other, more important men signed the Declaration, but there is an ample supply of their writings. This same pricing rule holds for more recent signatures, like those of James Dean or Marilyn Monroe.

Autographs and letters that have been forged, copied, or reproduced in some form have almost no resale value. You must own an original. Most libraries have excellent books about autograph collecting, which will offer many more hints about what is valuable. Autographs can be sold to local antiques dealers or to local antiquarian book dealers, or coin or stamp dealers who also handle autographed materials. If no local dealers are to be found, you may be able to sell important material through an out-of-town auction gallery. There are galleries that specialize in autographs and historic material. Out-of-town dealers who buy autographed materials will not buy from a description or photocopy. Carefully pack the material between pieces of cardboard, place it in a strong envelope, and seal with tape. Always get some sort of references before you send anything. Send the material first class, insured if it is worth under $300, or registered mail if it is worth more. Keep a photocopy for yourself as well as a list of what you sent. The dealer will usually send you a check. This is one of the very few areas of collecting where you are not expected to set the price.

ooo

Baseball Cards & Related Sports Collectibles

Even though the first baseball card was issued by 1887, age does not determine the value of a baseball or sports card. The price is determined by the condition, demand, and rarity. There are many price books for collectors. Most are available in public libraries and bookstores because baseball card collecting is a popular pastime for millions. Our son first entered the world of collecting when he was in second grade. He started saving baseball cards. His cards were traded, carried in a cramped pocket, "flipped" in a then-popular game, and finally stored in a shoebox. When one of his friends moved to Australia, he was given the treasure trove of baseball cards that belonged to the friend and his older brothers. Last year we rediscovered the

cards, which had been stored in our attic. Many are rare, but they are all in poor condition with scuffed pictures and ragged edges, and their value would be low.

Sort your cards by date and manufacturer. Match up the sets and put the cards in numerical order. Look at a current price book from your bookstore or library, and make a list of the cards you own and their approximate value. Always consider the condition when pricing a card. Note which sets are complete. Watch for error cards. The price books will comment on these. If you find a card that does not seem to be in the price book, look again. You may be looking in the gum card section and have cards that came with breakfast cereal.

There are several strange pricing truths. The earlier in a player's career the card was printed, the more it is worth. That means the rookie cards for famous players are high priced. Cards sell for more on the two coasts than in the middle of the country (so do many other collectibles). Cards sell best near the hometown of the team or player. Cards were numbered as they were printed, the high numbers released late in the season. Although for most antiques the lowest or earliest numbers are most wanted, for baseball cards it is the opposite. The high numbers bring the highest prices. This is because there were usually less of the high-numbered cards. Another odd pricing fact: if you add the price book prices for each card in a set, the

---

"You'll never guess what I found in my garage," the man said to an old friend at a summer barbecue. "Sheets and sheets of...what are they called? With the ballplayers' pictures on them?" The friend said, "Baseball cards?" The find was a stack of aluminum plates from an old printing plant. Each had a copy of the finished sheet taped to it. A bit of research in the magazine *Baseball Cards* revealed information about printing proofs. The discovery sold for over $5,000 to dealers who eventually sold the separate pieces for a total of about $20,000.

---

total is less than the listed price for the complete set. This is probably because buyers are more interested in completing a set than in buying a full one. Buyers will pay extra for a single card if they need it. Take your list to a local baseball card show. They are easy to find in all parts of the country. If you can't find one, check the ads that can be found in the publications listed in the Appendix.

Talk to the dealers. Show your inventory list and the cards. Be careful not to give a box of cards to a dealer and offer to sell a part of them. Hold out for an offer for all of them unless you want to set up your own booth to sell the collection individually. Good cards sell quickly. The others are worth very little and can be difficult to sell. Remember that a dealer is trying to sell and not just buy at a show. The rules of etiquette say you must never try to start selling your items to a busy dealer. Don't interrupt any ongoing conversations

in a booth. Wait until the dealer is free. You will find that stories spread quickly, and dealers and collectors will soon look for you and the possible treasure that might be in your baseball card collection. Expect to get less than half the price book value for a card, and remember to judge the condition accurately. If you are unsure, examine other cards. Never throw out a baseball card. Give it to a young friend.

Anything that looks like a baseball card or pictures a ballplayer has a value. This includes cigarette cards (usually from England), as well as small felt or silk pictures of players, candy boxes, bread wrappers, labels, ice-cream cup lids, and many other items. Most of the cards sell for under $2 each, but a box of hundreds has enough value to make it worth the effort. The dream of every collector is to find an old box with the fabled Honus Wagner card. (But be careful about finding the card of your dreams; the Wagner card has been faked in recent years.)

SPORTS OTHER THAN BASEBALL

Don't overlook the other sports-related items. Football, golf, tennis, Olympic events, soccer, and many other sports have serious collecting fans. Anything that pictures a sports activity, is used to play a sport (golf clubs or tennis rackets), is associated with an important player or winning team (photos, autographed footballs, Olympic medals,

programs), or even uniforms, children's games, and toys are wanted by
the right collector. The baseball enthusiasts gather at the baseball
card shows. Football cards and other sports cards can also be found
there. The specialty auction offering sports items developed in the
1980s. There are sales that include wooden-handled golf clubs, odd-
shaped gut-strung tennis rackets, and even cricket bats. Some of these
auctions are advertised in the general antiques publications, while
some are part of the auction schedule of the major auction galleries.
Ask a collector of any of the sports materials to suggest how to find
these auctions. Every item offered for sale belonged to someone like
you who wanted cash instead of an old football. Other potential buyers
of sports memorabilia are local sports enthusiasts and members of the
sports-related collecting clubs.

Don't forget the importance of college sports. The pennants, programs, and souvenirs are cherished by many alumni. Talk to the
university librarian or coaches to see if they have any sort of sports
trophy display. One family found their father's autographed baseball
from a 1914 university team. Instead of including it in the house sale
after his death, they gave it to the school sports department. It is
displayed in the case with an appropriate tag mentioning their father,
the winning pitcher. They also got a tax deduction for the estate.

ooo

Baskets

All baskets, from Indian and Nantucket baskets to Chinese sewing
baskets, are popular. The price is determined by quality, design,
maker, variety, and condition. Miniatures under two inches high and
the very large baskets always command a premium price. Amateurs have
a hard time pricing baskets. New African, Chinese, Filipino, South
American, Korean, Taiwanese, and other baskets are often made as exact
replicas of old baskets. Since natural materials are used, the design
is copied exactly, and the work is by hand, it takes great knowledge
to tell the old from the new. As a seller, you are only worried about
getting as much as possible. If you know the basket has been in your
family for fifty years, you know it is old, so you can price it accordingly. If you bought it at a house sale last year, you may not
have a valuable basket, and pricing could be difficult. Dealers in
baskets and good auction houses can tell the difference. Rather than
price your baskets too low, take them to an expert.

Prices are often listed by the maker in general price books. The most desirable baskets are by the Shakers, American Indians, or the Nantucket lightship makers. Added features like potato stamp designs, feathers or beads incorporated into the basket, or a strong history of maker and ownership will add to the price. Remember, baskets are of many shapes and sizes, from laundry baskets to toys.

ooo

Beer Cans & Breweriana

There are many collectors of beer cans, but most cans are traded and not sold. The best way to get rid of a collection is to go to a show-and-swap meet for beer-can collectors. The local papers and the beer-can collectors publications will list them. Cans are often sold in groups. Anyone who buys a six-pack has the start of a beer-can collec-

tion at almost no cost. Some of them can be traded for other cans, and there is still no cost. If you can sell some of the recent cans for anything, even 50¢, you have a profit. The best sellers are the cone-top cans. They are old and not easily found. Collectors prefer cans that have been opened from the bottom. Rust, dents, and other damage destroy the value of a common can and lower the value of rare cans.

Breweriana is anything related to beer and beer cans. This includes signs, labels, ads, coasters, glasses, hats, and the unpressed metal used to make cans. Breweriana will sell either at a beer-can collectors show or to the advertising collectors. For more information, see the section on Advertising Collectibles.

ooo

Black Collectibles

Anything that pictures a black person or is related to black culture is considered a "black collectible." This includes everything from early slave documents and photographs of life in earlier times to advertisements, figurines, and other stereotypical depictions. In a price book listing of black collectibles you will find items related to Aunt Jemima, the Cream of Wheat man, Amos 'n' Andy, a fast-food chain known as Coon Chicken Inns, and many nameless black people.

There are several books about black items and at least two special shows a year. But black collectibles are also bought and sold at any advertising or general antiques show. Black rag dolls are classed as both folk art and collectible dolls and are sold by dealers in both of these specialties. Some of the black material is derogatory, and you may be concerned about the propriety of offering it for sale. Remember, however, that the majority of the dealers who specialize in black items and the majority of the collectors of black items are themselves black. They want the pieces as part of their heritage, part of their history, and are eager to buy.

Because of the interest today, any item picturing a black will sell at a good price. The Amos 'n' Andy toys are worth 50 percent more than a comparable toy showing a white cartoon figure. Even small, dime-store, "joke" figurines of past years are selling for over $25 each. Be sure to visit an antiques show and check prices on black collectibles before you try to sell yours. Many sell for far more than the amateur would believe.

Books

Selling books presents different problems from selling other types of collectibles. Age is one of the factors that determine price, but it is not as important as people believe. Some books written during the past twenty-five years are worth more than books that are 200 years old. The value of a book is determined by rarity, condition, edition, and age. It is also influenced by whether it has the original wrapping intact, who owned it, if there is a bookplate or a signature, who printed it, and the subject. Books can be sold in house sales and auctions. They also can be sold to stores that carry used books and to antiquarian book dealers. It is necessary to think about a possible customer for your unusual books. For example, old local history books might be needed by a historical society library. If you are persistent and do the work, you can sell to private buyers.

If you have several hundred books that were purchased over a period of time by an average book buyer and not a serious collector, you can sell the group at a house sale. You can always call in a book dealer

Rare books, more than any other type of antique, often sell best to out-of-town specialists. If you want to sell your books to someone who cannot see them, you must list all the important information. Too long a letter, a rambling style, needless information, or poor handwriting can often discourage the buyer from even reading the letter. The shortest way of describing a book is the standard form used in bibliographies. List the author (last name first), title, subtitle, publisher, date, and place of publication. (If you enclose a photocopy of the title page, you will have given much of this information.) Include number of pages, number of illustrations, name of illustrator, type of illustration, description of binding, including color, and a short description of the contents. Emphasize the fact that there is a dust jacket, bookplate, autograph, inscription, interesting notes, or pre-1920 color pictures. These add value. Be sure to note all defects, including worn corners, weak spine, loose pages, water marks, or foxing (yellowish brown stains), writing or underlining, or any discolorations.

or friend to buy, but try to sell the entire collection. Otherwise you may find that the best books have been sold and the ones remaining have little value. If you have a number of rare books, contact an antiquarian book seller. They are listed in the Yellow Pages of the phone book or can be found selling books at one of the many book fairs. *Antiquarian Book Fairs and Antiquarian Bookseller Associations* is a pamphlet by Marjorie Parrott Adams listing all of these fairs. Another good source is *Buy Books Where - Sell Books Where* by Ruth Robinson and Daryush Farudi, an annual publication listing sellers of out-of-print books. (See listing in Appendix.) Most book collectors specialize by type or subject, and Robinson's book may give you some ideas about what is valuable.

First editions of important books are often valuable. To determine if a book is a first edition, look at the copyright page to see if it says "First Edition." Look on the title page to see whether the date agrees with the copyright date. Some recently published books list the numerals 1 through 10 on the bottom of the page. If the 1 is still in the list, it is the first printing. When there is a second printing the 1 is removed. By the tenth printing only the 10 remains. Books printed by certain small private presses and special printings of books are very valuable. Book-of-the-Month Club editions, special collector editions made in quantity, or reissues of old books have little value. First editions by the best 1930s and 1940s mystery writers are popular, but the books must have original dust jackets for highest value.

Bibles, encyclopedias, dictionaries, and textbooks have very low value. McGuffey readers, disaster books (describing a flood or earthquake), and books made into movies are of little value unless they are first editions or related to *Gone With the Wind*. The first McGuffey, the first edition of an important movie book, or a rare disaster book does sell well. Old cookbooks, decorating books, catalogs, horticulture and flower arranging books, sports books, history books, and early books on science and medicine have value. Very early children's books and illustrated children's books in good condition are wanted.

Books with unusual photographs, engraved illustrations, or other attractive pictures are worth money. Unfortunately, the pictures are sometimes worth more out of the book than the entire book is worth. That is why many nineteenth-century books of flower prints have been taken apart. Look for illustrations by WALLACE NUTTING, N. C. WYETH, ROCKWELL KENT, MAXFIELD PARRISH, BESSIE PEASE GUTMANN, and ARTHUR RACKHAM.

"Association" books are collected. Any book with a signature by an important owner or author or with an inscription to an important person has the added value of its association with that person. Sometimes the autograph is more valuable than the book. Some bookplates are also very valuable. A Charles Dickens or Paul Revere plate is worth hundreds of dollars.

Covers are important; leather bindings, elaborate gold-decorated bindings, and paper dust covers of special interest add value. Fore-edge painting (pictures on the front edge of the page) and pop-up illustrations also bring higher prices.

Paperback books that are first editions in good condition sell well. You can tell age by the price printed on the book and sometimes by low numbers used by publishers for identification. Early books had no bar code. Some collectors specialize, buying only books with lurid covers or with art by well-known illustrators. Worn paperbacks sell to buyers who want a good book to read at a minimum price. Condition is important for all types of books. Would you want a chipped cup? A torn book is the chipped cup of the book business. Transparent tape repairs also lower value.

If you mail a book to a buyer, wrap it in a padded book bag, and send it book mail, insured. The postage for books, magazines, and other printed materials is a bargain. Ask your post office.

ooo

Bottles & Go-Withs

Bottles can be divided into two separate selling problems. Modern figural bottles like Jim Beam, Ezra Brooks, and Avon have been collected for the past twenty years. There are several national collector clubs. The market has gone up and down, and today some people have large collections that are worth less than their original cost. Old and antique bottles are favored by a very different group of people. They are serious collectors who dig for bottles, trade bottles, belong to antique bottle clubs, go to shows, and think of bottles as a part of their own family life.

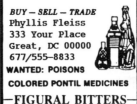

It is easy to price new bottles, but it is hard to sell them. The new figural bottles, including Avon and the liquor decanters, are listed in great detail and at retail price in the price books such as *Kovels' Bottles Price List.* You will be fortunate to get 50 percent of that price if you have a new bottle in mint condition with original labels. There are many national clubs for modern bottle collectors. An ad in the publications for these clubs is often the best place to sell. Some states have active collectors and clubs that sponsor modern bottle shows, but in other areas there is little interest. Make a list of your bottles. Only those in perfect condition sell. Damaged bottles are worth pennies at a garage sale. Determine the prices and offer to sell either to dealers or by mail to collectors who read the ads in the bottle and general publications.

Old bottles, especially rare ones, sell best at bottle shows and bottle auctions. Highest prices are paid by serious dealers and collectors. Many of these bottles are listed in *Kovels' Bottles Price List.* The listed price is very close to the price you should ask. Many types of old bottles are collected, including milk bottles, canning jars, inks, inkwells, medicines, bitters, sodas, poisons, whiskeys, figurals, and most desirable of all, historical flasks. Rare colors and markings indicate a bottle worth thousands of dollars. Common bottles can sell for a few dollars. Aqua-colored glass with bubbles is common. Desirable colors are cobalt blue, dark purple, honey amber, clear green, yellow, and sometimes white milk glass. A rough scar on the bottom of a bottle is called a pontil. This is usually an indication of an old hand-blown bottle. Seam marks on the neck of the bottle usually indicate a newer, machine-made bottle. Old is usually more valuable than new.

Machine-made bottles with no redeeming features sell best at flea markets or at house sales. Any type of perfume bottle sells well to dealers at any type of antiques show. The same is true for attractive figural bottles.

Warning! In some states it is against the law to sell bottles with

The basement of the newly purchased house was filled with old wine. Without a state liquor license, the wine could not be sold. Besides, the new owners of the house knew that the wine had been badly stored and was not fit to drink. A friend suggested they pour out the wine and sell the old labeled bottles to collectors. The almost 300 bottles brought over $3,000 from delighted bottle buffs at a bottle show.

---

the liquor still inside. It is illegal in every state to sell bottles that contain drugs such as opium or cocaine. These drugs sometimes remain in old bottles found in drugstores from the early 1900s, when the now-banned drugs were legal medicines.

Beginning collectors make several mistakes. Bottles are collected for their beauty and history. Fifteen years ago it was common to soak the labels off, but it is not being done today. Do not remove or destroy any paper labels, tax stamps, or other paper glued to a bottle or the original box, if available. The box and the labels add to the value. Uninformed collectors sometimes misunderstand the marks embossed on bottles. Don't think that the date 1858 in raised numerals in the glass of your fruit jar means that it is either old or rare. The date is the year the screw-top jar was patented, and the number was used for many years after 1858. Bubbles in the glass, "whittle marks," and pale aqua glass are not rare and are not indications of very expensive bottles. A nick or flaw is always significant in a rare bottle, and substantially lowers its value. Condition is important and a nick, scratch, or cloudy interior can lower the value by as much as 50 percent.

GO-WITHS

Anything that pictures a bottle or was used with a bottle is of interest to bottle collectors. This includes such things as bottle openers, jar openers, milk bottle caps, canning jar rubber rings and tops, corkscrews, fancy bottle corks, ads, and pamphlets. These items can all be sold. The corkscrew and bottle-opener collectors have very specific wants, and the best place to sell good examples of these is through the collector clubs and ads. Don't underestimate the value of old openers. The current record price for a corkscrew is over $1,000. Figural bottle openers often sell for over $25.

Bronzes

Bronze figures were very important decorative pieces in the 1880-1900 period, but then lost favor. A new-style Art Deco bronze, often set with ivory, became fashionable in the 1920s and 1930s and became popular again in the 1970s. The bronze figure was scorned for many years, so there may be some very valuable ones in your attic or living room. Some of the best bronzes were given to thrift shops or resale stores in the 1950s. They were purchased for a few dollars by some far-thinking collectors.

A bronze can be judged by the quality of the casting, the fame of the artist, and the appeal of the subject. Age is not as important as you might think. Many modern bronzes sell better than antique examples. Western subjects, the animal figures by nineteenth-century French artists, the Art Deco designs of the 1920s, and huge masculine subjects, such as nude males wrestling or warriors on horseback, are now bringing the highest prices. To check on the artist, see *Abage Encyclopedia: Bronzes, Sculptors & Founders* by Harold Berman. Look for names like FREDERIC REMINGTON, LANCERAY, CHIPARUS, PREISS, CLODION, KAUBA, MOREAU, BARYE, MÈNE, CARRIER-BELLEUSE, or NAM GREB.

A group is probably worth more than a single figure by the same artist. A marble base adds value. Generally the larger the bronze, the greater the value, although miniatures (under 6 inches) sell for surprisingly high prices. The artist's signature, founder's seal, number, and any other special marks increase the value.

Poor details, crossed eyes, dented noses, repaired fingers, missing parts, or cracks lower the value. If the patina has been removed or damaged, the value is lowered. Recast pieces have low values. If you discover a Remington or any other very famous bronze figure, take it to a qualified appraiser to learn if it is an old or new figure. Replicas have been made by using the original statue to make a new mold. The replicas will be slightly smaller than the original. An original Remington bust is worth over $100,000; a recast may sell for as low as a few hundred dollars.

Any auction house, antiques dealer, or art dealer can easily sell a good bronze figure, and you should have no problem selling yours.

●●●

Carousels & Carousel Figures

The hand-carved, wooden charging horse or prancing pig that was part of the amusement park merry-go-round is now classed as "folk art" and sells for thousands of dollars. This is one of the few types of collectibles that go up in value if the paint is new. A well-done repainted figure is worth more than an example with "park paint." Stripped figures are worth 25 percent less than park paint; repainted ones are worth 25-50 percent more. It is possible to identify the makers of some of the animals, and if the name of the amusement park that owned the merry-go-round or the name of the artist can be determined, the value goes up 50 percent.

The most valuable carousel figures are the most unusual. Menagerie animals are rarer than horses and usually sell for thousands of dollars. Tigers, polar bears, pigs, ostriches, giraffes, goats, and other strange animals are most desirable. The quality of the carving, very elaborate saddles and trappings, jeweled bridles, windblown manes, imaginative figures at the saddle cantles, and glass eyes add to the value. The figures in the outside row on the carousel were seen by the public and had the most elaborate decoration. The "lead" horse was the best. American figures, which bring higher prices in this country than European figures, are more highly decorated on the right side because the carousel goes in a counterclockwise direction. English carousels are the reverse. Horses are called standers (three or four feet on the ground), prancers (back feet on the ground), or jumpers (no feet on the ground). All are equally valuable.

Any part of the carousel will sell to a folk art collector. The trim above the center section, the carved carriage sides, even the signs of the maker have a value. Metal carousel horses also sell, but for much lower prices. There are many other carvings and decorations from amusement parks that are now wanted by collectors. The figures from the fun house, the painted canvas backdrops from the sideshow, carts, planes, cars, and other parts of rides, and the penny arcade equipment and gifts are now being bought by collectors. If you are lucky enough to own any parts of a defunct amusement park, be sure to check with local auctioneers and shops when selling your pieces. Carousel figures and parts are large and they are most often sold through well-advertised auctions.

The market is nationwide, and buyers will travel long distances to get a rare figure or even a complete carousel. The problem of moving a large item does not seem to bother the carousel collector.

Celebrity Memorabilia

Celebrity memorabilia is bought and sold in four major categories: items related to the movies; items related to TV, radio, and recording stars; comic-related items; and historic personality items. Each has a slightly different market.

MOVIES
Anything related to the movie business is in high demand: old props, costumes, lobby cards, still photographs, scripts, publicity packets, promotional giveaways, signs, objects (especially clothing) owned by a star, and of course the movies themselves. Even scrapbooks filled with newspaper clippings or the fan movie magazines are bought and sold. Although much movie memorabilia is sold through flea markets, antiques shows, and even auctions, these do not represent the major market. Several newspapers are devoted to buying and selling movie material. Special shows are held during the year, especially in California. There are also several special mail auctions of movie material. Fan clubs want appropriate items. Try to find the movie collectors in your area. If you have a tie that belonged to John Wayne, you can find the proper fan club and contact the members. To locate the star or fan club, look in *The New Address Book* by Michael Levine at your library. It is important to verify the authenticity of your movie memorabilia. Many autographs were not originally signed by the stars. Pictures were often signed by someone on the staff. Anything related to *Gone With the Wind*, Marilyn Monroe, Elvis Presley, or James Dean has added value.

In 1955 a fan bribed his way on to the set of the movie *Giant*. He had Elizabeth Taylor, Rock Hudson, and Jane Withers sign a 35-cent copy of the paperback book *Giant* he had with him. James Dean rarely signed his name, so at first he refused to autograph the book. He finally put his first name on an inside page, his full name on the inside cover. Dean died a few months later. The book was sold at auction in 1985 for the record price for a paperback, $1,263. The owner realized that the Dean autograph would generate national interest and sold the book through a nationally advertised auction.

TV, RADIO, AND RECORDING STARS
TV and radio materials are collected by fans and by those who are interested in old-time radio (see the section on Radio and Television). Contact these collectors through the radio publications, at the

special shops and shows, or at the large flea markets. "Star Trek" fans have special shows each year and buy and sell old scripts, tapes, and all sorts of memorabilia. Disneyana collectors are eager to buy Mouseketeers items. "M.A.S.H.," "Howdy Doody," "The Man from U.N.C.L.E.," and "The Honeymooners" also have special collector organizations. Old *TV Guides* and other magazines are also wanted.

Recording stars often appeared on TV or in movies, so there are several reasons their memorabilia would be collected. Try selling your items to dealers in records who also have "go-withs," or to the regular twentieth-century collectibles dealers. You should also check any local fan club members if you have some rarities or a large box of material.

COMIC-RELATED MATERIALS

Little Lulu dolls, posters of Spiderman, lunch boxes printed with pictures of the Flintstones, cookie jars, and anything else that shows a cartoon character are all collected by someone. The best place to sell these items is to the comic book and comic art collectors. (See the section on Comic Books and Comic Art.) Dealers at flea markets and shopping mall antiques shows are always looking tor these items.

HISTORIC PERSONALITIES

Charles Lindbergh, any prominent political figure, the astronauts, composers, scientists, explorers, notorious criminals, and many other people interest collectors today. Often the best place to sell "association items," like a chair that belonged to Teddy Roosevelt or

Queen Victoria's underdrawers, is through a national auction that specializes in autographs and historic items. Less important items can be sold through these same sales, through some of the mail-order auctions, or to dealers or collectors. Look for other possiblities. An astronaut's autographed picture might interest a collector of space toys. Lindbergh and his flight have fascinated airplane lovers for many years, and there are so many collectors that these items even have a special section in *Kovels' Antiques & Collectibles Price List.*

If you are fortunate enough to be the descendant of an important person or have acquired a large collection of material about one person, you might offer it as a collection to the historical society that would be most interested, one in the hometown, state, or center of activity of the famous person. There may also be a Hall of Fame that would be interested. Everything from aviation to rock and roll to football has a Hall of Fame.

A large collection should be sold as a unit to obtain the best price. In other words, the price for the whole is greater than the price for the sum of the parts. This means you must find a dealer or auctioneer who will take all of it. If you sell one or two important pieces you will lower the interest in the remaining collection.

ooo

Christmas & Holiday Collectibles

If your attic has been used for storage for the past thirty years or more, it probably holds some valuable holiday collectibles. Christmas ornaments, light bulbs, tree holders, cards, tinsel, Halloween papier-mâché pumpkins, black cats, skeletons, costumes, candy containers, even Fourth of July banners, or fireworks package labels, Easter bunnies, or foldout paper turkeys from Thanksgiving are eagerly collected. The prices paid for old Christmas ornaments are astounding. Do your homework. Look at the special books about holiday collectibles at your library. There are six or seven fine books with color pictures, descriptions, and some price information. There is also price information in the annual general price lists like *Kovels' Antiques & Collectibles Price List.* Don't just put out a box of ornaments at your garage sale; you might be giving away money. If you do not have time to do the research, take the holiday memorabilia to a local auction gallery or to a dealer who is already selling this type of merchandise. These pieces sell best the month before the holiday, so be sure to talk to the dealers several months earlier. Sell Christmas ornaments by October 1, Halloween pumpkins by August.

> Never throw out anything before you check the possible worth. After selling his house, the seller kept heaping trash on the front lawn. The astute collector next door checked the trash and salvaged three boxes of old Christmas ornaments worth over $300, a windup toy clock worth $15, and several other old toys.

In general, anything figural will sell well: Santa Claus, black cats, sleighs filled with toys, even bottles shaped like holiday symbols. Newer items are often made partially of plastic, so study anything you have that is made entirely of paper, iron, or tin. Early blown-glass ornaments are hard to date because they have been copied since the 1950s, but even relatively recent ones are worth money to the right person. Chains of bubble lights, working bubble lights, or figural bulbs, working or not, and all sorts of old paper and tinsel ornaments can be surprisingly high priced. The old chicken-feather Christmas trees are now classed as folk art and sell for hundreds of dollars even if they are only 12 inches high. Postcards and greeting cards sell as holiday items at regular shows and also do well at the specialty shows for paper items.

○○○

Cigarette Lighters

Cigarette and cigar lighters have been made since the late nineteenth century, but collectors search for the unusual pocket lighters made since the 1940s and the large electric-spark or kerosene cigar lighters that were kept on the store counter. The store lighters should be

sold to those interested in advertising and country store materials. (See section on Advertising.)

Remember those silver-plated Ronson lighters that everyone received as a wedding gift in the 1950s? They were unsalable until about 1985, when the Fifties room was being revived by avant-garde collectors, and the lighter was needed as a table ornament. Now all types of figural lighters are in demand. The bartender-behind-the-bar lighter of the 1930s, the Coca-Cola bottle lighter of the 1950s, or the dueling-pistol lighter of the 1960s all sell well. Any lighter with an ad or an unusual shape will usually sell to a collector or flea market dealer. The common urn-shaped Ronson lighters do not sell well. Silver and gold lighters, some with precious jewels, should be sold like jewelry.

Look for RONSON, figurals, the Kool cigarettes' plastic penguin, and large, figural, cigar-store lighters.

○○○

Clocks & Watches

According to some collectors, a home without a ticking clock has no heart. Clocks that *work* always sell well. It does not seem to matter if they are old, new, Art Deco, or eighteenth-century French. One problem with pricing clocks is that two clocks that look the same to a novice may look very different to an expert. Years ago we ran a picture of a clock owned by a reader of our newspaper column. It was an 1880 wall clock with elaborate ''gingerbread'' trim. We gave a suggested value. The day after the column appeared, we started to receive phone calls and letters from readers. We got another, clearer picture of the clock, and when we examined the trim very carefully, we saw what our clock-expert readers had noticed. This was a rare version of the wall clock, worth in the thousands of dollars, not just the few hundred dollars we had suggested.

Our rule for pricing antiques is that if it moves or makes noise, it brings a premium price. This includes animated alarm clocks, grandfather clocks with chimes, and any other clock that makes noise or has moving parts other than the hands. Figural clocks of any age sell well. Look for LUX on the label and double the price.

To identify a watch, you must open it and look for names, labels, and construction features. If you can't do it, ask a local jeweler to help. When you check the value in a watch price book, you must know the name on the dial or movement, the number of jewels, serial number, size of case, and if it is solid gold or plate. A clock must also be opened to see if there is a label and to check on the type of mechanism running the clock. If it winds, the key is important.

An old clock with replaced works is a "marriage" and is only worth from 10 to 20 percent as much as an all original clock. Grandfather or tall case clocks are often found in an altered state. During the past 200 years, owners have repaired or glorified the clock with additions or changes. If the feet or finials are new, subtract 10 percent. If the door is new, subtract 20-25 percent. If the base was shortened, subtract 30 percent. If the case was badly refinished or the carvings destroyed, deduct 25 percent or more.

A slightly restored *painted* dial or *minor* replacement of parts or case lowers the value by about 10 percent. If the dial is totally repainted, it lowers the value of the clock to the value of the case; the repainted dial is worthless. A restored, cracked, or damaged *enameled* dial lowers the value by up to 50 percent. If the face is old but a replacement, deduct 20 percent.

Wristwatches that look old-fashioned are in demand and are worn as jewelry even if they do not keep time because they have not been cleaned and repaired. Dealers who specialize in old watches or jewelry

will buy them. Look for these dealers at the shows or in the Yellow Pages of the phone book under "Watch Repair" or "Jewelry." Of course, solid-gold watches are far more valuable than gold-plated or chrome-plated ones. The names ROLEX, PATEK PHILIPPE, HAMILTON, VACHERON & CONSTANTIN, OMEGA, PIAGET, MOVADO, GRUEN, TIFFANY, LE COULTRE, and CARTIER add value. Diamond watches must be appraised by a qualified jeweler for the diamond and gold value. The wristwatch must sell for more than the "breakdown" value (see section on Jewelry). Winding stems positioned out of sight in the back and triangular or other odd-shaped cases add value. So do calendars, stopwatches, chimes, and other special features. Look for the special buttons or levers that indicate these items on the watches. Unusual watches with psychedelic dials, moon dials, cartoon characters, moving figures, or slogans are considered novelties and can be sold, but they usually do not bring high dollars.

Pocket watches are wanted by watch collectors but not necessarily by a jewelry buyer. This is a special market, and best prices are paid by the serious collector. A very low serial number adds to the value. When pricing watches, be sure to determine the difference between the markings on plated and solid-gold cases. The marks can be misleading. The words "Guaranteed 5 (10, 20, 30) Years" appear on cases that are gold filled or rolled gold. The karat mark with a year guarantee was used until 1924. After that, the government required the cases to be marked "10K gold filled" or "10K rolled gold plate." A solid-gold case will probably be marked with the karat mark and the words "Warranted U.S. Assay." A few are marked with hallmarks. Contact a watch dealer or an auction gallery if you want to sell a good, solid-gold pocket watch.

Antique grandfather clocks, especially American examples, should be examined by a qualified appraiser. If unaltered, they are usually worth thousands of dollars and should be sold by a professional dealer or auction house with national exposure for the best price. Also, be sure to check carefully on the value of carriage clocks, chronometers, novelty clocks, and elaborate clocks with ormolu or porcelain decorations. Many of these are worth big money.

ooo

Clothing & Accessories

There are old clothes and there are vintage clothes. The styles change so quickly that today vintage clothes can be twenty-five years old or more. Anything that is wearable, in good condition, with no permanent stains or damaged fabric, can be sold. The silly hats of the 1940s, the bowling shirts and Hawaiian prints of the 1950s, the plastic purses of the 1960s are in demand to be worn, not displayed. The white cotton petticoats and camisoles that were once underwear are now party dresses. Beaded flapper dresses or old lace wedding dresses are wanted for special occasions. Before you send old clothes to the local thrift shops, be sure they are not worth more money at a vintage clothing store.

Silk that is crumbling, fabric deteriorating under the arms, moth holes, and stains make a piece of clothing unsalable. Only pieces in good condition are of value. Lace trim, buttons, even special embroidery can be salvaged and sold separately. Vintage clothing with designer names can sell for thousands of dollars. Look for CHANEL, FORTUNY, WORTH, ADRIAN, CLAIRE McCARDELL, BONNIE CASHIN, and other important names.

Very small sizes are more difficult to sell because so few people can wear them. We often think our ancestors must have been tiny because so many dresses are size 6 or less. Remember, the waists were cinched, so an 18-inch waist was not unusual. It's easy to make a dress smaller, but more difficult to make it larger. Many dresses were remade for use by other family members, so each time a dress was altered, it was usually made for a smaller person. Accessories, including men's and women's hats, purses, fur pieces, scarves, and neckties, sell well. Cashmere sweaters and coats, men's or women's, sell quickly. Ordinary men's clothes do not sell at vintage clothing stores. Give them away to charity. Shoes are also difficult to sell.

ooo

Coin-Operated Machines, Jukeboxes, Slot Machines

There is a corollary to the joke among antiques dealers that anything that moves or makes noise has a value. They say that there is even more value to anything with a money slot. This includes most types of music-making machines, from nineteenth-century Swiss boxes to 1950s jukeboxes. Slot machines, gum ball machines, and all of the myriad types of gamelike machines known as "trade stimulators" or amusement park coin-ops are part of the valued "it moves and makes money" antiques.

If you are selling any type of slot machine or gambling device, be sure to check the laws in your state. It is not always legal to sell these items. Any machine that moves or makes noise is worth less than half if it is broken. Some types of machines are so difficult to repair that they are only worth about 20 percent if broken. But remember, many of these machines sell for thousands of dollars if perfect. The general rule is that the more neon lights and Art Deco trim there is on a jukebox, the more it will be in demand, and the higher the price. The highest prices paid for slot machines and coin-operated games are paid by the dealers and auctioneers who specialize in them. Contact these people at the appropriate shows or sales. They are listed in the antiques trading papers and in the magazines written for collectors.

There are many types of trade stimulators and penny arcade games. The granny fortune teller, horse race games, claw digger steam shovel games, love testers, Kinetoscopes (movie machines), and many others all sell well. Collectors do not differentiate as much by age as by "gimmick" value. A moving figure, unusual configuration, or very elaborate case will add value. Even perfume dispensers, match, cigarette, gum ball, or sandwich machines, and all types of games of chance sell well. Be sure the machine works on U.S. coins. Some English games have been imported, and the value is much lower.

The make, model, serial number, patent dates, address of the manufacturer, and other important information can be found on an identification plate under or behind the machine. A dealer or serious collector can identify your jukebox from a picture. (So can you if you get the right books from the library.) Even arcade games and pinball machines can be identified from clear photographs. Take a picture of the top playing area and another of the back glass area so all details show well. It is easier to sell a large game or jukebox by pictures and descriptions than any other way. Buyers won't travel to your house if the machine doesn't seem to be a good one. You must make the effort to take pictures and write letters, place ads, or talk to dealers, or

you will get very little for the machine. A neighbor may think it would be a nice toy for the basement, but only a real collector will pay top price.

ooo

Coins &
Other Numismatic Items

Do you remember going to the bank for rolls of pennies so you could search for the rare dates? Have you kept a box of foreign coins brought by traveling relatives? Collections of this sort, even those started by grandpa as a boy, have less value than imagined because of the poor condition of the coins. However, you can never be sure there is not a treasure hiding in with the ordinary, so you must examine coin collections carefully. If you have inherited a properly stored serious collection of coins in good to mint condition, you have even more reason to be careful about selling. We remember appraising an estate that had a library full of coin books. We asked about the coins, and the almost unbelievable answer was, "Oh, there were lots of old coins. I took them to the bank and deposited them into the savings account." That is exactly the wrong thing to do.

You will find many books in the library about coin values and the buying and selling of coins. The prices are the going retail prices, not what you will get for your coins from a dealer. You will probably be offered half of the listed price. The books picture coins and indicate prices for coins in all grades or conditions. The books refer to coins in proof (PRF), uncirculated (UNC or MS), extremely fine (EF or EX), very fine (VF), fine (F), very good (VG), good (G), or poor (PR) condition. Each book has a slightly different code. Beware! It takes an expert to know the condition of a coin. All you can do is learn the range of prices for your coin if it seems to be in excellent condition. That means it has the bright, shiny finish of a new coin, no scratches, no nicks, no overall wear. Never clean a coin! That lowers the value. The bright finish must be the original one. Remember, an old coin or bill is almost always worth at least the face

A recent coin price book listed these prices for a 1927 Mercury dime: G, $1.00; VG, $1.15; F, $1.50; VF, $3.75; XF, $5.75; MS60 (proof), $17.00; MS65, 65 (choice proof), $95.00; FSB (fully split bands, a special grade for this coin only), $525. If the dime has a D mint mark, the FSB price is $2,400. When determining proof or choice proof, the difference in grade for this coin can only be seen under a four-power magnifying glass.

value. Check the meltdown value of silver coins. When silver prices were very high in the 1970s, coins were worth much more than face value or even coin collectors' values. Many coins in poor condition were melted and sold as silver.

The most obvious place to sell coins is to a coin dealer. There is a listing of "Coin Dealers" in the Yellow Pages of the telephone book. Some large department stores have coin departments, and they will also be listed and will buy coins. Anyone who sells coins, buys coins. Auctioneers sell good quality coins. A local antiques auction gallery may also have special sales for coins or include coins in regular sales. There are also some nationally known coin auction houses. Some are listed in the Appendix, and others can be found through the advertisements in any of the coin publications. If you send your coins to be auctioned, be sure to ask who pays for insurance for the coins while at the gallery, photography of coins for the catalog, and any advertising. You must pay a fee to the auctioneer, and you should ask what percentage of the sale price that will be. Get a signed contract or agreement, and send the coins insured and with a full inventory list.

Information about coins and coin prices can often be learned by telephone. An accurately described coin can be looked up in any of the price books, and an approximate value can be given by phone. Some dealers will give the approximate price they will pay by phone.

If you inherit what appears to be a good collection, it might be advisable to contact a coin appraiser. They will be listed in the Yellow Pages under either "Coin" or "Appraiser." The probate court must use appraisers to determine the value of coins in an estate, and the names of these appraisers are known to the lawyers and judges in your city. A qualified appraiser should belong to some of the national numismatic organizations. The appraiser can also arrange for the sale of your coins. Be sure to ask the charge for appraisal and for disposing of the collection. We have found that an amateur does not do well trying to sell a collection of rare coins. It takes a professional auctioneer or appraiser to watch out for your interests.

Coins and paper money can often be sold to friends, to dealers at coin shows, or to jewelers who advertise for pieces for meltdown. We

A bronze 1943 Lincoln penny sold for $20,350 in 1986. It is one of perhaps twelve thought to exist. The United States Mint never admitted the coin was made, although several have been sold at auctions.

caution that before you sell by this method, you must be sure you do not have a very rare coin. It takes an expert to understand the difference in value between a coin with a mint mark and one without it, and any of the other details that determine great rarity and value.

There are many coin dealers who buy and sell by mail or through ads in the numismatic publications. We urge caution in these dealings. Most publications try to screen the dealers, but sometimes a dishonest person may offer to buy for months before problems surface. If you plan to sell to an unknown person, try to get references. Ask how long you must wait for your money and include a full list. If possible, have someone, perhaps a local collector, help you determine the condition of your coins. You could be wrong, and a fine-looking coin may only be extra good. An unscrupulous dealer could tell you that your coin is in worse condition than it really is. Sometimes you may have to wait too long for your money from the sale of your coins. Send the coins registered mail. Postal fraud is a crime, and even dishonest dealers try to avoid it.

There are many special categories for coins. You must learn what mint set, proof set, reissue, restrike, type set, and other words mean. If you have sets or rolls of coins, sell them as a unit, do not break them up.

Tokens and any other types of "money" have a value to a coin collector. Some specialize in store tokens, odd types of money that are not metal coins, mis-struck coins, and error coins. Even canceled and blank checks are wanted. Paper bills are very popular, and these should be researched and sold in the same way as coins.

Almost every type of "money," from wooden nickels to gold coins, has a value. If the money is an unfamiliar-looking American coin or bill, it is even more important to check the value. Medals are sold through coin dealers. Even jewelry made from coins can be sold through coin dealers.

Solid-gold coins present a special problem. They can be sold for the gold content or for the numismatic value. In recent years many investors have started to buy gold coins. The value changes daily with the price of gold. Look for nicks in the edges that indicate bits of the gold have been removed. This lowers both values. Coins mounted in bezels as jewelry retain numismatic value if they can be removed with no damage to the coin. Of course the coin may be scratched from wear. Coins mounted as jewelry with soldered links have lost the numismatic value even if the link is removed. The solder will damage the edge of the coin. Gold coins in good condition sell for the highest prices at coin shops and auctions.

●●●

Comic Books & Comic Strips

Action Comics No. 1 is the first superhero comic. In June 1938, this comic book introduced Superman. In fine condition the comic now sells for over $50,000. A copy of *Marvel Comics No. 1*, Oct.-Nov. 1939, in mint condition, sold in 1984 for $35,000. Most of the high-priced comics contain superheroes.

Age alone does not determine the value of a collectible comic. Comic strips started in 1896 with the introduction of the ''Yellow Kid.'' The first monthly comic book was the 10¢ ''Famous Funnies,'' which appeared in July 1934. Comics were popular with children, young adults, and especially servicemen during the 1940s. After the war there was a movement to censor comics, to remove the violence and sex, and many comic books were burned. The paper drives of the war and the reformation movement after the war mean few of the old copies remain. The newsprint used for comics is easily damaged by heat, light, and moisture. Those comics that were not destroyed by a series of young readers were often preserved until a tidy mother decided they were no longer worth saving. It is the lucky collector who finds a box of well-preserved, old comic books in an attic where they avoided house-cleaning days. Comic books are wanted by young collectors who specialize in superheroes, Westerns, funny animals, jungle, SF (science fiction), or special issues or full years of favored comics. They are also purchased by serious older collectors who have more money and more expensive desires.

Comic collecting became an organized pastime about 1960. Several

magazines and newspapers were started that discussed the history of comics, reported on new comics, and, of course, included buy and sell ads. Today there are comic shops and comic shows in most major cities. Reprints, price books, and research materials are available.

Most comic collectors are not children; they are adult, affluent, educated males. The easiest place to find old comic books is at the special comic book stores. You may be able to find one nearby. If there is no shop listed in the Yellow Pages of the telephone book, you could try selling at a comic show, a mall show, or a store that sells used books. Check the local papers or ask your friends' children. If you find a large collection of comic books, you should go to a comics convention. Trading takes place at the convention and in the rooms of the hotel during the convention days and nights. The standard comic price guides, including the original one, *The Comic Book Price Guide* by Robert Overstreet, list almost every title and issue. The prices are high retail, and dealers at a comic show often start out offering to sell you a comic at half the Overstreet price. You will get even less for your comics, though great rarities usually hold their value.

Condition is very important. A serious collector stores the comics in special plastic bags to protect them from added tears, cover bends, or spine damage. When pricing comics, remember to check condition. This is one field of collecting where finding a retail price is as simple as reading a price guide that is available in every library and most bookstores. The comic must be in original, unrestored condition. It should not be repaired by gluing, restapling, recoloring, trimming, or bleaching. Rusty staples, bad printing, creases, even yellow paper, will lower the value. Mint copies have almost-white pages and glossy covers. A good copy has only suffered from average use, slight soil, possible creases or minor tears, but has no tape or missing pages.

It is not only comic books that are collected but also comic strips from newspapers, the original art from comics and cartoons, and even the original celluloid drawings used to make animated movie cartoons. The Disney cels were offered for sale to tourists at Disneyland when it first opened. The framed cel was sold for about $15. Each cel was marked on the back with a short history of celluloids. Other cels were sold earlier by Courvoisier Art Galleries in San Francisco and each was marked on the mat framing the cel and on the back. A scene from

In the 1950s we visited Disneyland. We were given two Disney "cels" from the gift shop for our children. One pictured Donald Duck on a train, the other was Cinderella and the Prince. Each then cost $15. We were able to have them autographed by Walt Disney. Our children have been offered $5,000 for Donald and $3,000 for Cinderella, but they haven't sold the cels yet. The autograph adds value, but any cel is worth money.

Snow White showing the evil queen as a hag dipping the apple into a pot of poison sold in 1986 for $30,800. Other original comic art used for posters or publicity also sells for thousands of dollars.

The original art for comic books and comic strips was so undervalued before 1970 that it was often burned by the newspaper syndicates. The artists of the comics you read now usually own their art and either give it to special friends or sell it. A single strip is worth over $100 if it is the work of a popular artist, and under $25 if it's by a forgotten artist. The subject matter makes the difference in the price. Old political cartoons and sports cartoons for local papers are of minimal value. Any strip for PRINCE VALIANT, LI'L ABNER, or YELLOW KID is of value. All types of comic art sell at comic book shows.

It is easy to sell good comics by mail. Buyers look for comic books through the ads in the comic collector publications.

ooo

Decoys

In 1986 a duck decoy sold for $319,000. The same year, many decoys sold for under $25. Most were sold for prices in between these two amounts. Because decoys are collected as art, the most expensive are not necessarily the oldest. The quality of carving and decoration and the fame of the maker determine the price. Average working decoys in

poor condition sell quickly if they are reasonably priced. They should be offered through the normal antiques channels and shown to dealers, collectors, auctioneers, and friends. What is difficult is deciding if your decoys are just average or are "stars."

Once again we suggest you try doing serious research at a library. There are many books that picture decoys and tell about the important makers. Try to identify your decoys. Remember, the decoy was originally made to lure a bird, and your decoy should be an identifiable fowl. The nondescript, rough silhouette of a bird is not a valuable decoy although it will sell as a decorative piece of folk art. If your decoys seem to be valuable, you should take them to an appraiser or auction gallery to get an expert opinion. If you live in an area with no decoy appraisers nearby, you should be able to get enough information by sending a clear photograph to one of the auction galleries that regularly sells decoys. The most successful decoy auctions have been on the East Coast.

Decoy collectors are a special group with their own clubs, publications, and events. It is not easy to learn about them. However, many decoys are included in shows and sales that interest the folk art and "country look" collectors.

ooo

Firearms & Weapons

Never attempt to sell firearms, swords, dangerous war souvenirs, or other weapons before checking with local police about your city and state laws. The laws concerning the sale of guns are very strict. You could be subject to a fine or jail sentence, or even be held responsible for any death caused by a gun you sold illegally. Don't sell or trade firearms or weapons to friends or other collectors before you know the law. The safest way to dispose of a gun, rifle, or perhaps an eighteenth-century blunderbuss is to have it auctioned or sold by a

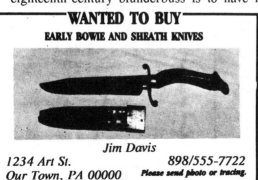

reputable firearms dealer. They will be listed in the Yellow Pages of the phone book under ''Guns'' along with antique gun appraisers. It pays to check on the value of any large collection before offering it for sale.

War souvenirs sell well, especially medals, books, historic documents, photographs, uniform caps and insignias, foreign flags, small firearms, and knives. Be very careful. Some types of knives are illegal and should not be sold as anything but collector's items. You must always conform with your local laws. Don't try setting up a table at a garage sale or flea market without knowing the law. Grenades, bullets, and other explosive objects are dangerous, and many become unstable with age. Never handle old explosives before you talk to the local bomb removal squad. It is amazing how often an old box of souvenirs has a dangerous grenade in it.

Never let children near any of these items.

There are many serious collectors of firearms and weapons. Early swords, especially decorated Japanese ceremonial pieces, military dress uniform swords, and any good sword made before 1850, command a high price. Kentucky rifles, muskets, Civil War weapons, dueling pistols, and even World War I and II guns are wanted. Well-made military knives can also be sold to collectors of weapons.

The buyers for these items are not usually found at the average antiques show. Some flea markets have a few tables of dealers who specialize in war materials. Ask the collectors and dealers in your area who sell weapons. They can tell you about the clubs, the shows, and the auctions that are the best for you.

ooo

Folk Art

The meaning of the term ''folk art'' has changed. In the 1950s it referred to stiff, formal American portraits done by itinerant painters of the seventeenth and eighteenth centuries, ships' carved figureheads, cigar store figures, weather vanes, and a few other large signs and carvings. In the 1970s an important book on folk sculpture was written, and folk art took on a new meaning. Large carvings that were often exaggerated or bizarre, duck decoys, quilts, paintings in the

FROM MICKEY MOUSE TO MASTERPIECE

EXCEPTIONAL PICTORIAL QUILTS FROM ALL PERIODS *WANTED*

Pieced and appliqued, Pennsylvania c. 1935

Baltimore Album Quilt, signed "Hannah Foote Baltimore 1850"
Both of these quilts have been sold prior to publication.

Michelle Sidrane Our Town, MT 00000 533/555-1580

Grandma Moses style, commercial weather vanes, carousel horses, and even printed advertising tins all became defined as folk art. The experts still debate the meaning of the words ''folk art,'' but for you, the seller, folk art is what the customer wants to call folk art. Age is of little importance. Decorative value, humor, the artist's fame, and some ''hype'' determine the value. We watched a prestigious dealer sell an 1890s iron-bladed lawn mower for several thousand dollars at a folk art show. It had a ''sculptural quality.''

Look at what you want to sell. If it is primitive, colorful, attractive, or very unusual, it will be purchased. Price is arbitrary for most items. There are listed prices for decoys, carousel figures, cigar store figures, quilts, and paintings by known artists or from known schools of painting. These pieces should be researched because treasures do indeed look like trash to the uninformed in this market.

There is almost no way to set a price by comparison on a hand-carved bird cage, a cemetery statue, a wooden maypole, or a cast-cement urn. It is one price at a flea market, quite another if anointed as "art" by a prestigious dealer. (There is growing concern about tombstones and statues removed from cemeteries. It is illegal to own or sell them.)

Look at the folk art books in your library. Visit folk art exhibits. Talk to the dealers and collectors at shows. If your object is large, colorful, and strange, price it a little higher than you might have thought possible. A collection of intricate carvings made by your grandfather or a group of nineteenth-century paintings by a distant relative should possibly be offered for sale through an auction gallery. It is the public that sets the price, and the gallery will show the pieces to more prospective buyers than you could. An appraisal of the collection will only be as good as your appraiser, and most appraisers who are not in the larger cities might not understand the market for unique folk art pieces.

An unusual piece of folk art will sell quickly. We were once offered a large cut-out tin sign of a black boy advertising a store in a small Ohio town. In two months it had been sold and resold to dealers five times until it finally appeared in an ad for a New York folk art gallery at twenty times the price we had originally seen. You will not be able to get the very top price for your folk art, but you should get a third of its retail value in the best shops. Don't ignore commercial items that might attract folk art buyers. That tin sign was a store ad. Side show banners and other circus memorabilia, chalk (plaster) figures, birdhouses, garden ornaments, fraternal order carvings and banners, even religious paintings, prints, and figures are considered folk art.

ooo

Furniture

The largest antiques you will have to sell are probably pieces of furniture. They are also among the most valuable. The size creates special problems and limits your methods of sale. Antique furniture, which includes anything made before 1960, has a market value that can be determined from price books, auctions, and shop sales. You will hear about chairs that sell for $150,000 each, even one that brought $2.75 million, but these are the great rarities of the eighteenth century. You probably have less valuable pieces.

Any usable piece of furniture has a resale value. Higher prices are paid for pieces in fine condition. Because new furniture is made with staples, glue, and veneers, well-constructed older pieces, even those in poor condition, can be sold. Study the price books and the reference books in the library to find out about your furniture. If you have an antique-collecting friend, ask for an opinion about the pieces. If you own furniture that is exceptionally large (for example, a large bed, a grandfather clock that is over eight feet tall, or a very wide desk), be sure to determine how it can be removed from the room. Maybe there is a removable finial or top cresting. Note this for the prospective buyer because wise collectors have learned the hazards. A 7-foot-ll-inch piece will sell for a better price than an 8-foot-1-inch piece because most of today's homes have 8-foot ceilings. Deduct 50 percent from the value if a bookcase, desk, grandfather clock, or bed is over 8 feet high or is too wide to go through an average door.

If you have any information about the furniture (old bills, where and when the pieces were bought, maker's labels, type of wood, or written family history), put it with the furniture for the prospective buyer. A label adds to the value by 10-100 percent if the piece is worth less than $20,000. On the superstars of the furniture world, the pieces worth over $20,000, a label can increase the price four to five times. The fame of the maker determines how much value is added. If you inherited the pieces from elderly relatives, search all seat cushions for hidden valuables. Look for hidden compartments in desks. Look underneath drawers or inside the furniture. Carefully slit the

backing on framed pictures and mirrors and look for valuable papers or money.

If you think there are some pieces of furniture over fifty years old, contact a local auctioneer and talk about the possible value at auction. The auction will advertise good antiques and get a higher price than you could through your own ads. If you are selling the entire contents of a house, a house sale might be best. The furniture may not bring top prices, but it will bring buyers, including antiques dealers, to the sale, and the other small items will sell for more. *Do not* invite a dealer in to pick out a few items if you are trying to sell the entire contents of the house. A smart dealer will buy the few good pieces, and you will have trouble getting anyone to come to see the remaining ones. If you advertise a sale, you need a few fast-selling items, like a rolltop desk or large dining room set, to entice dealers and collectors. Auctioneers will want the entire contents of the house only if there are some choice pieces.

Price your pieces for your local market. It takes an expert to determine the age of a piece in a period style. A Chippendale-style chair dating from the eighteenth century is worth $1,500-$150,000; a Chippendale style chair from the nineteenth century is worth $2,000-$3,000; a twentieth-century copy is worth $200-$500.

If you have good reason to believe that your furniture is antique and may not bring a good price at a local auction, write to an out-of-town auction gallery about selling it. Send photographs of the front, back, and bottom construction. Oak furniture sells best in the West, elaborate Victorian in the South, and Art Deco in the East.

For period or old reproduction chairs of average quality: A pair is worth three times as much as a single; a set of four is worth six to seven times as much as a single. Six chairs are worth ten to twelve times as much as a single. A set of eight chairs is worth twelve to fifteen times the price of one chair. A set of twelve chairs including two armchairs is worth twenty times the price of one chair. Dining room table and chair sets should be sold as a unit. The breakfronts and buffets may be sold separately for better overall prices. A bedroom set usually brings the highest price when sold as a unit. Don't split the set so a friend can have the dresser. Offer the full set, but take bids on the individual pieces in case you can't sell the full set at a high enough price. Sell a piano to a local piano store, or place an ad to sell it from the house. Unless top quality, pianos are very difficult to sell. The old square pianos do not stay in tune, sell low, and are usually purchased to be made into desks.

Serious collectors searching for pre-1875 painted furniture in original condition will pay a premium. Choice, painted furniture is worth 50 percent more than an unpainted similar piece. The paint was not as durable as polished wood so it may be in poor condition and may have to be sold at a lower price. Even black ebonized Victorian furniture, although old and in a popular style, is worth 30 percent less than a similar piece with an unpainted finish, unless the paint is in mint condition. It is very difficult to restore. If the original finish on a chair or table was painted and the piece has been stripped to natural wood, deduct 75 percent. In other words, a painted piece that is stripped is worth less than a similar piece that was originally made with a natural wood finish. Painted furniture of the twentieth century is not rare and not yet in great demand.

Wicker, twig, cast iron, and horn pieces are back in style and sell well. Furniture from the 1950s by important makers brings good prices at auction or from Art Deco dealers. Some pieces from the 1960s are gaining in value. Names like WOOTON, HERMAN MILLER, GUSTAV STICKLEY, LARKIN, HUNZINGER, HERTER, ROUX, NOGUCHI, and RUSSEL WRIGHT add value.

Do not worry too much about how to move heavy antique furniture. There are always local movers listed in the telephone book. There are also some long-distance moving companies that specialize in moving uncrated antique pieces. Ask any local antiques dealer for the name of someone in your area.

Most of the furniture that is bought and sold in America is English or American in design and manufacture. Other, less easily recognized types are also in demand. Pictures of all these types of furniture can be found in books at your library. Identify your piece from the pictures, then check in the price books for values.

IMPORTED

Oriental (18th-20th century). Dark woods, often teak or rosewood, oriental designs. Made in China, Japan, Korea, or India. Later pieces have much elaborate carving. Lacquer, stone inlay. Some pieces were made in European shapes but with oriental woods and decorations. All-wooden armchairs, screens, plant stands, large display cabinets.

Scandinavian (18th-19th century). Brightly painted peasant designs cover much of the wood. Blue and red preferred. Large cupboards, lift-top blanket chests, carved wooden chairs.

Dutch (18th-19th centuries). Traditional European shapes in Chippendale through Victorian styles covered with elaborate inlay in small designs. Chairs, tables, chests of drawers, cabinets.

French (18th-19th century). Louis XV style, rococo flowing lines, ornate curves, cabriole legs, asymmetrical; and Louis XVI style, dainty, neoclassical, straight legs.

Fantasy Furniture (1800-present). Egyptian, carved shell chairs, Greek, Persian-inspired accessories, Bugatti designs.

AMERICAN

Late Empire (1825-1850). Heavy; pillar and scroll design. Mahogany,

cherry, maple, solid or veneer. Chests of drawers, round wooden knobs. Scroll-arm, rolltop sofas, lyre-base tables, sleigh beds, wooden-back chairs.

Victorian Gothic Revival (1830-1850). Designs resemble gothic church arches; carvings, little upholstery. Walnut, rosewood, mahogany, maple. Straight-back chairs with carved high backs, settees, armchairs, washstands.

Victorian Rococo Revival (1845-1865). French-looking, onamented, curved, carved fruit and flowers. Rosewood, mahogany. Curved sofas, parlor sets, marble-topped tables, slipper chairs.

Eastlake Victorian (1870-1900). Rectangular furniture, contrasting color woods, incised lines. Walnut, burl, maple, veneer, oak. Highback beds, washstands, chairs, chests, and mirror dressers.

Colonial Revival or Centennial (1876-1950). Copies of the 18th- and early 19th-century William and Mary, Chippendale, Sheraton, Empire, and other designs.

Golden Oak (1880-1920). Mass-produced, heavy. Dark or light oak, ash. Asymmetrical cabinets, chests of drawers, rolltop desks, claw-feet or pedestal dining tables, press-back chairs.

Cottage (1890-1920). Painted Eastlake adaptations, marbleized or solid color paint, trimmed with lines, flowers, pictorial medallions. Bedroom sets, small tables, chairs.

Mission (1900-1920). Straight lines, solid wood usually oak, no ornamentation, smooth surface. Rectangular tables, chairs, sofas, bookcases.

Office Furniture (1900-1930). Mission-inspired working pieces made for the office. Filing cabinets, large rolltop desks, lift-up glass-front stacked bookcases, captain's chairs, children's school desks.

Art Deco (1910-1930). Straight lines, geometric. Light-colored wood or black lacquer finish, mirrored surfaces. Square pedestal tables, bedroom sets.

Twig or Rustic (1890-1930). Bark-covered branches joined together to form chairs, tables, beds, plant stands, smoking stands. Animal horns, antlers, other natural materials used regionally.

Country (1700-1950). A "look," unsophisticated, worn, simple, handmade, solid wood, faded paint. Tables, large cupboards and shelf units, wooden chairs, stools.

Waterfall (1930s). Patterned veneer on cabinet doors, tabletops, or bed backs placed to make V-shaped design. Rounded corners, round mirrors. Base woods are poplar or ash. Bedroom and dining room sets.

Moderne (1930-1950s). Sometimes called Hollywood Art Deco. The theatrical, modern-looking furniture seen in movies. Art Deco but a bit less severe and more dramatic. Coffee tables, dressing tables, glass-topped tables, rounded upholstered chairs.

Mid-Century Modern (1950s). Organically shaped, new materials and technology. Plastic, plywood, chrome, steel. Interchangeable units and stacked chairs, coffee tables, wall-mounted shelf units. Blond "Scandinavian" sets.

Wicker (1850-1930).

Brass and Iron Beds (1900-1920).

PRICING AND REPAIRS
Repairs seriously change the value of an antique or collectible. The rarer the piece, the more acceptable a repair. An eighteenth-century American table can have replaced casters, a spliced foot, or even a restored edge, with no great loss in value. A twentieth-century table should be in pristine condition. The supply is greater, and a perfect table probably exists. You should do easy repairs before you try to sell a piece. Dust and wipe off dirt. Rub the edges of drawers with paraffin to make them open easily. Reglue any loose parts or veneer.

Tighten knobs and glue any wobbly legs by forcing wood glue into the joints. Polish brasses if they need it. A light rubbing with scratch polish will often improve the look of the surface.

Sometimes an accurate restoration is impossible because there is no model to follow. We saw a Goddard block-front desk last year that should have been worth over $200,000. Unfortunately, all of the legs had been cut off in the 1880s, and new feet were made. There is no way to know what the original legs looked like, so the desk is worth about $20,000.

Formulas for pricing are only a guide and not infallible. These formulas are for pieces in attractive condition with almost invisible repairs.

Chest of drawers, good to excellent quality, pre-1850. If brasses are replacements, deduct 10 percent. If finish has been totally restored, deduct 10 percent. If one front foot has been replaced, deduct 10 percent. If two rear feet have been replaced, deduct 15 percent. If all feet have been replaced, deduct 70 percent. If important decorative carving has been replaced or if veneer is new, deduct 20 percent.

Chair, good quality, pre-1850. Look in a general price guide for a chair similar to yours. If the slip seat has been replaced, deduct nothing. If glued block braces (the structural supports under the chair) have been replaced, deduct nothing. If one or two leg brackets are restored, deduct nothing. If all leg brackets are restored, deduct 10 percent. If one leg is replaced, deduct 33 percent. If a splat or an important part of chair back has been replaced, deduct 33 percent. If top crest rail is replaced, deduct 10-15 percent.

Early nineteenth-century furniture with veneered fronts. If veneer is replaced, deduct 50-90 percent. Original veneer is an important part of the design of the furniture. A small, well-matched patch does not lower the value, but a totally new veneer surface cannot imitate the original appearance. Sometimes just one drawer has replaced veneer. If it is a well-matched piece of wood, deduct 50 percent. If all the veneer on the front of the piece is replaced, deduct 90 percent.

Eighteenth- or early nineteenth-century table, good quality. If top is replaced, deduct 50 percent. If one plain leg is replaced, deduct 20 percent. If all carved feet have been restored or replaced, deduct 90 percent. Watch out for "marriages," a top of one table put on the legs of another. Look underneath the top for signs of this. There will be unexpected screw holes or color variations.

Desk, pre-1900. If the interior compartments or drawers are missing, deduct 30 percent. If the interior compartments or drawers are accurately replaced, deduct 20 percent. If one interior drawer or drawer front is a replacement, deduct nothing. If the desk has been created from a reworked bookshelf cabinet (drawer removed, fall front added), deduct 75 percent.

Other. If the top of a table or chest is warped but can be fixed, deduct 20 percent. If the top of a table or chest is extremely warped or split, the sides split, or inlay or marquetry badly damaged, deduct 75 percent. If the top of a table or chest has been reworked, given rounded edges, extra trim or carving, deduct 50 percent. If the marble top of a Victorian table is badly cracked or damaged, deduct 50 percent.

Watch out for repairs that affect value on later pieces of furniture. Glass doors are more desirable than wooden doors because they are preferred for display. Add 50 percent to the value for glass. If the glass is a replacement for a solid wooden door, subtract 50 percent.

Welsh cupboards with original spoon holders are worth 50 percent more than plain cupboards. If the spoon holders have been newly added, price the cupboard like a plain one.

ooo

Glass

Glass is one of the most difficult types of antiques to identify and price. Few pieces are marked, reproductions abound, and quality is not always the reason for a price. All types of glass are collected: early blown and molded glass, colored art glass from the 1890s, cameo glass made of carved layers, cut glass, pressed glass, Depression glass, elegant glass of the 1930s to 1970s, modern art glass, studio glass, and even decorated drinking glasses with comic figures on them. A novice will have great difficulty (some experts do too) in identifying reproductions. It is a major task to learn the names of the many glasswares.

> A smart young man stopped by on the third day of a yard sale and bought a vase for $3. He found a signature, looked up the maker, G. Argy Rousseau, and later sold the vase at auction for $900. He did the research necessary to get the highest price.

First, sort your glassware. Sets of goblets, plates, and cups and saucers should be put in one group. Vases, figurines, candlesticks, and other decorative items should be considered separately. We wrote *Kovels' Know Your Antiques* and *Kovels' Know Your Collectibles* for the beginner. There is a chapter on glass in each book, written to help make identifying the type of glass a less complicated task. The colored art glass of Victorian times is described in terms of color and design. The names Pomona, Peachblow, amberina, Quezal, and others will make more sense after you study a little. You might also go to a large antiques show and look for glassware that resembles yours. The dealers will be glad to tell you what it is called. Then you can look up the prices in any of the books listed in the Appendix. Victorian glass has been reproduced and modern versions are made today. Milk glass, purple or blue slag glass (it resembles a marble cake), and many types of colored glass baskets, cruets, and plates are being made for the gift-shop trade. You probably can't tell the old from the new without expert help. If you know your glass vase belonged to a great-grandmother, you should research the value carefully. Some of the strangest looking glass pieces are of great value.

Almost all types of gold iridescent glass, one of the types made by L.C. Tiffany, is very valuable. Any piece of glass that can be identified as being from the Tiffany workshops has a high value. The signature on a piece doubles the value. Also look for STEUBEN, DURAND, QUEZAL, KEW BLAS, WEBB, and small trademarks like the fleur-de-lis or initials that identify the makers.

Blown glass of the eighteenth and early nineteenth centuries is older than art glass but seldom brings as high a price unless very rare. Although the English collectors eagerly buy goblets with blown and twisted stems and decanters with applied decorations, the American collectors have never been as interested. Many decanters from the 1820s sell for under $150. Early blown bottles are a whole different story. Very rare mold-blown whiskey flasks can sell for thousands of dollars. Even common ones sell for hundreds. (See section on Bottles.)

Cut glass, especially the very elaborate pieces known as "brilliant cut," was not easy to sell until the 1970s. Suddenly, after over fifty years of being out of favor, it was back in demand. The cost of making the glass was high, so the antique pieces began to rise in value. Today old cut glass is high priced, very much in demand, and, if in perfect condition, it sells very quickly. Small or large nicks lower value by 25-50 percent depending on rarity of design. If the glass is sick (cloudy) and does not seem to wash clean, deduct 40 percent. If the object is made of colored and clear glass, add 100 percent. If the glass is signed, add 25 percent. The signature can be difficult to find but is usually on the smooth surface of the inside of a bowl. Because the marks are acid-etched, they are very faint and can only be seen if the bowl is turned to catch the light the right way. Ask an antiques dealer to show you a signature on a piece of cut glass and you will quickly learn how to find others. Only about one in ten pieces is signed. There are several kinds of feet that could be put on a piece of cut glass. A round disc and short stem on a vase are common, but the same type of foot on a carafe, sugar or creamer, bowl, jug, decanter, or ice tub adds 15 percent. A tall foot on a compote is expected, but the same tall foot on a berry bowl, spooner, cologne, sugar, or creamer adds 15 percent. If there are decorations on the feet, add 2 percent more. Peg feet on a vase, bowl, bucket, creamer,

A green carnival glass tumbler, purchased at a lawn sale for 25¢, was kept on a window ledge in the kitchen of a Missouri home. The owner saw a report of an auction of carnival glass. Curious about the value of the kitchen tumbler, she called the auction house, then sent a picture. The tumbler was identified as the rare "Frolicking Bear" pattern and sold for over $4,000 at auction. If she had not checked on the pattern and value, the glass would have remained a pencil holder on the window ledge.

or sugar raise the value by 10 percent. Cut glass prices are listed in the general price books. It is best to try to determine the name of the pattern by looking at the cut glass picture books in your library. Even without the pattern name, you can decide approximate value.

Cameo glass and Art Nouveau- and Art Deco-inspired glasswares are very popular and very high priced today. Quality and signature are important. Often a small piece that will fit on a breakfront shelf is preferred to a very large vase since serious collectors run out of space. Cameo glass is made of several layers of glass of different colors. The design is made by cutting away the top color to make patterns. The French cameo glass was inspired by the Art Nouveau tradition. GALLÉ, A. WALTER, DAUM NANCY, ARGY-ROUSSEAU, MÜLLER FRERES, DE VEZ, DELATTE, and LEGRAS are names found on French cameo glass that add to the value. If cameo glass is signed by Gallé, add 100 percent. If the piece is signed by a less important maker, add 50 percent to the value of a similar unsigned piece. The best name of all, from a seller's viewpoint, is WOODALL. He was an English artist and his cameo glass vases are worth thousands of dollars. The American Steuben glassworks made an acid-cut, cameolike ware that sells well.

LALIQUE is another marketable name. Lalique glass is still being made. The older pieces, signed ''R. Lalique,'' were made before 1945 and are worth 100-500 percent more than the newer ones. (The pieces made after 1945 are signed ''Lalique.'') The best pieces of Lalique are the more uncommon colored pieces. Most of the glass was made in frosted, clear, or opalescent glass.

Pressed glass, made in Victorian times, was a very popular collectible in the 1930s but lost favor until the 1980s. It was inexpensive and easy to find, perhaps because the design was unfashionable or because almost undetectable reproductions were made. The prices remained low until collectors began to realize that the 1890 pressed glass goblet now sold for the same price as a 1930s Depression glass piece, and bargain hunters began looking for pressed glass sets again. To price these you need a good book listing patterns. Learn the name of your pattern, then look in the latest edition of a price guide for a retail value. Only perfect pieces sell because the supply is plentiful. Pressed glass sells best at a general antiques show or through mail-order ads.

Carnival glass, an inexpensive iridescent glass popular in the early twentieth century, can be sold to the interested collector or used as a decorative accessory for a home. The highest prices are for rare patterns and forms; punch bowls and certain pitchers and lamps sell well. Ordinary carnival glass is not high priced, so be realistic when you set your selling price. Check the carnival glass guides to see if you own a rare pattern or color. Most of the guides have sketches or photographs of each pattern. It is a bit complicated to understand how to identify the color of carnival glass. The color of the glass itself, not the color of the iridescence seen on the top, is the determining factor.

Depression glass began gaining favor with collectors during the 1970s. It was then that the pale pink or green lacy pattern pieces were first noticed. Sets were assembled from garage sales. A cup often cost a nickel and a plate a dime. Today there are many serious collectors of all types of Depression glass, from the pastels to the bright ruby, cobalt blue, or forest green. Hobnail, the Sandwich patterns, and even enamel-decorated pieces are wanted. The highest prices are paid at Depression glass shows. Try to find one in your area. Another good place to sell your glass is through the trade papers that specialize in glass. Prices are easily determined from the price books. Patterns are pictured and priced. There are at least ten current price books on Depression glass. A few reproductions of Depression glass have been made: some are sets for everyday use; some are copies of the rarities, like the pink Cherry Blossom cookie jar that sells for hundreds of dollars if original.

In the 1980s, a group of buyers appeared who were willing to pay good prices for the studio and art glass made from the 1950s on. VENINI, KOSTA, ORREFORS, HOLMEGAARD, and BODA are some of the most important foreign names. There are also American makers with names like EDRIS ECKHARDT, DOMINICK LABINO, and JIM LUNDBERG. In general, the more Art Moderne in appearance, the more abstract the forms and heavier the glass bodies, the higher the prices. Signatures are very important for these pieces.

One of the best-selling types of glass is that unnamed group made from the 1930s to the 1970s. It is sometimes called "elegant glass-ware." Included are certain patterns by HEISEY, FENTON, FOSTORIA, CAMBRIDGE, IMPERIAL, and DUNCAN AND MIL-LER. These and a few other American companies made fine quality, cut-crystal goblets, wines, plates, and figurines for the gift shop trade. Heisey is well known for both its decorated pieces and its heavy, modern, glass animal figures. Very high prices are paid for these figures and for the goblets with animal- or bird-shaped stems. Small is big with the animal figures; the small sizes sell for the most.

If your glass was inherited from parents or grandparents, you could easily have some of these pieces. They were sold in all parts of the country and were popular wedding gifts. The problem is identification. There is a Heisey glass museum and several clubs for the other types of glass. A clear photograph and letter to these groups may get you the information about age and pattern name that you need to determine a price from the price guides. There are books showing many of the patterns, but it is not a quick research project. A few of the pieces are signed with initials or insignia, but most are not. If you have this type of glass, go to the antiques shows and glass shows and ask questions to try to determine a price. Most small local auction galleries do very well with this type of glassware and get high prices for you. They should be able to identify it and tell you the approximate value. It is difficult to sell a partial set of drinking glasses because the new owner will not be able to fill in the twelfth for a party. All other types of glass made after the 1930s can sell for surprisingly high prices. We have seen and purchased many pieces of unmarked Heisey for under $5 at garage sales where they are often overlooked and underpriced by the amateur seller.

Glass candlesticks of any kind are now selling very well. They seem to have come back into fashion in the 1980s. Remember, even if your glass looks like dime-store junk to you, or like a misshapen ashtray made from a glob of glass, you are selling and not buying. To the trained eye your glass dish may be a treasure, and you must train your eye enough to recognize the high-priced items.

A list of glass matching services can be found in the appendix.

Don Hall of Rochester, New York, collected Depression glass as an investment, planning to sell it eventually to send his daughter to college. After twelve years, he sold part of it at auction and part by mail order and had enough to pay her tuition.

ooo

Indian Artifacts

American Indian artifacts sell well to the right collectors in the right areas. Indians lived in all parts of the United States, but the major dealers, collectors, and shows are in the Southwest. Arrowheads dug up on your farm should be sold to nearby specialists. Any Indian item sells best closest to its point of origin, if that is known. If you have a collection of baskets, clothing, or carvings assembled from many sources, you should contact a Southwestern or major Eastern dealer or gallery. A large collection or an important piece should be appraised by a competent expert on Indian art, a rarity in most cities. It will be of no help to go to the average appraiser of fine arts for values. Ask for references and be sure the appraiser has appraised Indian art before.

There are many laws about buying and selling Indian artifacts. It is illegal to sell or buy anything decorated with eagle feathers. Many Indian pieces have been illegally obtained from burial sites, and there can be problems. Mexican Indian pieces of importance are, by law, kept in Mexico, and smuggled items will be confiscated in both the United States and Mexico. Some items are religious, and the Indians themselves will try to force the seller to return them to the original tribal owners. For all these reasons we urge you to contact an expert if you inherit a large collection. You must be able to prove your right to the pieces if you try to sell them at any public show or auction.

Many baskets, dolls, and beaded pieces were made by the Indians to sell to tourists in the early 1900s. These all sell quickly at reasonable prices, and you can learn the values through the general price books. It is the unusual, a carved figure or ceremonial pipe, that is very valuable.

In the 1930s a seven-year-old child bought a mask at a churchyard sale. It cost 25¢. For the next ten years she wore it as a Halloween mask. It depicted a hawk, painted blue, with red leather eye flaps and beak, and had inset horsehair. A friend realized it might be an authentic Indian piece, so the mask was shown to an expert. It had been made by Northwest Coast Indians. When sold in 1985, it brought $45,100.

Look in *The Indian Trader* or other publications about Indian art. Dealers and shows will be listed, and if you live far away, you can offer your pieces with pictures by mail. Rarity, artistic value, condition, and age determine the price of an Indian artifact.

ooo

Ivory

All ivory does not come from elephant tusks. Ivory can also be from other animals, such as walruses, hippopotamuses, or whales. Some vegetable materials have a similar texture and density and may look like ivory, but it is possible to see the growth rings on a large piece of an elephant's tusk. Some types of plastic look very much like ivory. Determining whether you have ivory or plastic may prove a problem. The standard test is to heat a needle red hot while holding it with pliers. Press the point of the needle into the bottom of the ivory piece. Plastic will melt, but ivory will not.

The value of ivory objects is determined by the quality of the carving and the condition. If the ivory is milk white because it was washed, deduct 30 percent. If the ivory is noticeably cracked, deduct 75 percent. Oriental ivory carvings, from large elephant tusks to tiny netsuke (Japanese buttons), sell quickly to friends and dealers. New ones are being made, but premium prices are paid for the old ones. A signature adds 50 percent or more.

If you suspect you have an old, top-quality ivory carving, make an appointment with the proper person at your local art museum. You should be able to learn the age and the quality. Do not ask the value. A museum cannot appraise for you. Once you know the age, it is not difficult to compare your carving with others of similar quality that you can find at good shops, shows, or auctions. Price guides list hundreds of ivory items under such headings as Ivory, Scrimshaw, Netsuke, Carving, Orientalia, or Jewelry.

Scrimshaw is ivory or ivorylike material decorated or carved by sailors. It is a very popular, high-priced form of folk art and sells to maritime collectors and folk art enthusiasts at important shows and auctions. If you have some old scrimshaw, a carved tooth, a small box, tool, or a whimsy, it should be appraised by an expert before it is sold. Beware! Imitation scrimshaw, especially carved teeth, has been made for the past twenty years or more. Some plastic reproductions are so realistic they have fooled auctioneers. Even poor-quality, modern ivory carvings can be sold, but they have a low value, about half the retail price.

An English woman found a 7½-inch-by-3½-inch piece of carved ivory at a "jumble sale." She later took it to an auction gallery, and her Carolingian ivory plaque, made in the ninth century and carved with the figure of St. John, sold for a record price of $470,857.

ᴑᴑᴑ

Jewelry

Jewelry has a special monetary worth known in the trade as "meltdown." This is the value of the piece if it is totally destroyed and the wholesale price of the gold, silver, and gem is calculated. You must *never* sell for less than meltdown. It is like giving dollar bills away. Grandmother left you her heirloom diamond pin, probably dating from about 1910. It is made of white metal and has many small diamonds set in the old-fashioned way. You might be able to take it to a local jeweler to learn the meltdown value. "Jewelry Buyers" are listed in the Yellow Pages of the phone book, and the ads indicate those that buy "estate" jewelry and scrap. These are the people to tell you the lowest price you should take. They will test the metal to see if it is white gold, silver, or platinum; they will check the diamonds and then tell you what they will pay. Sometimes there is a small fee for this service. Most do not take into consideration the artistic value of the piece or the antique interest. These dealers will buy old jewelry, broken watches, gold teeth, anything that is made of precious stones or metals. This is the place to sell damaged silverware and jewelry.

Now that you have a base price, you can determine what a jeweler who sells antique jewelry will pay. This includes the added dollars offered for the artistic value. Of course, you can also sell it to a friend, to an antiques dealer, or through an auction house. Some jewelers will take the pieces on consignment.

Remember, styles in modern jewelry change and influence the value of antique pieces. In recent years large brooches have become stylish. Bar pins, which were unsalable as wearable jewelry in the 1970s, are now in demand. Large antique brooches have a low break-up value because the stones are usually small. The pins are especially attractive to the insurance-conscious, mugger-wary buyer, and they sell well. If you have decided it would be nice to make a modern pin using the old stones, be sure to check the prices carefully. It might be better to sell the old piece as an antique and buy a totally new one. The old stones are often of poor quality, and the expense of a new setting for the old stones may be more than the value of the finished, reworked piece.

Jewelry is one of the items that can easily be sold directly to a dealer. Often shops and jewelers who sell ''estate jewelry'' will make you an offer. Some large department stores sell estate or antique jewelry in a special department or at special sales several times a year. The buyers for these departments might want your jewelry. If you go to an antiques show and see dealers with pieces like yours, you can probably sell your items. Because most shops and dealers specialize, it is best to look for someone with jewelry like yours. A dealer who specializes in watches and gold chains may not want a small diamond pin.

One problem with selling antiques, especially jewelry, is proof of ownership. The buyer of your jewelry must be sure that you really own the piece and have a legal right to sell it. Many pieces of stolen jewelry are offered to dealers during the year. Have good personal identification with you and offer to show it. Don't send a teenager to

sell jewelry. The dealers are fearful that even if the jewelry belongs in the family, the seller is not the true owner.

There are often marks on jewelry that add to the value. A known signature adds up to 30 percent. Although most marks are found on the back of the piece, be sure to check the catch on a necklace and the sides of a large piece. If it says FABERGÉ (ФАБЕРЖЕ), you have a piece worth thousands of dollars. If the name TIFFANY, LALIQUE, FOUQUET, MARCUS, or CASTILLO appears, the piece is worth hundreds or thousands of dollars. If it is a piece of silver jewelry marked GEORG JENSEN or HA (Hector Aguilar), it may be worth hundreds of dollars.

Use a magnifying glass. The hallmarks used on silver or gold are a series of small pictures like this 🐟 🏺 Ⓥ ☾ . Check the meaning in the appropriate books. Some marks indicate the country of origin. This may be important in setting the price. Danish and Mexican silver has an added value for collectors. Some marks indicate the makers. The names that add to the value, especially the names of important designers of the Art Nouveau and twentieth-century Arts and Crafts schools, can be found in books. The library will also have books on jewelry makers and on silver marks. (Remember the words ''silver plate'' in an English publication mean solid silver, but in an American book they signify just a thin coating of silver over another metal.)

The words and symbols on jewelry can be confusing. Pure gold is 24 karat, but too soft to be useful for jewelry. 14K (karat), 18K, 20K, and 22K are gold quality marks indicating solid gold (not hollow). If it is 14 parts pure gold and 10 parts of another metal, it is 14/24 parts gold or 14 karat.

''Gold filled,'' ''gold plated,'' ''rolled gold,'' or ''gold overlay'' means your jewelry has limited meltdown value. It has only a layer of gold on another metal. Be careful, because sometimes the label is ''14K gold filled,'' which probably means it is classed as ''costume jewelry.''

''Sterling,'' ''coin,'' and ''800'' are desirable silver quality marks. Nickel silver and German silver are not silver at all. They are white metals similar to pewter. ''Quadruple plate'' and ''triple plate'' mean the pieces have only a thin layer of silver over another, less valuable metal.

Platinum may look like silver but is much more valuable. If it says ''PLATINUM'' in tiny letters on the back of the jewelry, take it to a jeweler for a professional appraisal before you sell it.

Prices are up for cultured pearls. Irregularly shaped freshwater pearls, baroque cultured pearls, and smooth, spherical pearls are in style. The graduated pearl necklace is temporarily out of style, and the best prices today are for strings of pearls of one size. Good pearls are always strung with a knot between each bead. There is a strange rule for drop-shaped natural pearls. If they are drilled end to end they are worth 40 percent less than if they are drilled at the top only. A black (ultraviolet) light will tell if your pearls are cultured or fakes. Cultured and real pearls look slightly fluorescent, but fake pearls glow a bright white.

The glow produced by the black light will also help show if stones are real or glass. If the setting of the jewelry is made of real gold, have a jeweler check any large stones to see if they are good quality diamonds, sapphires, or rubies, or just plain glass. Even experts are being fooled by zirconium, a diamond substitute. Gemstones are usually cold to the touch and very hard; a stone with worn edges is probably just colored glass.

Some stones, old or new, are doublets or even triplets. That means a piece of the colored stone is joined with clear stone. Almost all gem-quality opals sold today are doublets or triplets. We once bought an emerald, complete with a Colombian government guarantee of authenticity, for a bargain price. It turned out to be a clear piece of the mineral beryl, called an ''emerald'' when it is green. Underneath the clear part was a dark green piece of glass. The top tested as an emerald, the green glass improved the color. By making it a doublet, the color was enhanced and the finished stone looked dark green, but it had no gem value.

There are some styles of very early Spanish, Hungarian, and English jewelry made with foil-backed stones. A piece of silver or colored foil is set behind a clear or colored stone to enhance the color. These are wanted by collectors as examples of a rare type of antique jewelry.

Some types of antique jewelry are not being made today. Mourning jewelry was often made of braided hair set with gold trim as a memorial to the departed. Enameled rings with images of funeral urns and special rings given as gifts at funerals are also among the best known mourning jewelry. All these are wanted by collectors, although they are not considered popular as wearable jewelry. Berlin ironwork was made for a short time in the nineteenth century. It was actually made of iron, instead of gold, during a time when gold was needed for the war effort. This is rare and valuable to serious collectors. So are gold jewelry set with feathers from China and jet or black beads made

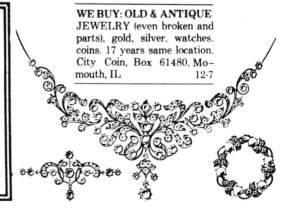

from composition material. Both were popular in the late nineteenth century. Hatpins, elaborate combs, watch-chain slides, studs, scarf rings, posy holders, watch fobs, and other similar types of jewelry are not worn much today but are wanted by special collectors.

The English made a special type of jewelry from carved quartz backed with a specially applied picture, often of a dog or horse. The finished stone looks like glass with a piece of paper behind it. It is actually a very valuable form, usually set in cuff links for men. The Chinese made clear quartz beads like miniature crystal balls set in loops of wire; they look like glass but are very valuable.

Cameos are of special interest. Agate or carnelian cameos have more value than shell cameos. The light pink and white shell cameos are easy to identify because the curve of the shell can always be seen. Stone cameos have flat backs. The quality of the carving and the setting help determine the value. The more detail, the better. Remember, beautiful women in the nineteenth century were chubby-faced and had full noses. Today's beauty is thin and pug-nosed. This helps to date a cameo.

Don't underestimate the value of old beads of amethyst, pink quartz, garnet, amber, or colored stones. It takes an expert to recognize the quality, so be sure to show them to a qualified appraiser before putting them in the junk box at your garage sale. Don't think that something you consider ugly, like lava stone (dirty gray), or a realistic bug pin, has no value. Gold pins and necklaces designed with snakes, beetles, and dragonflies are of extra value.

Some of the important early jewelry by innovative designers, such as RENÉ LALIQUE or many of the English Arts and Crafts artists, were deliberately made from worthless materials like glass, base metals, cut steel, inexpensive moonstones, and enamels. The quality of workmanship can make these as valuable as gold and precious stone jewelry. Look carefully for a name.

American Indian jewelry has a special market. If you can trace the history of an Indian necklace, pin, or ring back over fifty years, it may be very valuable. Try to sell it to Indian collectors or through Western dealers.

Compacts, lipstick cases, money clips, cigarette cases, and cigarette lighters are sometimes made of precious metals and stones. These should be sold like any other type of precious jewelry. Those made of imitation gold and silver also have a resale value, and they should be sold to costume jewelry dealers or to specialists who favor pens, pencils, lighters, and other ''smalls.''

COSTUME JEWELRY

Old beads, rhinestones, marcasite, enameled Art Nouveau and Art Deco, and plastic pieces are all in vogue. The major auction houses have even had sales of the costume jewelry made since the 1920s. Names that add value to costume jewelry are EISENBERG ICE, HOBE, SCHIAPARELLI, HATTIE CARNEGIE, KRAMER,

MATISSE, WEISS, VOGUE, HOLLYCRAFT, JOSEPH WIESNER, SARAH COVENTRY, REGENCY, VENDOME, and FLORENZA. MONET, CORO, TRIFARI, NAPIER, and KENNETH LANE are still working, but pre-1960 pieces by these companies bring premium prices.

Look at the new jewelry being offered in the department stores. Run-of-the-mill old pieces are worth about 60 percent of the cost of comparable new ones. Old rhinestones are probably worth more than new ones because old rhinestones are of better quality. Two- or three-color Bakelite plastic pins are worth more than new jewelry. So are many of the pieces with important makers' names.

Most ordinary old costume jewelry is sold for the best prices at house and garage sales, at flea markets, and to mall-show dealers or vintage-clothing stores. Rhinestone and plastic costume jewelry and good Art Deco designs are being sold at even the best antiques shows.

ooo

Kitchen Paraphernalia

Anything that was ever used in a kitchen, from a wrought-iron kettle holder of the 1700s to a 1960s juicer or reamer, has a sale value. Most buyers want something nostalgic and decorative to put in a modern kitchen. Any unusual object will sell quickly at a house sale or flea market or to friends. The antiques shops usually deal in utensils that were made before 1900 and in kitchen tools of the Art Deco period. Very modern-looking equipment, preferably chrome, bright-colored pottery or plastic pitchers, toasters, canisters, and a few other objects with Art Deco designs are in demand. The electric items of the past, such as old toasters, mixers, and waffle irons, have little value unless the design is very unusual and decorative. An electric toaster with a blue willow porcelain plaque on the side will sell. The

same toaster without the attractive sides is worth almost nothing. A rare glass iron sells for hundreds of dollars; an electric metal iron is unwanted.

Think of the kitchen gadgets in terms of "How will it look on a wall or shelf?" Anything with red and white or green and cream does well. These were the colors favored in the 1930s. Colored plastic handles add value to old eggbeaters and other utensils. Eggbeaters are very salable. The nineteenth-century ones are iron; by 1900 the eggbeater had an iron gear but stainless steel beaters. The beaters and gears soon became all stainless. Many eggbeaters have dates in raised numbers on the gears. Ice-cream dippers sell for much more money than seems possible. Check the price guides carefully. Almost any dipper manufactured before 1940 is worth over $50, many much more. Juicers or reamers also sell for high prices. Favored are those with colored glass or figural shapes. All out-of-production cookie cutters, molds, nutcrackers, openers, and apple peelers have value.

Mixing bowls of all kinds, pitchers, storage jars, and other ceramic kitchen items have a dual value. They are wanted by both the kitchen and the pottery collectors. (See section on Pottery and Porcelain.) Check the maker from the marks and look in both a general price guide and a kitchen price book.

Your mother's and grandmother's kitchens are still filled with treasures: scrapers, forks, funnels, dessert molds, ice-cream molds and pans, either purchased new or "borrowed" from an aging parent who no longer baked. Now that microwaves, electric burners, self-cleaning ovens, and dishwashers have changed the requirements, many old pots and bowls are out of favor with cooks. Don't throw anything away until you check on the value. Even molded-plastic string holders, clocks, and menu planners can have value. All salt and pepper sets and stove or refrigerator sets are collected.

Don't ignore the old stove, refrigerator, vacuum cleaner, or washing machine. If decorative, they will sell, sometimes to an appliance store that needs one for a window display. Cookbooks and recipe pamphlets sell well, too. (See sections on Advertising; Books.)

In general, the oldest sells for the highest price. Items that are figural or colorful sell well; so do plastic, brass, and copper. Anything that moves, like an apple peeler, will sell. Aluminum is just starting to interest collectors. Early wooden items are wanted by "country" collectors, but sometimes not-so-old, but well-worn, wooden cutting boards and knives are overvalued by novice collectors.

Watch for the names DOVER and ENTERPRISE on metal kitchen gadgets.

ooo

Labels

All types of labels can be sold: cigar box labels for the top and sides of the box, fruit crate labels, food can labels, labels for luggage, beer bottles, tobacco pouches, and brooms. Most of the labels you find offered by dealers were found in old print shops or factories. Thousands of a single design were found. These were then resold in groups to dealers, often for less than 5¢ each. They were eventually sold as single labels to the collector. All the sales and resales included markups, so if you are buying common labels, you pay far more than twice the amount you will get if you are selling common labels. If you are fortunate enough to find an attic filled with the remains of your grandfather's label company, you have a treasure that should be sold to the dealers at the wholesale level. If you have a few orange crate labels that were framed and hung in your kitchen, you should sell them to a collector friend or at a flea market.

There has been a lot of hype in the selling of "stone-lithographed cigar box labels" as rare and valuable art. Some labels are rare, but most were found in bundles of a thousand and are not rare. The framed, matted examples found in gift shops are priced as decorative pictures and do not have the resale value you would hope for in the antiques market.

The cigar box and fruit crate labels are the best known, the larg-

est, and the most decorative, and so sell the highest. The other labels, from broom handle to beer bottle, are often just traded or sold for a few cents. You will find more hints on where to sell labels in the section on Advertising and Country Store Collectibles.

ooo

Lamps & Lighting

All types of lamps and lighting devices, including candlesticks, rushlight holders, and railroad lanterns, can be sold. Buyers purchase electric lamps to give light and to be decorative. Earlier forms of lighting are purchased either as part of a historic collection or as decorative pieces. To sell rushlights, old candlesticks, or even flashlights, you must find the proper collector. There are many who collect whale oil lamps, sandwich glass oil lamps, or some other specialty. These lighting devices are over 100 years old, and they sell well to dealers and at auctions. Judge the market by the device's appearance. Some belong in a ''country look'' home, while others are for the more sophisticated home filled with English nineteenth-century antiques.

Lamp bases from the late nineteenth and twentieth centuries were often made by important glass, pottery, or metalworking firms. A Tiffany lamp has value as a lamp and because it is Tiffany. Consequently, it sells for 100 percent more than a comparable lamp without the Tiffany mark. Cameo glass lamps by Gallé are also priced at least 100 percent more than common cameo lamps. The signature of a less important cameo glass maker adds only 50 percent. Sell these lamps and

A Midwestern country club decided to redecorate, and the committee sold the unfashionable, old light fixtures, porcelains, and lamps. Instead of asking for expert advice from an antiques collector, the committee sold everything to a dealer who paid the asking price, under $1,000. The dealer sold two pieces of Chinese porcelain for over $8,000, the antique light fixtures for $800 each, and the other items for thousands more. The committee was embarrassed to later learn that many of the items had been sold to members of the club who knew the value of the objects.

other special types of glass-shaded lamps to glass collectors.

A pottery lamp base made by an important pottery firm sometimes sells best as a lamp; occasionally, however, a lamp base is sold as a freestanding figurine or as a vase. If a hole for wiring is drilled in the bottom of a vase and the lamp is dismantled, the vase has a flaw. Factories like Rookwood or Van Briggle often made the base with the hole. The glaze even shows it is still in original condition. But the collector still pays half as much for a vase with a hole in the bottom. Figurines can usually be removed from the base with no indication of their original use. Lamps often have decorative metal bases that hide any indication of the maker of the pottery. It is a gamble to try to see if there is a mark.

In general, table lamps, unless by known makers, do not sell well. The highest prices are obtained at house sales or flea markets. Lampshades have suddenly become of interest to decorators, and old fringed or parchment shades can be sold with or without the lamp. Brass floor lamps have become popular again because many of the new ones are not made of solid brass. They can be refinished, rewired, and resold for a good price, so some dealers will buy a good metal floor lamp in any condition. Special types of lighting, like chandeliers, wall sconces, and torcheres, have limited markets.

The highest priced lamps have leaded or painted glass shades. If the maker can be identified from either design or signature, the lamp has added value. Thousands of dollars are paid for lamps by HANDEL, TIFFANY, DIRK VAN ERP or PAIRPOINT. Lamps sell for hundreds to thousands of dollars if made by STEUBEN, BRADLEY AND HUBBARD, DUFFNER & KIMBERLEY, EMERALITE, or JEFFERSON. Be sure to check in the Glass and Pottery sections if your lamp is marked by a known glass or pottery company. Look in the general price books for the maker's name. If it isn't listed, the maker was unimportant. Outstanding Art Deco or 1950s lamps sell for good prices no matter who made them; price is determined by the appeal.

ооо

Locks & Keys

Locks and keys have intrigued collectors since medieval times, and today collectors want everything from wrought-iron door locks to brass-tagged hotel keys. Wooden locks were used by the Egyptians about 2000 B.C. By the Middle Ages, huge metal locks were made to keep intruders out of the castle. Collectors divide locks into types and often specialize in categories such as railroad locks, trick locks, ball and chains, institutional locks, combination locks, padlocks, or locks made by special companies or for special events. A few locks

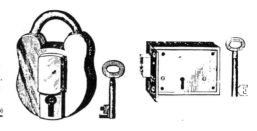

have historical value because they can be traced to a maker or historic building.

Locks sell well in flea markets and antiques stores, in restored and in original condition. Missing keys are not a problem. Best prices are paid for locks with special features, those with unusual mechanisms or rare logos, and those in pristine condition with the original box and key.

Keys are priced by rarity, shape, and age. Old iron keys are best, but some collectors now buy brass hotel keys either tagged or with the name on the key.

Look for the names YALE, VAN DORN IRON WORKS, and WINCHESTER.

ooo

Magazines

You may not be able to sell a book by its cover, but that is probably the best way to sell an old magazine. It is often the cover illustration that brings the money for old but not rare magazines. A picture of Marilyn Monroe on a *Life* magazine or a Norman Rockwell illustration on the cover of the *Saturday Evening Post* means there is more value than expected for the magazine. There are other parts of magazines that sell well: advertisements, paper dolls, and stories by famous authors. There is a moral dilemma here. Should you cut up the magazine and destroy it forever, or is it better to try to sell the parts? The whole magazine is often worth less money than the parts, but it does take time and extra research to know how to sell the individual pages. If you are selling the whole magazine, be sure that every page is still in your magazine. Missing pages lower the value dramatically. The first issue of any magazine has a value, even if the magazine is now unknown.

Collectors prize cover illustrations and the inside story illustrations by known artists. Names to look for are JESSIE WILLCOX SMITH, ROLF ARMSTRONG, HOWARD CHANDLER CHRISTY, PALMER COX, ERTÉ, HARRISON FISHER, J.C. LEYENDECKER, F. X. LEYENDECKER, CHARLES DANA GIBSON, JAMES MONTGOMERY FLAGG, KATE GREENAWAY,

WINSLOW HOMER, THOMAS NAST, ROSE O'NEILL, MAX-FIELD PARRISH, COLES PHILLIPS, ARTHUR RACKHAM, FREDERIC REMINGTON, PETTY, and NORMAN ROCKWELL. The early hand-colored fashion illustrations from the nineteenth-century *Godey's Ladies Book* or *The Delineator* are often torn from the magazines and sold separately. The woodcuts by Winslow Homer and other important artists that were in *Harper's Weekly* are also cut and removed.

Photographic covers and illustrations by less well-known artists can have extra value. A *Life* magazine photograph by ALFRED STEIG-LITZ or MARGARET BOURKE-WHITE adds value. A *Time* or *News-week* cover showing a baseball player, especially LOU GEHRIG, TY COBB, or BABE RUTH, a famous person from the 1920s-1940s, some World War II personalities such as ADOLF HITLER or GENERAL DOUGLAS MacARTHUR, or a famous movie star has added value. There is a special market for any type of Nazi and war memor-abilia.

Paper dolls are wanted by special collectors. The full-page pictures of dolls or the separate paper-doll books are collected and sell best at either doll shows or with other paper ephemera. Look for the dolls called LETTIE LANE, BETTY BONNET, KEWPIE, and DOLLY DINGLE.

Movie magazines are wanted by many of the buyers of other types of

---

4451   MAGAZINES WANTED

BUYING TEEN/ROCK & Movie Magazines (1950-86) Teen Screen, Teen Illustrated, Tiger Beat, Fave, "16", Dig, Movie Teen, Rave, Monkee Spectaculars, Rolling Stone, Creem, Circus, Rock Scene, Hit Parader, Song Hits, etc. Also Monkees & Beatles memorabilia, tour books, Fillmore posters, etc., etc. PH: **727/555-2040** Henke, Orchard St.

MONKEES AND Dark Shadows items such as magazines, gum cards, watches, paperbacks, toys, games, posters, TV Guides, movie items, etc. Send listing with prices. Rogosky, Box 1074. BG. Oaks, NY

RARE MONSTER magazines wanted: Demonique, Monster Parade, Monster Monthly, Witchcraft, Screen Monsters, Halls of Horror, Supernatural, Monster Mag, Best of Monster Times, etc. PH: **526/555-2378**. Mark Immen, Ford St.

HUNTING FOR back issues of magazine titled, gasm. Please quote. L.D. Dickart, Box 371106. **9999 First Street**

TREASURE & Western related magazines wanted for research. Condition not important. Send list to: JR Knight, Grass Lake

MOTION PICTURE Classic, January 1930. Send price: Roger Natteort 19th Ave. North, F Dodge **733/555-4321**

4441   PULPS WANTED

I WANT SF pulp. Buy or trade Japanese items. Masaakoka, 10-8569, Hyuga, Takatuki--Cho Japan.

MAGAZINES WANTED

COMIC BOOKS 1900-1960s, "Big Little Books," Sunday Funnies, Disney, Movie/TV Magazines. — Kenny, 10 Conacher, Ontario. M2M N6.
jly40081

OLD MAGAZINES PURCHASED: 1890s Thru 1970s; Movies, (Men's Girlie), Ladies, General, Price/Describe! - COLLECTOR'S, PO Box 1958382, Sequm, 98 WA
ap40081

TV GUIDES 1948-1985, Comic Books pre-1970, Vogue, Baseball Cards, Movie & TV Magazines, Doc Savage & Shadow items, Movie & TV paperbacks, James Bond, Avengers, & U.N.C.L.E. items. Send listing with prices. – Rogosky, Box 10, Glen NY
ap80027

OLD BUSINESS AND TYPEWRITER MAGAZINES WANTED

PHONOGRAPHIC WORLD (1885-1910)
PHONOGRAPHIC MAGAZINE (1886-1910)
TYPEWRITER TOPICS (1900-1930)

Any other 19th-century typewriter advertising, instructions, books.

I am also interested in the typewriters themselves.
Bryan Brady   12 Wrestling Trail
663/555-1698   Football, OK 00000

movie memorabilia. (See section on Celebrity Memorabilia.) We have seen recent ads placed by collectors trying to buy old *TV Guides*. There is also a rising interest in early sports and health magazines.

Magazines that have short stories by famous authors are collected by the same people who want old books. Often an author wrote the first version of a story in a magazine. Of special interest are science fiction magazine stories. These should be sold through antiquarian book dealers. (See section on Books.)

Girlie magazines or men's magazines are collected, but only the early ones sell for good prices. The collectors want special issues that feature BRIGITTE BARDOT, JANE FONDA, JAYNE MANS-FIELD, MARILYN MONROE, or CANDY STARR. *Playboy* generates the most interest. Because each issue includes comic strips, the comic magazine dealers often buy and sell the *Playboy* issues known as "fillers." These are the issues complete except for the center-fold.

Some collectors are searching for old advertisements. Best are the CREAM OF WHEAT ads by famous illustrators and the COCA-COLA ads that appeared on the back cover of *National Geographic* magazine for many years. Small ads from magazines which were published before 1940 are often cut out and sold as individual pictures to collectors, so you must sell car ads to car collectors, food ads to advertising collectors, etc. Each ad must be matted.

There is a special class of magazines known as the "pulps." These are magazines, often printed on poor-quality paper, that published mystery and science fiction stories. Pulps should never be cut. The value is greater for the complete magazine than for any combination of cut-up illustrations and stories. These magazines are usually wanted by book and comic dealers.

Don't be disappointed if your large stack of *Life* magazines or *National Geographics* is not worth a small fortune. It is rare for a magazine to sell at retail for over $5 unless it is mint, has an interesting cover or story and is at least pre-1960. Many magazines have no value at all. Still, try to sell your stacks of old magazines, especially *Life, National Geographic, Playboy,* and other similar magazines, decorating magazines like *House Beautiful,* gardening and cooking magazines, sports, movie, TV, automobile, and special interest magazines. If you have enough, you will find that even at less than $1 each, the value adds up.

ooo

Medical Antiques

The best customers for medical and dental antiques are doctors and dentists. Strange-looking old tools, dental chairs, examining tables,

advertising cards, catalogs, medicine bottles, and anything else related to medicine has a market. Dental items like shaving mugs, razors, barbershop signs (the old-time dentist and barber were the same man), extraction tools, and even false teeth are collected, usually by dentists. All early pharmaceutical collectibles can be sold easily. A small local shop or drugstore will often buy pieces for use in window displays. Decorative bottles (see Bottles section), cabinets, and early medicine labels and packets sell easily to general collectors. Quack medicine items like electric shock machines to cure rheumatism are of special interest to many. A different group of people will buy any drug-related items.

There are special dealers who conduct mail-order auctions of medical, dental, and drug-related collectibles. You can locate them through the general antiques publications ads. If you have a large collection, it would be profitable to take an ad in a professional magazine of interest to doctors, dentists, or lawyers. Locate these with the help of your local librarian.

Miniatures & Dollhouses

There are many collectors of dollhouses and miniature dollhouse furniture. The older and more complete the dollhouse, the more valuable. There is also an extra interest in wooden houses with lithographed paper exteriors made by BLISS. The name is often included on the dollhouse. Other important names are McLOUGHLIN BROTHERS, SCHOENHUT, and TOOTSIETOY. Dollhouses were made in many sizes. By the 1870s most of them were made on a scale of one inch to one foot. Dollhouses seem to sell best at special auctions; look in the section on Toys to learn where these sales are held. Local dealers can also sell dollhouses. Scale houses sell well, especially those made before 1930. Price new dollhouses at a toy store, and always price yours higher than the comparable new ones. Be sure the dollhouse will fit through a normal door. The price is 50 percent less if it must be dismantled to be moved or set up in a home. Do not attempt to restore or repaint a dollhouse before selling it. Keep all loose pieces, or glue trim back in place, but do nothing major. Most buyers will want to do their own restoration. We have even seen a dollhouse sold in pieces in a plastic bag.

Dollhouse furniture was made to the same scale as the dollhouses and is always the easiest miniature to sell. However, anything in miniature is in demand and can bring surprisingly high prices. Doll-size dishes or dollhouse-size dishes, doll-size chairs or dollhouse-size chairs, and any other decorative objects, from tiny needlepoint rugs

to silverware and vases of flowers, sell well. A fine 4-inch chair could sell for over $100.

Many antiques dealers have a case filled with what is called "smalls" by the trade. Smalls include all the tiny, expensive, and easy-to-misplace items. Always look for a dealer with dollhouse smalls. If you own a furnished dollhouse or many pieces of furniture, try talking to dealers at a miniature show. These shows are for collectors of old and new dollhouse items and are often listed in your local paper. The national collector groups and collector magazines for miniature enthusiasts have complete show listings printed each month. They often list prices for new miniatures that can help you set a price for yours. Prices for any sort of old dollhouse or furnishings are listed in general price books.

ooo

Musical Instruments, Player Pianos, Music Boxes

MUSICAL INSTRUMENTS

Everyone has heard of the Stradivarius violin that was sold for over $450,000. Unfortunately, very few people know that 99.99 percent of the violins labeled Stradivarius are nineteenth- or twentieth-century versions and are worth very little. Some old musical instruments have great value, but most of them should be priced as secondhand instruments to be used by young musicians. If you have an old violin or other musical instrument, the best way to start determining the value is to take it to a friend who is a competent musician. Don't forget that even the bow might be of value. Very good bows can sell for thousands of dollars. You might price a new violin and bow to get some idea of value. Anyone who plays the violin well will know if your violin is of good quality. If it seems good, take it to a local store that sells used musical instruments. They are listed in the Yellow Pages of the phone book. If it seems very good, you might try to contact a violin appraiser. This type of specialist is often listed in the phone book but is not found in every city. The only other way to sell old violins is through a local auction, through an ad in the newspaper, or even at a flea market. Few antiques dealers buy and sell average-quality musical instruments.

Collectible musical instruments are old, decorative, and often unusual in appearance. Some are no longer made or used but are often playable. These instruments might include a sarrusophone (used in marching bands from the 1860s to the 1920s) or an American harp-guitar (popular from 1800 to 1925). Banjos and mandolins with carvings and mother-of-pearl inlay appeal both to collectors who want something

decorative to display and to musicians who are looking for instruments. Look for the names of major manufacturers such as GIBSON, VEGA, or EPIPHONE. Look at the construction of the instrument. Like fine furniture, it should be well made and have crisp detail. Inlays and carvings are often signs of quality. Collectors pay a premium for original condition and original cases, but musicians don't seem to mind restorations if it is a fine instrument that can be played.

Because pianos are so large and difficult to move, they present some special problems. Fine pianos with elaborately painted cases are very popular with decorators, especially for large apartments. The decorative value of the piano as a piece of furniture, as well as the quality of the instrument, is considered in determining the price. "Reproducing pianos" bring high prices. Any top-quality piano will probably sell best at a well-advertised antiques auction. If there is no gallery nearby, it can be sold to a piano store to be resold. An average-quality piano can be sold at a house sale, through an ad in the papers, to a music store, or through an auction. The best method will depend on what is available in your area. Square pianos, the 1880s type with rosewood case and heavy carved legs, are the most disappointing to sell. The square piano doesn't remain tuned very long. It is not a good instrument for a musician. Most of these pianos are finally sold for a few hundred dollars. The insides are removed and the case is remade into a desk.

Small musical instruments, like harmonicas and kazoos, sell at flea markets for prices a little lower than the cost of new ones. Unusual designs, extra large or small examples, or other odd features will raise the price.

PLAYER PIANOS

Player pianos are wanted for entertainment. If your player piano works, it will sell quickly at a good price. The more attractive the case, the higher the price. Well-finished wood and stained-glass panels add to the price. If the piano does not play, have it checked by a piano restorer. It may not be salable because the repairs are too expensive.

MUSIC BOXES

All music boxes, from the early cylinder types with bells and dancing figures to a ten-year-old musical powder box, are in demand. However, age, rarity, and the quality of the box are important in pricing it for sale. The nineteenth-century boxes that play using cylinders, teeth, and combs have values from hundreds to thousands of dollars. The REGINA boxes that play flat metal disks are also high priced and easy to sell. Go to a serious music box collector (your town may have an active chapter of the Musical Box Society International) or to your library. There are many books about music boxes that will help you decide if yours is average or special. The price books also price many of the boxes. Look for anything that moves, like bells or dancers, a selection of tunes, or an elaborate case. Some boxes play paper "rolls." These are old and, if working, should sell well. Very large cylinder boxes (over 3 feet long) are usually of top quality. Small boxes, 12 inches long or less, were usually made for tourists and are not as well made. Musical, animated birds are always popular with buyers. Any moving bird sells for hundreds of dollars. Twentieth-century music boxes include carved wooden figures that turn their heads and whistle tunes, musical powder boxes and jewelry cases, even carved chairs that play when you sit on them. Anything that moves and makes noise is popular with collectors.

Paintings, Sculpture & Other Original Art

Original art can be the most valuable and the most complicated antique to sell. You must be able to tell if it is an oil painting, a print, an original Remington sketch, or just a photographic copy. Find a friend who can tell you which pieces look authentic. It might be a local artist, craftsman, or photographer who can recognize quality. Then try to check on the artist before you offer the piece for sale.

If you live in or near a big city, ask whether the local art museum schedules a day for authenticating works of art for the general public. Many museums will tell you the age of the piece and information on the artist, but none will estimate price. Watch for an appraisal day at local auction galleries or at fund-raisers. Take the piece to the appraiser. If it is too big, take a black-and-white photograph.

The work of any artist listed in *Thieme-Becker Lexicon, Dictionnaire des Peintres, Sculpteurs, Dessinateurs et Graveurs* by Benezit, *Dictionary of American Painters, Sculptors and Engravers* by Fielding, or *Mallet's Index of Artists* has a value. Look in the library for copies of these books. Check prices for the past ten years in the yearly *Annual Art Sales Index* edited by Richard Hislop or in *Leonard's Price Index of Art Auctions*, also found at your library or at your local art museum library. You can also write to the Smithsonian's reference service, The Inventory of American Paintings, to learn about paintings by American artists. Photograph the piece, write a description, copy down the artist's name, and contact a local or out-of-town auction gallery or any dealer to sell the item. Before you decide how to sell your artwork, it would be prudent to go to some local auctions and see if the art sells for good prices. Sometimes a

small local gallery does not get high prices for good art, because it specializes in furniture, country antiques, or other types of sales.

Be careful if friends or dealers seem very interested in buying the piece. Good original paintings or sculptures sell for thousands of dollars. A small bronze only 6 inches tall could be worth more than a thousand dollars. Western subjects, American folk paintings, ancient and oriental bronzes, scrolls and woodblocks, and other unfamiliar items can be very valuable, but can look unimportant to someone who is not an expert. We went to an auction at a beach house to look at some of the rustic furniture mentioned in the ad. Four bronze figures, possibly Siamese, the largest 5 inches tall, were offered in one lot. The estimate was $20-$40. The bidding was quiet until it reached about $80. Then two bidders in the audience began to show determination. The final bid was over $1,000. We later asked why. One of the bronzes was very early and of very good quality. The other three were twentieth-century gift shop items. Obviously, two dealer-experts in the audience recognized the fine antique bronze. If only one knowledgeable person had been there, the figures would have sold for $40. When you have a piece that seems to be old and authentic, it is always wise to have an appraisal by a qualified art appraiser before you sell it. If you decide to sell it through an auction gallery, no appraisal is needed. The gallery should be able to tell you the approximate value. It is important to know the history of family pieces. Many good pieces of art "liberated" by soldiers during World War II are now appearing in house sales and estates. Many times, the value is unrecognized by the present owners. Some were obtained illegally and might still belong to an overseas owner, so a gallery might want to check it out.

Age does not always determine the value of fine art; but condition, quality, and the prestige of the artist do. You may think a painting is ugly, but someone else may pay important money for it. The size of an average-quality painting helps to determine the price. It should fit over a fireplace or sofa. If too high and narrow, it is worth 30 percent less. If the subject matter is unappealing (dead bodies, gored matadors, or unattractive factory views), the picture will not sell as easily as landscapes, seascapes, or still lifes by the same artist. Animals, beautiful women, sweet children, Jewish subjects, nudes, oriental views, and Paris street scenes are good sellers. Historical

A 4-by-8-foot painting hanging in a religious center in Grand Rapids, Michigan, was given away to Francesca Alvarado when the center closed. In 1981, Francesca gave the painting to her sister, Isaura Vela. Four years later, the painting by Guido Reni was sold for $600,000. Francesca sued for part of the money, claiming that she and Isaura had a verbal agreement that both would share in the profits if the picture was sold. If you give art or antiques to your friends before you check the value, you are really giving away dollar bills.

events, military battles, and Bible subjects are not as popular. If a landscape of a town can be identified, the value is at least doubled. A good gold-leaf frame is of added value when selling a large painting. Most buyers plan to hang the picture on a wall, and if they have to spend extra money to restore or frame a painting, it is worth less. Rips and damage in the main part of the painting (on a face, for example) are considered serious problems. Small tears in the background area are not serious if the painting has value. If the pictures were in the home of an elderly relative, be sure to check under the dust cover paper on the back for hidden money or stock certificates. The labels and writing on the back may also help with the history.

Don't be discouraged if friends tell you what a "bad" painting you have. Beauty is in the eye of the beholder. Respectable copies of famous paintings, decorative subjects, very primitive-looking pictures, and huge pictures (especially of food) that are suitable for restaurant walls will all sell. They are bought and sold, not as great art, but as decorations for boring walls or dark corners. They may even be purchased because the new owners like "kitsch," something that is so bad it has charm.

Always try to check the importance of a signed marble or bronze sculpture. (See Bronzes section.) Even unsigned figures, if well made, sell for hundreds of dollars today. Fine marble and bronze figures have been re-created in other materials such as spelter or plaster. The most famous of these are the JOHN ROGERS groups, figures made in late nineteenth-century America. They sell quickly if the original painted surface is in good condition.

ooo

Paper Collectibles & Ephemera

Paper collectibles were almost ignored until the 1970s, when the word *ephemera* came into common use. If you have a bookplate that belonged to Charles Dickens, a 1910 gum wrapper, a bill of sale for a slave, or an 1890 menu, it is called ephemera. They were throwaway bits of history. We seem more aware today that these bits are of historic importance. In earlier generations paper was not common and very little ephemera has remained. We have no accurate idea of what the Pilgrims wore on their feet because we have no photographs or personal letters. We can only make educated guesses about many of the everyday activities of the past. The history of the rich and famous remains in paintings and documents, but the everyday ephemera is gone.

Menus, newspapers, maps, ration books from the wars, personal letters, letterheads, diaries, children's lesson books, paper end-labels

A Midwestern housewife was cleaning the attic and almost got rid of a shoebox of old maps. A closer look told her that the maps were from the Lewis and Clark Expedition, and she sold them for $3,000.

from bolts of cloth, wallpaper, fabric sample books, and instruction books for obsolete machinery are among the items of interest to the ephemera collector. There are collectors of local history ephemera in every part of the country. Any paper item with a city or state name can probably be sold, and it will bring the best price near the city named on it.

Old newspapers are *not* very valuable. The paper is acid and "self-destructs" after a number of years, becoming brittle and falling apart. Many libraries are selling old newspapers and replacing them with microfilm, so the supply is larger than the demand. Most papers are worthless unless sold as a full-year set. A few special papers reporting interesting events are worth up to $15-$20.

Sort through boxes of old papers and "junk" you may find in the attic. Try to imagine who would find it useful. The best way to sell many special paper items can be found in the various appropriate sections of this book. Other items can be sold through mail-order ads in the general antiques publications. Ephemera is usually small, lightweight, and easy to mail to a buyer. There is even an international club of ephemera collectors and a newspaper devoted to the subject. Look at the want ads and try to find just the right person for your ephemera. When all else fails, place a box filled with the papers on a table at a flea market and lightly pencil a low price on each piece. Guess the value from the subject matter. Single pieces of paper over fifty years old can be worth from 10¢ to a few dollars even if they seem of no consequence to you.

♦♦♦

Paperweights

Newspapers are always reporting the high prices of antique French paperweights. For many years the value was rising so quickly that paperweights were considered a better investment than stocks or real estate. Unfortunately, few of us will ever discover the rare antique paperweight in fine condition that would sell for over $143,000 (a record price set in 1983). The paperweights we might own could be average-to-good antique French, English, or American weights, modern weights, Chinese or Italian copies of old weights. They could also be the many paperweights that are not all glass: the snow weights, advertising weights, and others.

The Paperweight Collectors Association newsletter had these words for members: "Fortunate indeed is the collector whose heir will enjoy and continue to develop the collection. Many families are faced with the problem of disposing of a collection. One collector told me that he enjoyed his paperweights so much that he was going to take them with him when he went, but he never gave me the secret of how he proposed to do this. Another collector, who has since learned the wisdom of his words, said that he had never seen a U-Haul trailer behind a hearse." The newsletter continues with good advice: "If you want to sell a collection for the highest dollars, you must find a collector who wants each weight and sell it directly. Of course, this is time consuming, if not impossible. You might consider donating the weights to a museum and taking the tax deduction. This has been done by several well-known paperweight collectors and the collections can be seen by those who want to learn how to recognize a fine old weight of value. Auctions are a good method but don't expect the high prices announced for the best weights. A minor difference in color, design, or any flaws can alter the value. If you have rare weights, the auction, even with the seller's fees and other costs, is a good way to sell. The rare weights are advertised to a worldwide group of collectors with money and an interest in buying more weights. You might want to sell to a paperweight dealer. There are a few who sell old and new weights but many specialize. Some will buy the weights outright, some will take your collection on consignment and send you the money as the weights are sold."

A list of dealers can be found through the *Paperweight Collectors*

Association Newsletter. Some advertise in the antiques publications. Modern weights are sold by gift shops as well as antiques dealers, and some of these shops may be willing to sell your weights on consignment. Chinese and Italian paperweights were made in the twentieth century to look like older, better weights. These can be very confusing for a novice. Ask an expert in paperweights, preferably a dealer, appraiser, or auctioneer who sells fine paperweights. They will be glad to show you what characteristics of the glasswork are important. In general, if the weight is made of small "canes" that look like hard candy, the canes should be very crisp and clear with no blurring of color or distortion of edges. The clear glass should be perfect, with no bubbles, flaws, or discoloration. The bottom should be ground flat. If there are flowers or animals inside, these too should be made with precision, no blurred edges or blurred color. Flowers and insects should be lifelike. If you remember that each color is made from a single strand of glass that has been worked by hand, you can understand the artistry in a single paperweight.

Advertising weights, small metal figural weights, and other collectible but not artistic weights sell through the regular antiques dealers and auction houses, flea markets, and sales. Because weights are small, you can take them to these sales and discreetly try to sell them to dealers who have some others in stock. Remember, the best way to sell any antique or collectible is to find someone who has already shown an interest in and a knowledge of the item. Any dealer who sells an antique has to buy that antique from someone.

◖◖◖

Pewter, Copper, Chrome & Other Metals

Eighteenth- and nineteenth-century iron, brass, tin, toleware, pewter, and copper utensils have always been popular collectibles and are easily sold to dealers, decorators, and collectors. The fashion for the "country look" has added to the popularity, and any old tool, trivet, or kitchen utensil that can be put on a shelf or hung on a wall is wanted. Fine old American examples, especially those stamped with a maker's mark, sell for hundreds to thousands of dollars. These early pieces can be sold through mail-order ads, at auction, or to collectors or dealers. They are part of the general merchandise found in most antiques shops. (See section on Kitchen Paraphernalia for additional information.)

Twentieth-century metalwork is sometimes mistakenly sold for low prices at garage sales because the uninformed don't realize that many recent pieces have a great value in the collectors' market. Iron door-

METALWARE. Pewter, copper, silverplate and metalwork, 1880s to 1920 period, especially pieces marked "Liberty", "Tudric", "WMF", "I/OX", "Kayserzinn", "Osiris", "Orivit", "Isis", "Cymric", also bound copies "The Studio", same period. J.R. Tonkin, Yorks Avenue, Romby. Tel. 0069-59571.

MOLDS FOR CASTING pewter spoons, bowls, plates, and other practical items (no soldiers) wanted by Edward Mar, Dunterry Vir. **666/555-4444**   My

In 1954 a collector bought a large copper bowl at an antiques store in Hinsdale, Illinois. The new owner paid $250 for "an antique Russian copper champagne cooler" she could use as a planter. After she died, her sister took it to a free appraisal clinic in San Francisco and it was identified as one of eight urns in a set made by Frank Lloyd Wright. One sold in December 1984 for $93,500. Three more remain to be discovered.

stops have sold for over $1,000. Heavy, solid copper cooking pots are also selling well. Price these by comparing them to new ones available in gourmet cooking stores. Art Nouveau and Art Deco pewter, chrome, or copper are in demand. Hammered aluminum from the 1940s and 1950s has some value if it is in very good condition. Of special interest are chrome cocktail shakers, Art Deco pieces with Bakelite (plastic) handles, and Arts and Crafts hammered-copper bookends or vases. Look for these names: pewter, KAYZERZINN, TUDRIC; copper, NEKRASSOFF, DIRK VAN ERP, HEINTZ, ROYCROFT, STICKLEY; chrome, CHASE; hammered aluminum, WENDELL AUGUST FORGE, STEDE, FARBERWARE, RODNEY KENT.

Cloisonné is a form of enameled metal. Small strips of wire, or cloisons, are applied to a metal (usually brass) vase. Enamel is then floated between the strips. The finished vase is smoothed until the surface shows the pattern of colored enamels and brass lines. All oriental cloisonné is now selling well. Age and quality determine the price. Any damage or dent lowers the value as much as 90 percent because repairs are difficult. Good quality old cloisonné should be sold to a top antiques dealer or by an auction gallery. The new cloisonné is very similar to the old, and it takes an expert to evaluate the piece.

ooo

Phonographs & Records

RECORDS

Enrico Caruso was a great opera singer, but his records are not all worth thousands of dollars. One very early European record has a high value. The others are probably only worth a few dollars. Price is determined by demand. Today's collectors are more interested in "My Bonnie" by Tony Sheridan and the Beat Brothers (early Beatles) on the 1961 Decca label than they are in Bing Crosby singing "White Christmas." Probably the rarest record is "Stormy Weather" by the Five Sharps, auctioned for $3,800 in 1977. It may not sell for as much today. Fairly recent records worth over $1,000 include Elvis Presley's "Good Luck Charm" and "TV Guide Presents Elvis Presley," both on the RCA label; "Anna" by the Beatles, a 1963 45 rpm; "The Sound of Leadership," a 1956 RCA sales convention souvenir; "Can't Help Loving That Gal of Mine," a 45 rpm by the Hideaways; "I'm Down in Honolulu Looking Them Over" by Al Jolson; "It's Too Soon to Know" by Sonny Till and the Orioles, on the Jubilee label; and "Starting from Tonight" by the Royals, on the Federal label.

Sad but true, most 78s (a standard size after 1926, but almost completely replaced by 1957) and strange-looking early records are not of great value. Cylinder discs for the pre-1906 phonographs are usually worth just a few dollars in the shops; flat, one-sided records (made until 1923) are also of very limited interest to collectors. The 33⅓ rpm record was developed in 1930, but was not popular until 1948, the same year the 45 rpm record was introduced.

Most records sell for low prices if they can be sold at all. Condition is important, and any record that has overwhelming surface noises, a label in poor condition, cracks, chips, or deep scratches is not salable to anyone. Records in mint (never played) to very good condition can be sold. Try playing the record before you sell it, unless you are sure it has never been played.

The picture sleeve is important and adds to the value. The value of albums is sometimes determined partially by the picture on the album cover.

Pricing records can be difficult because it is not just the artist and the song, but also the label, that determine the value. The best price books about records include pictures of the labels, so you have no problem identifying what you have.

The most valued 78 rpm records were made between 1915 and 1935. Unfortunately, if the same record was reissued on a 33⅓ or 45 rpm disc, the earlier record is of less value. The Enrico Caruso records with low values are now available in reissue with enhanced sound

quality, so the 78s do not sell well. Some combinations of artists are treasured but were recorded without listing all the artists' names on the record; some artists are valued highly only on particular labels (Al Jolson on Columbia or Brunswick); and some artists recorded under many names. Many 45s have been bootlegged or illegally copied, and these copies are not of great value. These factors show that it will take real study to know your records and to set a sensible price. The library and the price books will help.

Collectors specialize, so your records can be sold not only by artist and song, but also by type of music: rock, jazz, big band, blues, country, Western, etc. If you plan to sell the records yourself at a show or house sale, be sure to sort them into separate boxes to make it easier for people to find the type of music they are interested in.

If you have some rare records, perhaps the best way to sell them is through the dealers who specialize in records. The price books and the publications listed in the Appendix include many ads by these dealers. If there is no one near your town, you can call or write about what you want to sell. If you just have a pile of old records in poor condition, you may find it doesn't pay to spend the time researching and selling them.

PHONOGRAPHS

We are constantly asked the value of old phonographs. The early type with the large horn is probably the most valuable. Least desirable are the Mission-style, oak-cased phonographs from the 1910s to 1930s. They may play, but they are not attractive, and the quality of the music from the old records is poor. Phonographs are listed in *Kovels' Antiques & Collectibles Price List* and in several special price lists devoted to phonographs. The general rule is to check carefully if the machine has an exposed horn or unusual turntable arrangement with obvious pulleys and belts. Lower your expectations for enclosed machines, even if they are floor models. Many of the old phonographs are found with records. If the records are unusual in size or shape, cylinders or "fat," one-sided, flat records, you probably own an old machine. A collector may want it if it is unusual and still in working condition. Even if it is not working, a collector might be able to fix it and be willing to buy your phonograph.

ooo

Photography

CAMERAS

Any old camera has a value. So do stereo viewers and cards, screens, darkroom equipment, most professional photographs, and amateur photos taken before 1918. Most working old cameras can be sold at your local camera store, which is a better place than an antiques shop to try to sell a camera. An old camera can often be traded in for a new one, and this might be a good way to gain cash value for your collectible.

There are camera and photography clubs in most large cities. The members of these clubs buy many types of cameras, photographs, and photographic equipment. Call some local camera stores or the museum or historical society and ask for information on local camera clubs. Then call a member and describe what you have for sale. Often the members will help you price the items, will offer to buy them, or will tell you about dealers who might want them. Most large cities have camera and photography shows, and you can find customers for all types of photography-related items. Even film boxes, tripods, lenses, slide mounts, darkroom equipment, screens, and other photographica are wanted.

A working 35-mm camera made after 1950 can be sold to most pawnbrokers. More unusual cameras probably cannot. There are publications for the photography collector with interests in cameras, vintage pictures, 3-D, or other related subjects. Most of these publications have buy and sell ads and wanted lists. It is always best to read these for information on prices and possible customers. Cameras and exceptional pictures, daguerreotypes and daguerreotype cases, stereo viewers and stereo pictures (3-D), glass plate slides, and twentieth-century photographs by well-known photographers are often sold by antiques and art auction houses. Fine photographs are often sold in art galleries.

We have found that information about old cameras and photographs spreads well by word-of-mouth. If you have time to wait to sell your items, try this subtle form of advertising. Go to the flea markets and the shows, and tell your local camera store and friends exactly what you have to offer for sale. Give them a list of the items, including brand names, condition, and identifying numbers. When describing a camera, include the manufacturer's name, serial number, words written near the lens, type and condition of case, and any instruction books, lenses, or other parts that are included. Even the original bill and box are important. The word will be spread to other collectors, and one day you will receive a phone call from an unknown collector searching for just the items you have.

Any camera that seems unusual to you may have a value. Very old cameras, pre-1900, are of special interest. Unusual shapes, even a Mickey Mouse-shaped camera, extra large or extra small cameras, and of course cameras of exceptional quality sell well. Condition is impor-

tant. Wear, scratches, and minor, repairable problems lower the price by 25-50 percent.

PHOTOGRAPHS

Early pictures, daguerreotypes (silver image on glass), ambrotypes (glass negative backed with dark paper), tintypes (photo printed on black tin), and other pictures that were not printed on paper have a special group of customers. Some want to add to their "country look" decorating. Some want pictures for historical reasons and search for street views, war views, pictures of soldiers, miners, or people in other occupations, children with toys, or interior shop scenes. Some seek the most artistic photographs by the often nameless but skilled photographers. All types sell unless they are badly damaged. Restoration is next to impossible. Cartes de visite (2½-by-4-inch photographs on cardstock), cabinet cards (4-by-7-inch photographs on cardstock), album photos of grandparents, and other Victorian pictures also sell, but often for low prices.

Modern art photographs by artists like ANSEL ADAMS or DIANE ARBUS sell for high prices in the galleries. There has been some speculation that the price structure at auctions has been unduly influenced by some preplanned bidding, but whatever the reason for the ups and downs of this market, your picture will have a value if it is an original. Wallace Nutting "prints" are really hand-tinted photographs taken in the early 1900s. They picture views of early homes, landscapes, and interiors. Mr. Nutting sold hundreds of thousands of these pictures, each signed with his name. Collectors rediscovered them in the early 1980s.

Some collectors are interested in the oddities, the photos printed on porcelain dishes or enameled on plaques for tombstones. Stanhopes

---

The Stereo Realist camera, a special screen, large projector, glasses for viewing, slides, and slide mounts were all taking up space in the back closet. The equipment was no longer used. Jim first thought of donating it to a photography museum but the screen was 8 feet long and difficult to transport. He made a list of the items. At every show and flea market, he left his name, phone number, and the list with any dealer selling old cameras. A year later a call came from a collector 300 miles away. They made a package deal for everything, including some special lenses, instruction books, and a slide box. The collector drove all day to pick up the equipment in a rented truck. He was a member of a serious group of stereo enthusiasts and was delighted to have found some rare equipment. Jim got over $1,500 for collectibles that couldn't be sold in his town. If you know you have a rare collector's item and can wait, the collector will find you.

---

are tiny pictures seen through peepholes in canes or charms. These and other older oddities also have a market.

EQUIPMENT

Once at a house sale we watched a teenaged friend of our son buy a strange metal and glass object for a quarter. He told us later that he took it to a camera store and sold it for $50. He had recognized the close-up lens for a special make of camera. At the same sale we saw a happy collector buy an old wooden tripod, oak cases for slides, and other 1910 paraphernalia. He wanted it to decorate a room. Anything connected with photography will sell. There is new interest in old magazines and trade catalogs on photography. The collectors will buy it all. Your job is to find the true collector of photographica.

STEREO VIEWS

Stereo view cards are often found in boxes. Sets from the 1920s were often sold with a photograph of the family who bought them. There was one picture of some children, then boxes and boxes of educational scenes. These are of very low value. The stereo card has two almost identical pictures mounted on a piece of cardboard. The cardboard corners were square from 1854 to 1870 and sometimes the cardboard was colorful. Round corners were favored from 1868 to 1882. The curved cardboard mounts used after 1880 were usually buff, gray, or black. Thin cardboard was introduced about 1900. Colored pictures were made from 1900 to 1929.

Prices vary with age and subject. Views sell best near the area they picture. It may pay to try to sell out-of-state views by mail. Dealers at flea markets and postcard shows, as well as general antiques dealers, sell stereo views, so any of them might buy yours.

ooo

Political Memorabilia

Every fourth year, when a presidential race is filling the minds and newspapers of Americans, the price of political ephemera rises. The political buttons, banners, and oddities are suddenly discovered by a new group of collectors. Of course, there are many serious collectors who seek political items every year. The hobby has a national club, publication, shows, and a built-in publicity possibility that encourages new collectors and higher prices regularly. To a collector there are two kinds of political memorabilia: authentic items and ''brummagems.'' The brummagems are the tourist-trap pieces, made because they will sell. Most of the buttons with off-color or insulting slogans were made to be sold by hucksters, and they are not true political pieces.

In the back of the drawer at Grandfather's house you found a treasure trove that includes some John Kennedy campaign buttons, a cake of soap shaped like a baby but labeled McKinley, a pencil that says ''Win with Willkie,'' ''I Like Ike'' cigarettes, a newspaper telling about the death of Lincoln, and a Teddy Roosevelt bandanna. Are they really political items? Are they rare and valuable? The record price for a campaign button, set in 1980, was $33,000 for a Cox-Roosevelt celluloid button, 1¼ inches in diameter. Both candidates are pictured on the button. It is a type known to the trade as a ''jugate.'' In general, a jugate or picture button is of much more value than a button with just the names of the candidates. A button for two candidates is priced higher than a button for a single candidate. Buttons promoting a candidate for mayor or senator are of interest locally, but if your candidate eventually ran for president the button may be high priced. Buttons for candidates for the smaller parties are often high priced because they are rare. Buttons that promote both a local candidate for Senate or Congress and a national candidate for president also have a good value. Foreign-language buttons are scarce and sell well.

There are many books about political memorabilia. They include a set of three books on buttons, one on textiles, and several on the general subject. Most of these books include prices. Unfortunately, since the general price guides do not have room for complete descriptions and pictures, they are of limited use. The buttons are priced differently for slightly different print style, color, size, photo, or other feature. The American Political Items Collectors, whose membership represents the serious political buyers in the country, publish material on real and fake political pieces. If you have rarities, their members are your best prospective customers.

Buttons are small and easy to store, so most collectors have many. Other items are often rarer and bring high prices. Political bandannas, jewelry, knives, cigars, trays, dishes, dolls, umbrellas, canes, and posters are all collected. Anything that pictures a candidate running for office is salable. Anything that pictures an elected president or vice-president is in demand among regular political collectors and other groups of collectors. In recent years there has been active interest in campaign material for women who ran for office or the wives of elected officials. Older items are usually of more value than the newer ones. Never discard anything that mentions a politician. It can be sold.

Kleenex had a national promotion in the 1970s that included reproductions of many old campaign buttons. Several other similar promotions have offered repros since then. These buttons are marked on the edge with information about the reproduction year and company. Even these are now worth a few dollars.

But what about Grandfather's treasures? The Kennedy button and the Willkie pencil and Ike cigarettes are probably worth under $10; the baby-shaped soap with the original box is worth over $75; the bandanna, like most textiles, has an even higher value. The newspaper about Lincoln's death is worth only a few dollars.

ooo

Postcards

The first postal card with a printed stamp was issued in Austria in 1869. The idea proved to be so profitable for the government that it was quickly copied by many other countries. The United States used its first government postcard in May 1873. (A card dated May 12 or 13, 1873, would be a very high-priced rarity.) These early cards had printed messages. Personal messages were charged first-class rates. It was not until May 19, 1898, that private postcards were charged at a lower rate. A postal card has a preprinted stamp. A postcard has a space for an adhesive stamp.

It seems as if everyone's elderly aunts saved boxes of picture postcards sent to them by friends and relatives. A card can sell for anywhere from 5¢ to over $500. It pays to study before you take an offer for the whole box. First examine the stamps and check on the value of any unusual ones. The postmark and amount of postage will

POSTAGE RATE TABLE

1872	1¢	1928	1¢	1968	5¢	1976	9¢	1985	14¢
1917	2¢	1952	2¢	1971	6¢	1978	10¢	1988	15¢
1919	1¢	1959	3¢	1973	8¢	1981	12¢		
1925	2¢	1963	4¢	1975	7¢	1981	13¢		

help to date the card. Look for any strange stickers. Christmas seals, parcel post stamps, TB or Red Cross stickers, Easter seals, and others can add to the value of your card. There are collectors who want just the stickers.

There are seven periods of postcards for a collector: *The Pioneer Era Cards* (1893-1898) are the oldest available and bring high prices. *Private Mailing Cards* (1898-1901) have the words ''Private Mailing Card - Authorized by Act of Congress'' printed on the back. These cards also sell for premium prices. *The Undivided Back* period is from about 1902 to 1907. These cards were printed so that only the name and address, no message, could be written on the back. Next was *The Divided Back* era (1907-1915). *The White Border* period (1915-1930) had many printed cards of poor quality with white borders. *Linen Cards* (1920-1950) were printed on paper with a linen-textured surface. These were often bright colored cards with cartoons or jokes. *The Photochrome Cards* (1939 to present) are those seen today. Color film was available for these glossy cards. Cards made before 1900 were often drawn by an artist. Color lithographed cards were popular until about 1914. Photographs or pictures printed in black and white or sepia were used on cards in the early 1900s. Prices are high for any types of cards made before 1915.

Some collectors seek postcards made of unusual materials. Birchbark,

POST CARD

FOR CORRESPONDENCE   FOR ADDRESS ONLY   STAMP

woven silk, leather, feathers, fur, peat moss, mother-of-pearl, celluloid, real hair, fabrics, wood, and paper were used for cards. Some cards, called "mechanicals," were made with a metal spring to produce some action. A donkey tail might wag or a head nod. A few double cards were made that squeaked when pressed. Foldout, see-through, hold-to-light, and puzzle cards were made. All these novelty cards should be priced higher than a regular card made after 1915. Condition for these cards and all others is very important. A very worn card is of little value.

Manufacturers and artists with famous names add to the value of your cards. Look for RAPHAEL TUCK, ELLEN CLAPSADDLE, BERTHA CORBETT, HOWARD CHANDLER CHRISTY, HARRISON FISHER, LANCE THACKEREY, GENE CARR, LOUIS WAIN, and FRANCES BRUNDAGE. Add to your price if the card pictures coins, stamps, famous or infamous people, kewpies, blacks, advertising, disasters, animals dressed like people, fruits or vegetables that look like people, World's Fairs, expositions, or holidays. The best holidays are Halloween and Christmas, especially any card that includes a full-length picture of Santa Claus. All types of patriotic cards, including those featuring Fourth of July and political events, are in demand. Early planes, early autos, fire equipment, and other types of transportation are always wanted. The larger the picture of the car, the better; the largest are the so-called "close-up" transportation cards. Photograph cards of streets filled with stores, advertising, people, cars, or special events are collected. Extra-large cards or sets of cards bring a premium. Unpopular cards include views of woods, parks, rivers, mountains, churches, residential street scenes, and other scenery with few buildings or people.

After you have some idea of the value of the postcards, you have several options for selling them. A private collector may want your cards. Expect to get 50-75 percent of the published retail value. If private collectors were to pay 100 percent, they could buy it retail from any dealer's stock. If you sell just a few to a collector, you may find you are left with a relatively unsalable collection.

There are many postcard shows. Collectors and dealers usually pay well for rare cards. Go to a show and mention your collection. Decide if you want to sell single cards or the whole box. Make that decision before you sell the best ten items and then find that no one wants the rest. If you have time, you can sell the ordinary cards at any flea market or house sale. They can often be sold from a box labeled "All cards one price." Dealers tell us to use the prices 5¢, 10¢, 25¢, 50¢, etc. Never price at $1.25. There is a psychology to pricing merchandise, and for some reason, postcards sell best for one coin or bill. 45¢ or $1.25 are just not good prices.

Most serious dealers sort the cards by subject and state and display them in boxes or plastic mounts. Most collectors only want a special type of card and won't look through too big a pile.

If you don't want to work at selling each postcard, offer them as a lot to a dealer. There is a rule of thumb. A dealer can usually pay you 50-75 percent of the retail value of a card worth $1 or more, but can pay only 25 percent or less for the less expensive cards. The work involved in mounting, showing, and carrying is the same and most dealers prefer selling the better cards.

You might send the postcards to a mail-order auction that specializes in postcards. These auctions sell the best cards individually and the others in groups or lots. You will be paid for the lots that are sold and all the unsold items will be returned. It can take from three to six months to get your money after you send the collection to a mail-order auction. There is usually a 20-30 percent fee charged. The postcard publications list many possible places to sell cards.

The best advice we've heard regarding the pricing of cards came from a dealer who said, ''Ask yourself, which would the customer prefer to have in his pocket, the card or the money?'' The value is not like the value of gold or silver; it is a matter of demand. The value is in the eye of the buyer. Look at the price books, but they are only guides.

ooo

Pottery & Porcelain

An aunt left you her household belongings representing fifty or more years of accumulation, including figurines, lamps, kitchen mixing bowls, pottery crocks that held pickles, flower vases, dresser sets, ashtrays, three sets of dishes, and serving pieces. How would you sell everything for the best total price? Age and quality of ceramics do influence price, but a 1950 Hall pottery pitcher could be worth more than an 1850 German bowl. The whims of collectors determine the value, and sometimes the fashion of the day makes originally inexpensive pieces more important. The stone crocks that were cheap food-storage containers during the 1800s, yellowware, the Art Deco dishes of the

---

When Mother's house was closed after her death, vases filled with chicken wire and pin holders for flower arranging were found in the basement. The children and heirs didn't want any of the vases, but one grandchild liked a cream-colored bowl with a dancing lady standing in the center. She took it home and showed it to her sixteen-year-old friend, who mentioned it to her mother. The vase was Cowan pottery, worth over $150. The other vases were also examples of art pottery, and eventually the family sold them to a dealer for over $1,000. A rare Rookwood vase was donated to a museum in Mother's honor.

> A blue and white floral dish in a plain brown paper bag was brought to a free appraisal day at a small museum. The experts decided it was a fine fifteenth-century Ming porcelain, and the owner had it auctioned for over $40,000.

1920s, the nineteenth-century R. S. Prussia pieces decorated with voluptuous women, and some recent art pottery sell for higher prices than fine wares from the eighteenth and early nineteenth centuries.

If you are fortunate enough to have a close friend who understands antiques and collecting, call for help. Few collectors are experts in everything, but many of them can make good guesses about what might have value. A collector has been to the shops and shows and absorbs much information about what sells. If the task of identification seems overwhelming, you might want to send the contents to a consignment shop. These shops sell good-quality items and usually charge about 25-35 percent commission. The shop knows the highest retail price to ask, and even if a few things do not sell, you will have most of your money in a few months with very little work on your part. If you consign your dishes, be sure the shop has insurance. Get a signed contract describing the items (including any damage) and stating the terms of sale and the commission you will be charged.

You could sell your items through your own house or garage sale, or through an ad in the local paper. If you are offering the items through an ad, be sure to follow the sensible rules of safety: Never admit a stranger when you are alone in the house, take only cash and not checks, and watch for theft when strangers are inside. It might be wise to put all "for sale" items in the garage and let no one enter your house.

> An English housewife made her rice pudding in a china dish that had been in her family for years. One day she took it to an appraisal day to learn how old it really was. The ovenproof baking dish made of slipware had been manufactured in Staffordshire about 1720. It sold for over $40,000 at auction. Many kitchen bowls have been given from mother to daughter through several generations. If you have an old bowl, be sure to check the value.

If you sell most of the items to an antiques shop, you face the problem of what price to ask. To decide, you need a knowledgeable friend, a book like *Kovels' New Dictionary of Marks — Pottery & Porcelain*, a few other price books, and a working idea of the going prices in the gift and china shops. A simple rule of thumb is to compare your prices against those for similar pieces of new china. Most buyers will never pay more than 50 percent of china store prices

WANTED: Steins, Mettlach, military, pewter, glass, etc.. James Derry, Box 76, East Stevens, N.H. Phone 733/555-4321

SEBASTIANS WANTED

Old. Marblehead Sebastian Miniature Figurines by P. W. Baston. Willing to buy any quantity. Top dollar paid.

C. RAY
822/555-4777

GLASS AND CHINA WANTED

WANTED: FLOW BLUE China Albany pattern. Mfg. Johnson/Bros. Send item description, cost and condition to – Les D'Alo, U.S.M.C.A. HLN, Box, A.P.O. N.Y.

ap10021

ROOKWOOD POTTERY RARITIES – will pay highest prices; describe fully and price; include photo. – R buth's Antiques, Box 3, Scorough, NY

ap40891

ROYAL WORCESTER and Royal Doulton artist signed. Hand painted cabinet pieces wanted. Royal Doulton Dewars whiskey flasks wanted also. Top prices paid. Write– Lester Barre Antiques, GOP. OF Melbourne, Australia, or 3 E. 5th St., Apt. 4429 New York, NY   Telephone 626/555-0634

HISTORICAL STAFFORDSHIRE CHINA wanted in dark blue and lighter colors. Arms of the States by Mayer. Erie Canal and Liverpool pitchers wanted. State condition and price. – W.R. Kura P.O. Box 06, Jackson Heights

my120279

WANTED! We buy black memorabilia, cookie jars, Disney ceramics, Ceramic Art Studio, Hull Red Riding Hood, Florence ceramics. We buy collections or one piece. Judy Poe, Box 11, Teaneck, NJ **00000** Ph. **726/555−0855**

(6/5)

DISCONTINUED PATTERN of the forties — Name "Albemarle" #2012 marked Royal Worcester. Bone China, made in England. Particularly need cups and saucers, but will be interested in all items of this pattern. Good condition only. Please write: Bob's Place 87 Windemere. Across Town CA

12-4

McCOY COOKIE JARS. I am trying to get every McCoy jar, pattern and color. Write for my list of wants. Harold P.O. Box 1, Ames, IA 00150.

12-4

INTERESTED IN BUYING occupied Japan Blue Willow dinnerware. Mary Grer, P.O. Box 6, White City, IL Need serving pieces also.

· 12-4

WANTED: STUDIO POTTERY marked Vivika plus Otto, Deutch, Pitney, Cox, Natzler and McIntosh. Also want items marked ISC/Ames. Richard Harrider, 29 North Blvd., Suite 65, Phoenix, AZ

HAVILAND MATCHING. Match or buy French or American patterns. Send Schleiger number. SASE. E.C. Burt, Anderson, IN 771/555-6040

12-11

WANTED: OLD AMPHORA. Bretby, Fairyland Lustre, Gouda, Royal Dux Birds. Bizarre ceramics. Cliff Doson Hernon. Shreveport. LA 333/555-1782 (after 7 pm C.S.T.)

OCTAGON SOAP COUPON Dinnerware: Made by Homer Laughlin ca. 1933-50. Pierce Prairie Jr., Box 55, Sauda, CA 00000   149/555-4789

12-6

CHINA, STONEWARE, earthenware, crystal, stemware, sterling, silver plate flatware, many patterns needed. Coins, gold, silver, jewelry, postcards, unusual crocks. W. Sales, Lincoln, NE

12-8

GREEN PARROT DINNER Plates (10¼"), tumblers (4¼") or hot plate/trivet. Hasell's Antiques, Sonoma Road, Mountain Rosa, CA 733/555-4321

12-6

WANTED — LARGE Antique Bisque Piano Babies especially Heubach. Large Bisque Figurines of Children and Toddlers. Also a Heubach dog with a bandana around his head and a pipe in his mouth. Poteat, P.O. Box 2, Franklin,

12-6

and usually pay only 30 percent of retail prices. Some new sets can now be purchased for less than retail at discount stores. Antiques dealers are interested in what sells quickly, so they want attractive, undamaged figurines, lamps, vases, and the currently "hot" items like FIESTA (bright colored pottery of the 1930s), ROYAL DOULTON, and HUMMEL, country-look crocks and bowls, and marked art pottery.

The auction house offers another way to sell a house filled with ceramics. It is a good method if you can't take the time to separate the good from the bad. The good pieces will be sold separately. The best pieces may even be pictured and described in a brochure or catalog. There is a charge for pictures. Sets of dishes sell, but for low prices. Odd dishes can be placed into box lots and sold. Once again prices will be low. The auction house pays within three to six months, and its employees do all the work. Be sure to get a signed contract before leaving your merchandise. Have a written description of the items, including damage and repairs, and all terms of the sale.

> The nuns at Mary Seton College in Yonkers, New York, found a way to finance their work. They hired an appraiser to look at the art in the college. He found they owned a Medici porcelain bowl that was later auctioned for $180,000.

Sets of dishes can be sold to any one of the many matching services. There are many dealers throughout the country who make a living by selling matching pieces for sets of dishes, silver, or glassware. They are listed in several places, and many advertise in antiques publications and decorating magazines. These dealers always have customers waiting for dishes, and if your set is a popular pattern or in demand you can sell the set for a good price. The price a matching service is willing to pay is often better than an auction price. Send a description and a photograph or photocopy of a plate, front and back, and indicate the colors. Offer your set for sale. Be sure to include a self-addressed, stamped envelope.

Modern-looking, bright-colored dishes like FIESTA sell easily through newspaper ads, garage sales, and flea markets, or to dealers. Only perfect pieces can be sold. Chips and scratches make a difference. If the piece is twentieth century and common, a chip lowers the value by 90 percent. If the piece is rare (a Rookwood vase decorated with an Indian), a chip lowers the value only 10-20 percent. Prices are easy to find in the general price guides. AUTUMN LEAF pattern, WILLOW WARE, and LENOX china also sell easily. Anything by CLARICE CLIFF brings high prices.

Lamps are always hard to sell. If the ceramic base is not by a well-known art pottery, ROYAL DOULTON, or a name artist, it will sell simply as secondhand furniture.

Figurines of top quality from the eighteenth and early nineteenth centuries sell well. Look for the crossed swords mark of MEISSEN, the anchor of CHELSEA, or other symbols. Art Deco figures are popular now. Names worth extra money are GOLDSCHEIDER, CORDEY, WIESELTHIER, and ROBJ. Staffordshire figurines of dogs or unidentifiable people, romantic bisque Victorian men and women, and copies of eighteenth-century pieces sell for less than most think. We often hear descriptions like ''I know it is of value because every fingernail can be seen.'' This is not always true. You can often see every fingernail on a poor-quality figurine. The very best figures do sell for hundreds of dollars, however, and it might pay to take a clear picture or the actual figures to an auction house, dealer, or appraiser to learn the value.

''Country look'' pieces are the most confusing to a novice. Grand-mother's yellowware mixing bowl or blue spatter butter jar can be worth hundreds of dollars to the right collector or dealer. You must go to the shows and see the types of wares that are now popular and high priced. Stoneware crocks get publicity because examples with cobalt blue decorations of birds, people, or animals sell for thou-sands of dollars. Plain crocks are not expensive. The modern-shaped, bright red, cream, or blue pottery dishes made during the 1940s to store water or leftovers in the refrigerator sell well. So do some of

> The strange-looking Hummel figure was not illustrated in the price book. By calling a collectors club and a few serious collectors located through the club, it was found to be one of the rare "Hungarian" Hummels originally identified in 1976. It was then sold by mail for $6,000.

the salt and pepper sets, cookie jars, and canister sets of the 1920s-1960s.

Ashtrays don't sell well unless marked with a famous maker's name. Plain bowls, trays, and candy dishes sell for low prices unless by big makers. Beer steins of any type sell well; best are those by METTLACH. Novelty items, like figurines with nodding heads, open-mouthed monsters that are toothpick holders, fairings, and trinket boxes, GOSS souvenirs, small figurines of blacks, and "pink pig with green basket" figures, are all in demand.

How do you tell if you own a piece by an important factory in high demand by collectors? Look in the general price guides under the names you might find on your dishes. For example, R. S. PRUSSIA, NIPPON, ROYAL DOULTON, WEDGWOOD, SUSIE COOPER, HALL, HULL, McCOY, ROSEVILLE, WELLER, ROYAL BAYREUTH, HAVILAND, MINTON, LOTUS, NORITAKE, OHR, ROYAL COPENHAGEN, and many others are listed by name. If the factory is listed by name, the collectors are buying it. Some types are listed but not marked, so look at the shows and in the books until you can recognize SATSUMA, BANKO, SUMIDA GAWA, CHINESE EXPORT PORCELAIN, STAFFORDSHIRE, GOUDA, YELLOWWARE, SPATTERWARE, STONEWARE, IRONSTONE, PATE SUR PATE, and MAJOLICA. The collectors also look for the names of countries, such as OCCUPIED JAPAN and CZECHOSLOVAKIA.

Art pottery from the United States and England has become popular since the 1970s. Prices are steadily rising. The best of ROOKWOOD, and it may date from the 1930s, can sell for thousands of dollars. There are several books about art pottery that list names, patterns, and marks. The art pottery that many collect today was the florist's flower container of yesterday. A vase, filled with chicken wire so it could hold flowers, may still be in your mother's basement. When we wrote our book *Kovels' Collector's Guide to American Art Pottery*, we shopped at various garage sales and rummage stores and found choice pieces for a few dollars because they were unknown at the time. Books have now made the dealers and collectors experts, and they are willing to pay top prices for good pieces.

If the original cover for an art pottery or other type of ceramic jar is noticeably missing (some jars are made to be complete in appearance without a cover), deduct 50 percent. If a vase is decorated with, or shaped like, a pig or a snake, add 25-100 percent.

A 50¢ vase bought at a garage sale in Niles, Michigan, was thought by the new owners to be a fifteenth-century Ming porcelain. They told the newspapers it was worth $63,000. A week later, when an expert appraiser was called, it was found the vase was really worth about 50¢. Not everything is a treasure.

The ROYAL DOULTON and HUMMEL figurine craze may have made your 30-year-old figurine worth thousands of dollars. Doulton character jugs and series wares sell well, but the dinnerwares are like any other sets of dishes. The price books give retail prices, so you can easily price the figures and jugs by name or HN number. They sell quickly to dealers or at auction. Anything marked ''Goebel Hummel'' sells, although collectors prefer pieces with the old marks. If two figurines look exactly alike, the value may be different because of the small black V and Bee on the bottom. Marks, figurines, plates, and values are easy to find in the price books. The high prices will amaze you, and rarities sell quickly.

Limited edition collector plates are a problem. Many of them were made and sold. There is a small resale market for most of them. A few have gained in value. Look in the plate magazines listed in the Appendix for prices and dealers who buy plates. Talk to the local gift shops that sell plates or to those that handle what is known as the ''secondary market'' plates. Go to the shows. There is a huge swap meet at each national convention; if you can't sell your plates, perhaps you can trade them.

Anything oriental sells. If the marks are Chinese or Japanese characters, they are a mystery to most of us. They are not only hard to read but were often copied and put on the bottom of later porcelain pieces. It is said that 80 percent of the Chinese porcelains have ''retrospective'' marks (for example, an eighteenth-century copy with a sixteenth-century mark). If the piece has a retrospective mark, deduct 75 percent. An unmarked piece is usually of more value than a piece with an earlier, but retrospective, mark. The very old pieces (old is over 250 years old) sell to museums and serious collectors. This type of porcelain should be sold through a major auction house or top-priced dealer. Only experts can recognize the difference between old and more recent oriental pieces. Since the 1970s, quantities of average-quality blue and white nineteenth-century china has been shipped from China and Hong Kong for sale to collectors. These pieces are salable as decorative items, and they should be priced accordingly.

Chinese Export porcelain includes the dishes made in China in the eighteenth and nineteenth centuries to be sold in America and Europe. The dishes can be very valuable. Their gray-blue color can be easily recognized. Important tureens or platters with elaborate decorations or with a famous owner's initials can sell for thousands of dollars. A plain cup and saucer could be worth at least $100. If you have a set of export dishes, have them appraised before offering them for sale. Other oriental wares are also popular. The early, sophisticated Satsuma, the cruder, twentieth-century Satsuma, pieces made in Occupied Japan after World War II, and almost any other oriental porcelains sell quickly and for more money than comparable English or American pieces. Try to find someone to identify your pieces, and then check the prices in the general guides.

The family thought the figurine was ugly, but Mother always said it was valuable, so the children took it to an auction gallery. The marked Goldscheider figure of "The Butterfly Girl" sold for $3,100. "Beauty is in the eye of the beholder."

Blue and white dishes seem to be a favorite of collectors. Staffordshire "flow blue" was made in many patterns. Look for pieces without the word "England." They are usually older and should be worth more. If the center design is an American or Canadian architectural or historical scene, it is part of what collectors call "historic blue," and it can be worth a high price. The more common, fanciful oriental scenes, flowers, or other center designs are on the average-priced pieces. Platters, pitchers, and service bowls sell well because so few can be found. A soup tureen with an American view would be the best of all. It would sell for thousands of dollars. There are auctions and dealers who handle historic Staffordshire exclusively. ROWLAND AND MARSELLUS made a similar twentieth-century blue and white ware that is gaining in value. They made "rolled edge" plates with views of towns and cities for the local tourist trade. Collectors want the hundreds of different examples. Other popular blue and white patterns are IVANHOE, GIBSON GIRL, and the special plates made for colleges and universities by WEDGWOOD.

If you have a few dishes, spend a little time and do the research to be sure that you are not selling a treasure for 50¢ at your garage sale. If you have a houseful of dishes, you may have to sell them through a dealer or auction gallery and hope to get the best price for everything. Even the experts miss a few of the best items at times.

A list of china matching services can be found in the appendix.

°°°

Prints, Woodcuts, Posters, Calendar Art

It is difficult to sell black-and-white prints, etchings, and engravings. They are not popular now, and only very special prints in excellent condition by known artists will bring good money. Many prints that are attractive if framed have no antiques value. Some are just pages taken from old books. It takes an art expert to evaluate art prints. Your local museum may be able to help you identify the artist and age. Then the research needed to determine how to price the print is the same as the research needed to price a fine painting. (See Paintings section.) There are many terms that have meaning only to an expert. You don't need to know the difference between first strike, restrike, foxing, edition, steel engraving, etc. Unless you plan to go into the business of selling prints, the subtleties of these terms are too difficult to learn.

Japanese woodblock prints are popular and sell quickly. The prints were available immediately after World War II for only a few dollars each, and many soldiers brought them home. Today, some of the old prints in fine condition can be worth thousands of dollars. The colors should be bright, the paper untorn and without stains. If the print has been glued to a backing, it has lost its value. Several books are available to help you identify prints, but once again it takes an expert to know whether the woodblock print is worth a few hundred or a few thousand dollars. If you have had the prints for over thirty years, it would be wise to have an appraisal by an expert.

Other types of pictures can be more easily priced for sale. Movie, travel, and other posters are listed in price books and are easier to identify. The only hazards are the reproductions. Many old posters have been reissued and reproduced. There are clues, especially for movie posters, and easy research in the library will help.

Travel posters and circus posters sell at highest prices as decora-

tive pictures. Large colorful posters with interesting subjects sell quickly if in very good condition. Torn, faded posters do not sell. French posters by well-known artists, advertising posters, and posters printed by important companies are bought by specialists who will pay more than the average poster price. Check the value in a general price book or look in the catalogs sent out by the mail-order poster dealers. These dealers also have to buy more posters, so they could be your customers.

Calendar art, the pictures printed for the tops of wall-hung paper calendars, is a new area of collecting. Pinup girl prints by PETTY, VARGAS, and other artists working after 1940 are in demand. Sentimental pictures of children by early 1900s artists like BESSIE PEASE GUTMANN or ROSE O'NEILL sell well. Landscapes by R. ATKINSON FOX or Art Deco prints by MAXFIELD PARRISH are also desirable. Old CURRIER &

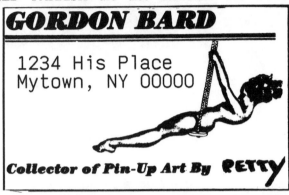

IVES prints have always been popular. Action scenes and outdoor scenes are priced the highest; religious subjects, vases of flowers, and portraits of children are priced low. Be careful, because there have been many reproductions. Look in *Currier & Ives Prints: An Illustrated Check List* for the exact size of the original of your print. Then look up the value in the general price books. Hand-colored bird prints by JOHN GOULD or JOHN JAMES AUDUBON, botanical prints, interior room views, architectural drawings, military scenes, and many other prints removed from nineteenth-century books are sold by special dealers at most large antiques shows. These may be the dealers who will buy your prints.

ooo

Radio & Television Sets

RADIOS

The streamlined, colored-plastic creations of the 1930s are the most wanted radios. More recent figural radios, especially those patterned on Disney characters, are selling for high prices. The blue mirror-covered EMERSON is worth money, even if it is not in working order. Brown plastic-cased radios, wooden radios, and large elaborate floor models made after 1935 are of limited value even if they are in working order. Some floor models are considered furniture, and the insides are removed and replaced with a stereo. If your radio is the proper size and shape for this, it has some sale value. Sets with added value are FADA, EMERSON, and crystal sets.

The old radio didn't work too well, so it was put in the basement about 1950. When the owners moved to a condominium in 1985, they noticed the radio and offered it to a grandchild. He asked permission to sell it to a collector friend; the red plastic radio then sold for $500.

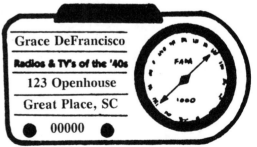

TELEVISIONS

Only the very early TV sets, those made before 1950 with screens of 2 inches or less, are of interest to collectors. Even these do not sell for hundreds of dollars, and it is difficult to find the right collector. Unfortunately, your old TV has very little value, especially if it is not working. The earliest sets worked on a chemical battery that requires maintenance.

Do not plug in the radio or TV to test it. You may cause damage or a fire. Just look for obviously missing parts. The serious collector will be able to judge value better than you. Even the tubes could be of use to repair other sets.

ooo

Rugs

Everyone knows that oriental rugs have value, but it is almost impossible to determine the value unless you are a rug expert. If you inherit a large, old oriental, have it appraised by a rug dealer or sold through an auction gallery. Never ask a rug dealer to "make an offer." If you were in the business of selling old rugs, wouldn't you offer as little as possible so that you could make a larger profit? The actual worth of the rug and the offer may have little in common. It is better to pay for an appraisal from a competent person and then try to sell it elsewhere. If you sell it as part of a house sale, be sure to learn the proper name for the rug, and be sure you have an expert set the price. Many things affect rug prices: the condition (no worn spots, stains, or missing fringe), the color (unfaded), the number of knots to the inch, the material (silk or wool are best), and the design and overall quality. Size is also important. Room-sized rugs and stair runners sell quickly. Very large rugs, 18 feet by 30 feet or larger, can only bring good prices at a well-advertised auction or from a major rug dealer.

Chinese rugs, especially those with Art Deco designs and pleasing colors (purple and chartreuse are hard to sell), any type of pictorial rag rug, needlepoints, dhurries, Navaho rugs, and almost any other type of usable floor coverings sell for good prices. If you have no guidelines and your rug is in good condition, measure it, determine the number of square yards, and price it at a little more than good new carpeting.

Sheet Music

Sheet music is collected for many reasons. Some want the music, but most want the old covers to frame as pictures. Others want covers that are celebrity or movie related. So there are several ways to sell the sheet music you might find in a box or a piano bench. A few pieces of sheet music may not have great value, but a pile of the music could add up to considerable money.

There is added value to covers illustrated with an old car, a train, a political event, a Gibson girl, blacks, well-known movie stars, Elvis Presley, or even a war scene. The general rule is the smaller the picture on the title page, the older the sheet music. Only historians want the early pieces. By the 1870s, the cover was a full picture, which was almost always lithographed. Photographs were used by the early 1900s. Sheet music was printed on pages measuring 13½ inches by 10½ inches before 1917. Most sheet music was published on sheets measuring 12 by 9 inches after 1920. Collectors like covers made before the 1930s.

The best prices are paid for music with all the pages intact and untrimmed. After 1920 the old music was often cut to fit in the piano bench. Dust the music and carefully erase pencil marks and smudges with an art gum eraser before you sell. Transparent tape and tears always lower the value, sometimes to a few cents. Dealers in shops and flea markets sell most of the music. It doesn't sell well at auctions.

Collectors and dealers of sheet music advertise in the general antiques publications and the paper ephemera publications. There are several dealers who sell music through the mail using monthly lists. They could be your best customers.

●●●

Silver

An old sterling silver teaspoon is never worth less than its meltdown value, which is the weight of the spoon multiplied by the going price of silver bullion. The number is reported in the daily newspapers on the stock quotation pages. If a dime is old enough to be made of a silver alloy, it could be worth more than 10¢ in meltdown value based on the price of silver. Most antique silver is worth more than the meltdown value, but the value is often calculated from that figure. Some appraisers weigh old silver and multiply the result by two times the meltdown; some use other formulas. Jewelry stores, coin shops, and "Gold, Silver, and Platinum Dealers" are listed in the phone book, and they will weigh and buy for the meltdown value. This is actually the lowest price you should receive for your pieces. Don't forget that some pieces of old silver, especially candlesticks, are "weighted." There is a heavy material in the base that keeps the candlestick from tipping. The meltdown buyers are interested in what the thin sterling shell weighs after the weight is removed.

A delivery boy in New York was given pawn tickets by an old lady he had helped by carrying her groceries. She kept telling him she was giving him her treasures. When she died, his family used its savings to redeem the pawned items, which turned out to be valuable silver. Instead of selling the silver immediately, they took it for a free appraisal at an auction house. The boy received over $50,000 from his benefactor's legacy of silver.

"Coin," "Sterling," and "925" are all indications of solid silver. The number 925 means 925 parts silver for every 1,000 parts of metal. It is marked on what is called "sterling silver." The word "coin" is stamped on nineteenth-century pieces that were made from melted coins. The silver content varies from 800 to 925 parts of silver. Many European silver pieces are marked 800. All these pieces are wanted for meltdown. Silver plate, A1, EPNS, triple plate, and other similar terms mean that the piece is made of a base metal and is covered with a thin layer of silver. The word "Sheffield" has several meanings. If it is stamped on the bottom of your piece, you probably have an item that is silver plated. None of the plated pieces have a good meltdown value.

Makers' names and hallmarks are very important in determining value. The names GEORG JENSEN, TIFFANY, MARTELE, LIBERTY, and (PAUL) REVERE, or the initials of the famous English silversmiths, like PAUL STORR or PAUL DE LAMERIE, add to

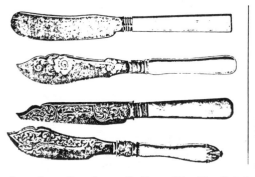

the value of a piece of silver. The English hallmark system of four or five small marks looks like this 🦀 🏰 Ⓥ Ⓞ . If the king's head looks to the right, the piece was made before 1850 and probably has added value. Queen Victoria's head faces left. Queen Elizabeth II's head faces left. The lion is an indication of sterling quality.

The showiest pieces of silver, such as the tea sets, punch bowls, epergnes, and large candelabra, always have a good resale value. Elaborate English pieces dating from 1850 to 1900 are usually "ball-park" priced from five to seven times the meltdown value. If the work is exceptional, if the silversmith is well known, or if the history ties the silver to a famous family or event, it could be worth as much as ten to twelve times the meltdown price. The condition is always important. There should be no dents, broken handles, or alterations. Tea sets of any description usually can be sold, even in poor condition. Twentieth-century plated or sterling sets should be priced at less than half the modern department store prices. Sterling sets must be priced with the weight considered. Earlier sets are worth more than modern sets. The price is determined by age, artistic value, and the maker. Silver tea services sell best at important house sales. Contact local house sale managers to see if you can have it sold by them at someone else's house. Silver-plated trays, small dishes, and flatware have a very low resale value, especially if they are not in mint condition.

Ordinary silver made after 1900 usually sells for about twice the meltdown price. If the decorations are lavish or if the piece is a very desirable shape, such as a punch bowl, it might sell for four times the meltdown. Very large or very decorative pieces can bring up to ten times meltdown. Pieces with a special meaning, such as Jewish religious items or historic pieces, sell for even more. Commemorative silver medals and modern limited edition sets sell for meltdown.

Very ornate Victorian silver is back in fashion and "more is better" when it comes to pricing. All sterling serving spoons, forks, asparagus servers, fish servers, grape shears, and other large serving pieces sell at prices comparable to modern examples. Very small pieces, like nut picks or pickle forks, do not sell as well. Pieces with elaborate, crisp, bright-cut designs sell well. Those with worn bright cutting are not in much demand. Figural napkin rings and souvenir spoons have a special value to collectors, so the meltdown value is in no way related to the price.

Sterling silver flatware in good condition is always worth more than meltdown. Sell it through an auction or offer it at a house sale at a price from 30 to 50 percent less than the department store price for a similar set. It can also be sold to a silver matching service. (To find matching services, visit large antiques shows or look in publications in the Appendix.) Send a photocopy of the front and back of a spoon or fork if you don't know the pattern name. Include a list of pieces and a stamped, self-addressed envelope. A monogram will lower the value on a set of silver less than 100 years old, but a crest or elaborate monogram on eighteenth-century or early nineteenth-century silver adds to the value. You do not have to remove a monogram; doing so is expensive and can cause damage. The market for silver flatware is many leveled. If the retailer, department store, or gift shop gets $5,000 for a new set of silver, a discount store might get 25 percent less or $3,750. The antiques shop or auction gallery would probably

> A well-informed American tourist at a London flea market paid
> about $70 each for two old tarnished, battered silver cups. The
> new owner took them to an auction gallery. Eight months later
> they were sold for $22,000 each. It wasn't just luck. The tour-
> ist realized that the hallmark *IC* in a fleur-de-lis was used by
> John Coney, a Boston silversmith who died in 1722. The cups
> were sold in New York, where American silver is appreciated.

ask 50 percent of retail, or $2,500, for a used set. The meltdown
would be half of that, $1,250 or even less. You determine your price
by where you plan to sell the set. Silver plated flatware is also
collected and can be matched but sells for low prices.

Early Sheffield plated silver, made before 1840 by rolling a thin
layer of silver on a copper base, has a special value for collectors.
Good pieces are worth thousands of dollars. If the copper shows because the top layer of silver is worn, the value is at least 50 percent less. If a piece of early rolled Sheffield is replated, deduct 90
percent.

If a piece of electroplated silver made after 1840 needs resilvering, deduct 50 percent. If a piece of electroplated silver has been
replated, deduct 5 percent. If the handle of a piece has been replaced, the feet redone, or any other part totally replaced, deduct 75
percent. If the piece has been reworked (a stein made from a vase),
the result is worth meltdown value plus about 10 percent.

A list of silver matching services can be found in the appendix.

ooo

Stamps

There have been stamp collectors since 1840, when the first postage
stamp was introduced by Sir Rowland Hill of England. It is a very
specialized field. Stamps should be examined by a dealer in stamps or
an auction house that knows that market. A large, serious collection
requires an expert. Condition, rarity, and demand determine the
prices. A stamp should have its original bright color, a centered
design, and wide margins. There should be no defects, full gum on the
back, no hinge marks, and only a light, clear cancel mark if used. It
should have no tears, dirt, creases, pinholes, or uneven perforations.
The average child's collection is rarely very valuable, but it should
always be checked.

The post office sells corner blocks of stamps to collectors every
day. These have been put away as an investment by many casual col-

lectors who have little understanding of the market. Most of the blocks under thirty years old only sell for their face value. Check with a stamp dealer and then use them on letters. Many sheets of commemoratives are equally unsalable for more than the face value. If you have blocks or sheets or sets of stamps, be sure you determine the value before you split them up or use them.

Don't ignore the stamps on old postcards and letters. Even printed stamps on postal cards could have a value. First day covers have a special value, and the stamp should not be removed. Sell the entire envelope. Envelopes with stamps postmarked before 1900 should be checked for value. Those dating before the Civil War should be appraised by an expert. Letters mailed without stamps for special reasons (during the Civil War) can be very valuable. Never remove a stamp from an envelope to sell it. Sell the envelope and stamp together.

Dealers are listed in the Yellow Pages of the telephone book. Clubs, shows, and meetings are listed in the philatelist publications in the Appendix. The best way to value or to sell stamps is with the help of experts. You may want a formal appraisal before you decide whether the collection should be auctioned or sold to a dealer. It is rarely a good idea to break up a collection and sell the stamps yourself unless you are a serious collector who has purchased through clubs and shows. The stamps are too small and too fragile to be handled over and over.

ooo

Stocks & Bonds

It seems that everyone who survived the stock market crash of 1929 had some stocks or bonds that, although worthless, were saved. Today there are two possible values for these old stocks. A few might have value due to a merger or acquisition. The worthless company or mine may have merged, been sold, found gold, or become part of a valuable company in some other way. To learn if you own stocks or bonds of value, first try your library. Look in *The Directory of Obsolete Securities* (Financial Information, Inc.), *The Capital Changes Reporter* (Commerce

Clearing House), or even try tracking mergers through the *Standard & Poor's* or *Moody's* directories. There are also several companies that will research your stock for a fee. (See Appendix.)

If your stocks have no value as part of a company, they still have a value for collectors who specialize in the scripophily market. (That's the formal name for the collecting of stocks and bonds.) Old certificates were decorated with elaborately engraved vignettes. Some were fanciful pictures of Liberty or other symbols, some pictured the industry with oil wells or smokestacks, while others were a combination of these. These certificates are sometimes framed and sold as gifts to collectors. For example, a picture of an oil well may intrigue a car collector. Railroads, mines, airplanes, and automobiles are favored. If the certificate is signed by a famous person, such as Thomas Edison or John D. Rockefeller, the price is higher. Some certificates have revenue stamps, and rare ones are purchased by stamp collectors.

Condition is always important; clean, crisp certificates are worth more than creased, worn examples. Hole-punched cancel marks lower the value. Other fiscal paper, such as mortgages, checks, and legal documents, may also have value. (See Paper Collectibles section.)

ooo

Telephone Collectibles

If you have anything old that has the word "telephone" or the familiar bell symbol pictured, it can be sold. Everything from telephone booths to telephones to telephone insulators is collected. The highest-priced phones are those that look old and that can be altered to actually work on today's phone lines. Blue glass paperweights, banks, enameled signs, and anything else marked with the Bell Telephone logo are purchased. Prices can be found in the general price books.

Telephone insulators are the glass, dome-shaped objects found at the top of telephone poles. Most insulators are found by digging in dumps or near old poles; selling is usually done at special shows for insulators or at the bottle shows. Only unusual or rare insulators in perfect condition sell for over a few dollars. Insulators are priced in many general price books, but it takes some special knowledge to recognize a treasure. If you have a basket of old insulators, take them to a show and talk to the collectors. They will tell you what the insulators are worth, and the show is the best place for you to dispose of them.

ⴲⴲⴲ

Textiles — Samplers, Quilts, Printed Fabric, Lace

The women's movement sparked an interest in the work of women from past centuries. That seems to have started the amazing rise in the price of old quilts, woven coverlets, samplers, and other examples of feminine handiwork from the past. The country decorating magazines added to the interest, and it wasn't long before collectors wanted open shelves piled high with examples of quilts and homespun cloth. Quilts are hung like huge pictures on the walls behind beds heaped with white work pillows and covers. Paisley shawls have become tablecloths. All of this means that any type of old textile that exhibits some handiwork can be sold.

SAMPLERS

The sampler originated in England. It was literally a sample of needlework done by a young girl. We must remember that hand-loomed sheets, covers, towels, and underclothes were expensive. In the legal accountings after a death, the linens were among the most valuable items in an eighteenth-century home. Every girl was expected to weave and sew enough for her future home. It was considered an important part of her dowry. Each item was embroidered with letters and numbers as part of an inventory system. Samplers had the alphabet, numbers, some symbolic pictures, and perhaps a motto or favorite saying. It was then proudly signed and dated by the girl who had stitched it. Samplers were made on homespun fabric, and the thread was often home-dyed. These materials discolor and fade, so condition is very important. A sampler with clear colors and a light background is worth from five to ten times as much as a similar sampler that is brown and faded. American and Canadian samplers are priced higher than English examples. You can sometimes identify the country of origin from the wording and designs. Crowns usually indicate an English sampler.

Seventeenth-century samplers are long and thin. In the eighteenth century the sampler became more rectangular. Nineteenth-century samplers have pictorial and memorial designs. Some "darning" samplers were made. Holes were cut and then darned. These were often from Holland. Italian samplers were frequently fringed instead of hemmed, and they often featured religious motifs. German samplers favored very small designs, often made with wool thread. Spanish samplers were almost always square, with a center design and borders.

Age can influence the price. The older, the better, provided the condition is good. Repairs lower the value of a sampler, and you should never repair an old one before selling it. Leave that to an expert. The history of the family of the maker always adds to the value. If your sampler was made by a distant relative, write down all the information you know, including the name, birth date, and venue of the maker. Attach the history to the back of the frame. The sampler would be even more valuable if your great-great-aunt had been part of a presidential family or had roomed with Nellie Bly. Any verifiable facts that connect the sampler to local or national history add to the price. Eighteenth-century American samplers sell for very high prices. If you are selling, try to have an appraisal by an expert before setting the price. Early nineteenth-century samplers are high priced; the handiwork of a 1920s child, however, is of a limited value.

QUILTS

If you can call it a quilt, you can sell it. The newspapers often report sales of quilts for thousands of dollars, but these quilts are exceptional. Age influences the price, but the most important factor is skill. The better the quilt design and stitching, the higher the price. Quilts are judged like fine paintings. Experts look for good design, originality, and unusual fabrics. There are several kinds of quilts. Some are pieced with many small patches stitched together. This large composite piece is then used as the top layer of a sandwich with a plainer bottom layer and a cotton filling. The three layers are then quilted together into one useful covering. The design and skill of this stitching or quilting is important in determining the value. Small stitches and attractive curved patterns in the almost invisible quilting are the key to a top-quality quilt. The very late or very simple quilt "sandwiches" may only be held together with knotted threads placed at intervals. Machine-stitched quilts were made in the late nineteenth century and after. The earliest quilts had a large center design. By the Civil War it had become fashionable to use overall repetitive designs that became known as Four-Patch, Log Cabin, Pineapple, and Sunburst.

Many fine quilts can still be found today in attic trunks. The mountain areas of West Virginia and Kentucky seem to furnish an endless quantity to the "pickers" who supply the best shops with antiques. The Amish from all areas made quilts of geometric blocks and

dark colors; these quilts have become fashionable and expensive. You must beware, as there are still skilled needleworkers making Amish and other quilts. The fabrics are probably the best guide to age.

It is possible to do an almost undetectable restoration on a quilt if you can find the proper fabric. Local quilting groups often repair quilts; if you have some minor damage on a quilt, you might check on the cost and quality of repairs before you sell. The usual rule for antiques is never to repair before you sell, but if the quilt is to be sold at auction, it will probably pay to have it in usable condition.

The libraries are filled with books about quilts and quilt values. Quilts are considered ''folk art'' and sell quickly. There will be quilts of all qualities at almost every antiques show. We went to a tailgate show in Indiana one weekend, and a single dealer had 150 quilts hanging on a fence. The supply seems endless, but there is a real shortage of top-quality pieces. They sell well everywhere but sell for the most money at the trendy New York shops. If you find twenty quilts made over eighty years ago by a very talented relative, it might pay to take them to New York.

COVERLETS AND HOMESPUN

Early fabrics were often completely handmade, from the growing of the cotton or flax to the cleaning, clipping, spinning, dyeing, and weaving of the finished thread. Homespun cloth was usually made in subdued shades of blue, green, brown, or red. Checked or striped patterns gained in favor and price during the 1980s. The faded, country look was ''in.'' Modern copies of the fabrics have been made, but collectors will always pay a premium for the real thing. Prices are standard and are easy to determine from a careful look at an antiques show. If your homespun is of similar size and condition, it should sell to a dealer for about half the retail price asked at a show.

Coverlets are more complicated to price because the condition, design, and maker's signature are equally important. Many coverlets have a name and date woven into the corner. These names can be checked in *Checklist of American Coverlet Weavers* by John W. Heisey. Coverlets by some weavers and coverlets with special borders, like a train, boat, or building design, are popular and expensive. Check in the price books and at the shows to learn more about their value; books list coverlets by maker pattern. Coverlets sell well at shows and auctions or to private collectors.

PRINTED TEXTILES

Printed textiles sell to a very small group of collectors. An old textile, such as a piece of drape, bedspread, or valance that is over 100 years old, is sometimes valuable because the print is historically interesting. Scenes of the death of Washington, fabrics used in political campaigns, World's Fair mementos, or important, early, roller-printed fabrics are high priced. They sell best in pieces that can be framed and hung as pictures. The entire repeat of the pattern should be included. Some newer fabrics are in demand for use as upholstery materials or for pillows. Art Deco and Art Nouveau designs, the free-form patterns of the 1950s, or bright Hawaiian Deco prints sell to the right person. The fabrics probably have low value if there is not sufficient yardage for at least one chair. The same collectors want historical handkerchiefs to frame for pictures. A good fabric "picture" is worth hundreds of dollars. Look in the library for books that picture old roller-printed fabrics. Many modern reproductions have been made, but if you are selling fabric found in an old attic trunk, you probably know if it is old or new. The dealer buying it will certainly know. Just remember, don't throw away any fabrics before you try to sell them.

LACE

There are probably fewer experts on old lace than in almost any field of collecting. Pieces of very old lace, such as collars, cuffs, or bits of trim, sell for thousands of dollars in Europe, where lace has been recognized and appreciated. There are few collectors or dealers in the United States who are interested in lace of that quality. Only the museums seem to be knowledgeable. If you have a box of your mother's old lace, chances are it is not over fifty years old and is of value only in the places where vintage clothing is bought and sold. If your mother made lace, or came from Europe and possibly saved the lace from her or her grandmother's wedding dress, you might have some valuable pieces. Take the lace to be appraised by an auction gallery if possible. Ask if they sell much lace and what prices they seem to get. If they can't identify old lace, ask for the expert at your local museum. The museum can't give a price, but an expert can tell you if it is old, handmade, and rare. Large lace pieces might sell for good prices to the vintage clothing shops that sell elaborate, redesigned, lace blouses or wedding dresses. If you have lace that a museum identifies as made before 1750, contact a major auction gallery.

We have tried to understand lace for years. We are able to tell handmade from machine-made and good from bad, but we still are not able to distinguish great from good. It takes an expert with experience. Pricing is even more difficult, so if you have any suspicion that your lace treasures are old and handmade, take them to an expert dealer, appraiser, museum curator, or auction gallery for an opinion.

The collectors of fabrics also buy Stevengraphs and other silk woven fabric pictures, good examples of needlepoint and Berlin work, and the many tools used in sewing, lacework, and other needlework. If you find an old, filled sewing basket, you have a treasure. There are buyers for thimbles, tape measures, buttons, trim, half-finished embroideries, and even the sewing basket.

ooo

Tobacco

Tobacco, like beer, seems to be a popular collecting area for men. Anything that has a picture of tobacco or held tobacco has a market. Labels, ads, tobacco cards, felts, tins, pipes, tags, and other smoking memorabilia sell well to general antiques dealers or in any of the usual ways one sells antiques. (Look in the sections on Advertising and Labels for some special suggestions.) A large collection of tobacco-related material might do well at auction. A small collection could be sold quickly at flea markets and shows.

A nonsmoker is amazed that old pipes sell for high prices to men who want to use them or display them. Lighters, cigar clippers, tobacco stamps, and cigar and cigarette cases are wanted for use. Prices can be found in the general price books. These are items that also sell well to friends who are smokers.

000

Tools

A few tools hung on the wall as sculptural decorations are often seen in the decorating magazines. Old tools can be sold to any friend or antiques dealer. There are also many serious tool collectors who specialize in one type of tool, such as wrenches or planes, or who have large general collections. If you have a toolbox filled with old hand tools, it would pay to try to find the dealers who specialize in tools or to contact the members of a tool-collecting club. There are some auction houses that have special tool sales a few times a year. If you have only one item, it is probably best to sell it locally. Many old-looking tools have minimal value, but some special tools are worth hundreds or even thousands of dollars.

Look for the name STANLEY. It adds to the value, and there are several special price books for Stanley tools. Also look for KEEN CUTTER, WINCHESTER, and stamped names and locations that were sometimes put on the early handmade tools by the makers. The most popular tools seem to be axes, planes, and rulers.

There is a disagreement among collectors about the desired condition of tools. Some clean and wax the wood and clean the metal. Others will not buy a tool that has been newly waxed or varnished. It won't hurt to remove the major dirt with a quick washing, but don't wax, scour, or use rust remover. Let the new owner make that decision. If you do it, you are taking a chance of losing a sale.

000

Toys

Don't discard any old toys. Even a Barbie doll's girdle has value to a collector. The best-selling toys are antique dolls, teddy bears, nineteenth-century iron toys, robot and space toys, pedal cars, and scale model autos and trains. Dollhouses and dollhouse furnishings, dolls from the 1930s to the 1960s, including Barbie and her accessories, banks and lithographed tin toys are valuable. Games, game boards, celebrity items, and farm toys are good sellers. Any toy that is out of production and mint-in-the-box has a resale value to collectors. Any old toy in good condition has value. The only toy that can be tattered and torn and still worth big money is a teddy bear over fifty years old; collectors seem to think it proves the bear was "loved." Other badly worn toys are of little value except for use as parts for repairs.

There are special antique toy and doll shows. They are the best places to sell old toys. Dealers at these shows sell for the highest prices and can usually afford to pay the highest prices. The shows are listed in the general antiques publications in the Appendix. Doll hospitals are listed in the Yellow Pages of the telephone book, and the owners often buy dolls and doll parts. General antiques dealers buy many types of toys. Look around in the shops and offer your toys to the dealer with toys like yours. It may be embarrassing to think that your childhood toys are antiques, but age is not the only factor determining value. The most desirable robots, space toys, and Barbie dolls from the 1960s sell for hundreds of dollars. Big isn't necessarily better. Size doesn't determine the value. All types of miniatures and dollhouse items are in demand. Lead and even plastic soldiers sell well if they are rare and in good condition. Look for the name BRITAINS.

MODEL TRAINS AND CARS

Big is better for electric model trains. The most valued are the Standard Gauge (2⅛ inches between the rails), then 0 gauge (half as big as Standard Gauge). There are special train collector shows in many cities and they provide the best place to sell an old train and its accessories. Even the houses, lampposts, trees, and figures made for elaborate train landscapes are selling well. Names that add value to trains include LIONEL, AMERICAN FLYER, CARLISLE AND FINCH, DORFAN, REVELL INC., MECCANO, and PLASTIC-VILLE.

All sorts of small and large automotive toys are wanted, from miniatures to pedal cars large enough for a child to ride. Look for the names: BUDDY L, TOOTSIETOY, DINKY TOY, CORGI, HUBLEY, GREY, KENTON, MANOIL, and ARCADE. Some very well known toy makers produced a great variety of toys for many years: wooden, iron, battery-operated, tin, slush-cast models, and windups. Collectors recognize the most famous of these companies and sometimes specialize in their products. This means there is added value to early toys marked MARX, BING, CHEIN, IVES, LINEOL, LEHMANN, MARKLIN, SCHUCO, STRAUSS, and STEPHENS AND BROWN.

Don't repaint, restore, or redress an old toy before you sell it. You could destroy all the value for a collector. If an iron or tin toy is repainted, deduct 75 percent. If a small piece is missing, such as a driver of a wagon, the wheel of a car, or an arm from a figure in the Dogpatch band, deduct only 20 percent. These missing pieces can be found.

BANKS

Bank collectors search for old mechanical banks and iron still (or nonmechanical) banks. A mechanical bank usually moves when a lever is pressed. Many of these have been reproduced and have the words "Book of Knowledge" on the bottom. Other reproductions are unmarked. Even the reproduction can be sold, but for a low price. There are books that tell which banks have been made recently, how to tell a fake by checking the bottom marking, and other clues. If there are indications that your bank has been altered on the bottom, it is probably a recent copy. "Recent" means after 1930. The "age of mechanical banks" was from the late 1890s to World War I. Mechanical banks have sold for hundreds to thousands of dollars since the 1970s, so collectors have now started to buy iron still banks. Several special price books picture and price hundreds of these banks. Repainted banks are worth much less than examples with old, worn paint. New paint could even hide identification marks of a recent copy.

DOLLS

Dolls are easy to sell, but hard to price. Rare, old French and German dolls from the nineteenth century bring thousands of dollars and should be sold to a top doll dealer or through an auction gallery. Several galleries have sales devoted just to dolls. The major collectors, with the most money and the best dolls, go to these auctions and pay high prices. Some sales even include lots of doll bodies, legs, arms, and eyes from old dolls, which are valued for repairs. We have seen a headless body sell for over $100.

Collectors divide dolls into several general categories. Antique dolls are seventy-five years old or older. Collectible dolls are from twenty-five to seventy-five years old. Modern dolls are those made during the past twenty-five years. Contemporary dolls are those still being made. The general rule is that it takes twenty years for a doll to start to go up in value, so the dolls whose prices are rising today are Barbie and other dolls of the 1960s. The most valuable Barbie is the first model. It has holes in the feet because it was made to fit on pegs on a stand. If your dolls are not rare and over seventy-five years old, they will probably sell well in shops that deal in dolls. The collectible foreign dolls of the 1930s to 1950s were difficult to sell for any price until the 1970s. Now they are found at most shops and doll sales. Stuffed cloth dolls, advertising and comic figures, composition dolls like Shirley Temple dolls, dolls that are replicas of famous people, characters from literature or movies, and, of course, the teenage dolls sell quickly if they are priced properly. These are all moderately priced dolls.

Many dolls are marked by the manufacturer. Look at the back of the neck, on the shoulders, or on the head of a hard porcelain or composition doll. Sometimes there are labels on the bottom of the feet, on the chest, in the clothes, or on extra tags. A few dolls can be accurately identified by the shape of eyes, face, feet, hands, or other parts, or by some peculiarity of construction. A doll expert can easily recognize these features. Look for twentieth-century dolls marked MATTEL, MADAME ALEXANDER, RAVCA, STEIFF, SCHOENHUT, LENCI, VOGUE, and STORYBOOK. Any KEWPIE or RAGGEDY ANN is worth money. Earlier dolls are often marked with initials or symbols. Look these up at your library in the *Collector's Encyclopedia of Dolls*, 2 volumes, by Dorothy S., Elizabeth A., and Evelyn J. Coleman.

Save all the boxes and hangtags that come with the doll. They add to the value. Always save all the accessories. The tiny pair of ice skates or the straw hat can add much to the value. If you should find the printed fabric that was sold to be made into a stuffed doll, don't cut and stuff it. It is worth more uncut. Paper dolls are worth more uncut. Don't restore any damaged dolls. A collector prefers to see the doll before restoration. A dealer can have the restoration done at a lower price, so the economies of the market make it smarter to sell a doll "as is."

Doll accessories sell well. Old clothing, doll carriages, chairs, and even old photographs of children with old dolls sell quickly. The celluloid pin found on the original Shirley Temple doll is so important that it has been reproduced. Barbie's clothes, including shoes, purse, and sunglasses, are valuable.

If you have an antique doll or a collection of 1930s dolls, you have a valuable asset, but you must set the price to sell it. Dolls that are to be sold through a major doll auction need no formal appraisal. Just photograph the doll dressed and undressed. The pictures should show details of construction, a close-up of the face, and any marks or damage. Send the pictures and a description to a doll auction house. If you want an appraisal so you can sell the doll to a dealer or friend, you can pay for one from a local doll dealer or doll hospital. Some of the doll auction galleries will do appraisals by mail for a fee. Local members of the major appraisal societies (listed in the Appendix) should be able to tell you the value of your dolls. Doll appraisal clinics are held in many parts of the country in conjunction with a sale; professional advise is available either for a small fee or free. Some doll shows give verbal appraisals for a small fee. There are several good books that list doll prices (see Appendix); your bookstore or library will have them. Study these books carefully. You will usually find a doll similar to yours, but you will rarely find exactly the same doll. Even so, the prices are a guide. Condition is important. Even minor cracks and repaints lower the value of pre-1920 dolls by 50-75 percent. Although original clothes are preferred, replacements that are old do not lower the value. Once you have a general idea of the value of your doll, you can sell it through an auction, to an antiques or doll dealer, in a shop, at a special doll show, at a house sale, or by any of the other methods dicussed in the Introduction. There seems to be an emotional "something" that influences buyers of dolls and toys, so pricing is sometimes best set by determining how "lovable" your toy might be.

A word of caution! If you send your doll to a dealer on consignment or to an auction, always be sure to keep a complete pictorial record and a written description. Have the dealer sign and return your record after examining the doll. Too often there is an argument later about the doll's condition if the doll is returned because it couldn't be sold. There is a classic horror story told by doll collectors about the doll that went to a doll hospital to be repaired. When it was returned, it appeared to be a totally different doll, with a new head, new body and arms. The doll hospital insisted that it was the old doll repaired. The collector was certain that the old doll was so valuable the dishonest repairer switched the parts. This is a legend, but there is a possibility of a misunderstanding anytime you give your valuable items to another person. Keep accurate pictures and records. Repairs, new parts, and replacements sometimes seem to "appear." It is like hanging new curtains in a room. The room looked fine before, but after fresh, bright curtains are added, the woodwork and walls look nicked, smudged, and in need of paint and the carpet seems faded. Set dates for payment or the return of any unsold dolls. Many doll hospitals insist on this sort of written record to assure customer satisfaction.

It is difficult to discuss doll and toy sales because absolutely every toy older than five years is wanted by someone. Even the early computer-type games are collected. (They have to work.) Tin windup toys are wanted, but prices are 75-90 percent lower if they have a broken spring. If you have boxes of toys in the attic, be sure to check carefully on their possible value before you sell.

TEDDY BEARS

Condition is important when selling old toys, games, or dolls, but collectors do not seem to mind how worn or tattered a teddy bear may be. Poor condition lowers value a little, but not as much as it does for any other type of antique. We have seen teddy bears with no eyes, worn "fur," and arms torn off and hanging sell at auction to a dealer for over $300. The first teddy bear was made in 1902. Early teddy bears often have longer noses than the new ones have. Some have added features like electrically lit eyes or internal music boxes. There seems to be no explanation for the teddy bear mania of today. Any bear made before 1950 is worth over $100. Some are even worth thousands. There has been so much interest in teddy bears that there are clubs, calendars, contests, newspapers, magazines, and books on the subject. If you have an old bear, everyone will want to buy it. Try to find a trusted collector friend or a qualified appraiser who will know if you own a fortune or just a nice bear. Look for the name

STEIFF (and a tag in the ear), for long noses, and for unfamiliar types of fur.

GAMES

Games have a special appeal for collectors. If you are lucky enough to have a very early baseball game, it may be of more value to a baseball card collector than to a game collector. The Lindbergh games based on his airplane flight, the games with ads for products like Coca-Cola, and the celebrity or TV-related games like Star Trek sell for more money to the specialist than to the game collector. If Orphan Annie, Jack Armstrong, Charlie Chaplin, or Disney characters are on the game or box, you have a high-priced item.

Collectors divide games into types. "Name Games" are those that are collected for their association with well-known events, people, places, or collecting areas. The theme of the game is important. Remember, the collector is not buying the game to play it, but rather to display it. The graphics of the board, the box, and the shape of the playing pieces add to the value. Look for anything that includes pictures of advertising, airplanes, animals, automobiles, bicycles, blacks, cartoons, circus themes, fortune-tellers, motorcycles, movies, political themes, radios, Santa Claus, sports, the Statue of Liberty, TV, and war battles.

Game collectors want what one expert calls "Game Games." These games are collected for their graphics, their parts, or their historic value. Unless early (pre-1910) or exceptionally decorated, "Game Games" do not sell as well as "Name Games." The companies that made these games are important. Those marked MILTON BRADLEY, McLOUGHLIN BROTHERS, IVES, PARKER BROTHERS, SELCHOW & RIGHTER, BLISS, E. I. HORSMAN, CLARK & SOWDON, and WEST & LEE are popular and usually high priced. The first board game, "Mansion of Happiness," was manufactured in 1843 by W. & S. B. Ives. Other "Mansion of Happiness" games were made by Parker Bros. in 1894 and by McLoughlin in 1895, but they are not as valuable as the Ives example. A very rare game may not be more valuable, because collectors prefer games by well-known companies.

Games were bought for children. They were usually loved, used, abused, and eventually damaged. Condition is important; a pristine game is always more valuable. A large piece torn from the graphics on the front of a box can lower the value by 30 percent. Metal games are worth more than lithographed paper and wooden games. Wood is worth more than cardboard. A few games have playing pieces made of metal, Bakelite or other plastics, ceramics, or even ivory. Pewter is worth more than wood. Modern plastic is of no extra value. Sometimes the playing pieces are of special interest because they are small toys or marbles that have a resale value even when separated from the game board. Unusual spinners, ivory dice, play money, and uncommon designs on the playing cards add value. Unusual playing cards over fifty years old have special buyers and clubs.

All these are just hints. The market for games is strictly supply and demand. A collector eager for everything ever made about the Dionne quintuplets will pay a premium for the right game picturing the babies. You must price your games with this intangible in mind. It is often not the age or beauty alone that determines the price of a game. In the late 1970s the country-look decorating magazines began to show rooms with checkerboards and backgammon boards hung like rare paintings. Today no old, wooden game board is too shabby or too crude to demand a high price as "folk art." Don't discard any type of game board; it will sell.

Another toy that has found favor as folk art is the wooden sled. The best example we have seen sold brought over $30,000 at auction. Most ordinary sleds sell for under $100. It pays to check the market. Old sleds should have handwrought iron runners and painted wooden bodies. A date as part of the decoration is a plus. Other toys that have gained in value from the "folk art" tag are decorated drums, whirligigs, rag dolls, especially black and Amish examples, and doll quilts.

There are specialists who want almost every type of toy or game. Try to find the right dealers, collectors, and clubs. Marbles, sports-related toys, celebrity toys, puzzles, magic tricks, cars, military toys, even toys in special shapes, like dogs, cats, or particular breeds, are bought by these specialists.

ooo

Transportation, Automobiles, Planes, Trains

The larger an antique, the harder it is to sell to an out-of-town customer. That is the general rule, but for cars the rule does not hold. A car in working condition can be driven or hauled to its new home with a minimum of problems. This means that antique and classic automobiles have a national market. To get the best price for a car, first check the guides used by automobile dealers and wholesalers when they make an offer on your secondhand car. After you have established these prices, get a copy of *Hemmings Motor News,* the newspaper for car collectors, and check further.

There are car swap meets and sales in every area of the country. Any old-car owner near you can tell you how to find these rallies. This is the best place to sell a car if you know the value. If you don't, it may pay to visit a rally and ask for some opinions from collectors.

They are always happy to help. An ad in the local paper sells classic autos just as well as it sells used cars. If you own a desirable antique auto or an expensive classic, it will sell well at an antique car auction. They are listed in *Hemmings* or in the other car publications found in your library.

Full-sized airplanes, boats, trains, and farm machinery present problems. They are huge, difficult to transport, and of limited interest. They can be sold to one of a small group of interested collectors. Sometimes they can be sold to a town restoration, a large outdoor village museum, or an amusement park. An ad in the antiques papers, a specialized publication, or even a local newspaper might bring results. The best customer for you is someone who has previously purchased a full-sized vehicle. There are meets for owners of farm equipment, especially steam-powered equipment, and for train, boat, motorcycle, firefighting, and airplane enthusiasts. Locate the meets, attend (if possible), and explain what you have to sell.

The smaller transportation collectibles, such as light bulbs, paint, floor mats, hubcaps, hood ornaments, instruction books, or anything else needed for a car, sell well through the regular antiques dealers and shows, as well as at the special car meets. A car meet usually has tables for dealers or collectors who want to swap or sell parts. You can sell your items at the meet to dealers or collectors. Don't forget old license plates and gasoline station memorabilia like gas pump globes.

Transportation memorabilia like railroad bells, uniforms, menus, china, replicas of trains, ads, boating brochures, spark plugs, motors, makers' nameplates, and farm machinery parts, especially cast-iron seats, are easily sold if you locate the right collectors. Toys related to all these collections also sell well through the meets and publications and through the regular toy shows.

The same rules apply for large horse-drawn carriages, sleighs, popcorn wagons, old farm equipment, or any of the oversized riding antiques. There are clubs and meets for collectors of everything from full-sized trains to steam-operated farm equipment.

ooo

Western Art

Western art is a special field of collecting. Old and new pieces made by artists in the Western and Southwestern states are very much in demand. Everything from typical furniture with a Spanish influence, Indian artifacts, bronze figures of Western subjects, cow-horn furniture, prints, cowboy boots, rugs, pottery, and even spurs and saddles sell well. The best prices are paid in the Western states. Houses there are often decorated with fine arts of the region or with a Western-flavored country look.

The major dealers in this field attend the special shows featuring Western art. If you live near one of these shows, it is the best place for you to sell anything Western in origin. If you live in the East, you could probably find an auction gallery that advertises nationally or a visiting dealer who might be interested in buying your pieces. The places that sell Indian art and collectibles usually sell cowboy art and collectibles. (See section on Indian Artifacts.)

Indian objects, including tourist baskets, cow-horn chairs, and Navaho rugs, as well as cowboy equipment, including elaborate boots and belts, and prints, paintings, and bronzes depicting horses and horsemen of the West, all came into favor in the 1960s and prices have continued rising. Don't underestimate the value of any collectible that pictures a cowboy or Western scene. It is difficult to sell good Western art for the best possible prices in the East or South, but it can be done with a little study and effort.

ooo

And All the Rest

Over twenty years ago we wrote: "There is a time in everyone's life when you must decide what to do with an attic, basement, or even a drawer full of odd bits of small 'junk.' Don't throw anything away. More good antiques have been lost because of an eager housewife than by all the other ways combined. Open all boxes and sort the contents. Stop for a moment and think, study, read, and ask lots of questions. There is a collector for almost anything. We have known of individuals and organizations that want matchboxes, playing cards, racetrack betting tickets, theater ticket stubs, theater programs, postmarks, Masonic items, erotica, gambling chips, trunks, Christmas seals, funeral invitations, old valentines and greeting cards, ads, trading cards, military insignia, railroad passes, coffin markers, newspapers, sheet music, comic books, magazines, almost anything (including the box it came in). Be patient! No item loses value with age. If, after looking around, you can find no value for the items, give them to a collector, historical society, or even a neighbor's young child. It will go into another box of 'junk' to be saved for another generation of collectors. Maybe in twenty-five years it will have a value, and for the next twenty-five it will give joy to the child who received it."

The advice was good then and is still. Notice that many of the things we mentioned then that were considered worthless, such as greeting cards, ads, and comic books, are valued today, some even worth thousands of dollars. It's impossible to mention everything you might have that could be sold through the antiques market. We have tried to discuss selling most types of collectibles. A few other specialized collecting interests that are important enough to have created a club or publication include animal license tags, lightning rods, badges, barbed wire, bells, buttons, buckles, fans, umbrellas, police insignia, Girl Scout and Boy Scout memorabilia, and World's Fair and exposition items.

One word of pessimism: there are a few things that are poor sellers. They are often not worth the time required to find a buyer. These include most old Bibles and religious items, encyclopedias and dictionaries, typewriters, flags, sewing machines, and swizzle sticks. In our book written over twenty years ago we had a list of things the country store collectors ignored. Included were brooms, turkey-feather dusters, soapstone foot warmers, and typewriters, all still not very easy to sell. But we wish we had the rest of the list: bathtubs, candy-making tools, early electrical equipment, egg carriers, egg-beaters, flour sifters, gas mantels, glass rolling pins, graniteware (enamel on metal dishes), iceboxes, ice-cream makers, ice-cream scoops, needle cases, peanut butter pails, and pencil sharpeners.

Our last bit of advice about selling is the "Damn Fool Theory": "REMEMBER, IF I WAS DAMN FOOL ENOUGH TO BUY THIS ANTIQUE, SOMEWHERE THERE IS ANOTHER DAMN FOOL WHO WILL BUY IT FOR MORE MONEY." So don't throw anything away. A buyer is out there somewhere; it just takes time.

A California-born woman, when a little girl, had saved the small toys from her Cracker Jack boxes along with her dolls' clothes and other childhood mementos. When she rediscovered the box of "treasures" in her attic, she went to a nearby advertising show and sold them to a dealer at the going price, $5 to $25 each. She had a $700 find.

Appendix: Books, Clubs, Reference Sources

All the books listed below can be found, but some are privately printed or out of print, and it may take extra effort. Ask at your local bookstore or library. A bookstore can order books if they are still in print. This list gives all the necessary information about publisher and source, even for privately printed books. The full address information for publishers of books listed can be obtained from your local library or bookstore. Go to the library, and if necessary, ask the librarian to help. Many libraries still have the old-fashioned card catalogs. You can find the book either by author's name or title. The new computer catalogs are a bit tricky. There are at least two alphabetizing systems. If you type *KOVEL'S* instead of *KOVELS'*, the computer may not find the book. Any minor mistype or confusion of punctuation can cause problems. With some systems you must omit all punctuation and spell it *KOVELS*. There are also special rules about *the*, *a*, and *and* as the first word. Check with your librarian. If your library does not have the book, it can find out where it is available for loan. Ask the librarian to locate the book through interlibrary loan. Many libraries belong to networks which share books without charge to the patrons. The smallest library can make interlibrary loan arrangements even if it does not have a computer hookup. Don't ignore the libraries in museums and historical societies. Most major libraries have a copy of *The Encyclopedia of Associations*. This book lists many clubs with addresses and phone numbers.

Books listed here are recent price books. We have written to every club and publication to verify the address and other information. Any that did not write back to us were not included in this list. If we can't get information by mail, we presume you can't get information either. The abbreviations used in this list are MAG for magazine, NP for newspaper, and NL for newsletter. The listing is alphabetical by name or title. First we list clubs with the names of their publications. Then we list publications that are not connected to a club.

GENERAL

Publications

Almanac (MAG), Franklin Center, PA 19091.
American Collector's Journal (NP), Box 407, Kewanee, IL 61443.
American Heritage (MAG), Forbes Building, 60 Fifth Avenue, New York, NY 10011.
Americana (MAG), 205 West Center Street, Marion, OH 43302.

Antiquarian Magazine (MAG), Box 798, Huntington, NY 11743.

Antique & Collectables (NP), P.O. Box 1565, El Cajon, CA 92022.

Antique & Collectors Fayre (MAG), Quartet Publications, 149 North Street, Romford RM1 1ED, England.

Antique & Collector's Guide (NP), 8510 Frazier Drive, Beaumont, TX 77707 (guide to Texas & Louisiana).

Antique Collecting (MAG), Journal of The Antique Collectors' Club, 5 Church Street, Clopton, Woodbridge, Suffolk 1P12 1DS, England.

Antique Collector (MAG), Quadrant Subscription Services Ltd., Ground Floor Post Room, Oakfield House, 35 Perrymount, Haywards Heath, West Sussex, RH16 3DH England.

Antique Collector and Auction Guide (NP), P.O. Box 38, Salem, OH 44460.

Antique Dealer & Collectors Guide (MAG), Freepost 1061, Haywards Heath, West Sussex RH16 3ZA, England.

Antique Gazette (NP), 6949 Charlotte Pike, Suite 106, Nashville, TN 37209.

Antique Market Report (MAG), P.O. Box 12830, Wichita, KS 67277.

Antique Monthly (MAG), P.O. Box 884, Farmingdale, NY 11735.

Antique Press (NP), 12403 North Florida Avenue, Tampa, FL 33612.

Antique Review (NP), Box 538, 12 East Stafford Street, Worthington, OH 43085.

Antique Shoppe (NP), P.O. Box 2335, Inverness, FL 32651-2335.

Antique Showcase (MAG), P.O. Box 260, Bala, ON P0C 1A0, Canada.

Antique Trader Weekly (NP), *Antique Trader Bi-Monthly Price Guide to Antiques* (MAG), P.O. Box 1050, Dubuque, IA 52001.

Antiques Advertiser U.S.A. (MAG), 37419 Hwy 45, Lake Villa, IL 60046.

Antiques & Art Around Florida (MAG), P.O. Box 2481, Fort Lauderdale, FL 33303-2481.

Antiques & Auction News (NP), P.O. Box 500, Route 230 West, Mount Joy, PA 17552.

Antiques & Collectibles Buyer (MAG), P.O. Box 320014, Tampa, FL 33679.

Antiques & Collectibles Magazine (NP), P.O. Box 268, Greenvale, NY 11548.

Antiques & Collecting Hobbies (MAG), 1006 South Michigan Avenue, Chicago, IL 60605.

Antiques & Fine Art (MAG), 255 North Market Street, Suite 120, San Jose, CA 95110.

Antiques & The Arts Weekly (NP), Newtown Bee Publishing Co., 5 Church Hill Road, Newtown, CT 06470-9987.

Antiques Trade Gazette (NP), 17 Whitcomb Street, London WC2H 7PL, England.

Antiques West (NP), 3315 Sacramento Street, #618, San Francisco, CA 94118.

AntiqueWeek (NP), P.O. Box 90, Knightstown, IN 46148.

Antiquing U.S.A. (NL), Route 2, Box 11, Fontanelle, IA 50846-9702 (Iowa edition).

Apollo Magazine Ltd. (MAG), The International Magazine of the Arts, P.O. Box 47, North Hollywood, CA 91603.

Arizona Antique News & Southwest Antiques Journal (NP), P.O. Box 26536, Phoenix, AZ 85068.

Art & Antiques (MAG), 89 Fifth Avenue, New York, NY 10003.

Art & Auction (MAG), 250 West 57th Street, New York, NY 10107.

Arts & Crafts Quarterly (NL), Station E, P.O. Box 3592, Trenton, NJ 08629 (Arts & Crafts movement).

Auction Forum U.S.A. (NL), 341 West 12th Street, New York, NY 10014.

Buckeye Marketeer (NP), P.O. Box 954, Westerville, OH 43081.

Canadian Antiquer & Collector (NP), P.O. Box 70, Postal Station Q, Toronto, ON M4T 2P1, Canada.

Cape Cod Antiques & Arts (NP), Register Newspaper, P.O. Box 400, Yarmouth Port, MA 02675.

Carolina Antique News (NP), P.O. Box 241114, Charlotte, NC 28224.

Collector (NP), 105 South Buchanan, Box 158, Heyworth, IL 61745.

Collector (NP), 1535 West Holt Boulevard, Pomona, CA 91768.

Collector Editions (MAG), 170 Fifth Avenue, New York, NY 10010.

Collectors' Classified (NL), P.O. Box 347, Holbrook, MA 02343-0347.

Collectors Connection and Registry (NL), P.O. Box 54, South San Francisco, CA 94083-0054.

Collector's Exchange (NP), P.O. Box 306, Oak Hill, WV 25901.

Collectors Journal (NP), P.O. Box 601, 421 First Avenue, Vinton, IA 52349.

Collector's Marketplace (NP), P.O. Box 25, Stewartsville, NJ 08886.

Collectors Mart (MAG), Old Railway Station, Horringford, Arreton, Isle of Wight P030 3AP, England.

Collectors Mart (NP), 650 Westdale Drive, Wichita, KS 67207.

Collector's News & The Antique Reporter (NP), P.O. Box 156, 506 Second Street, Grundy Center, IA 50638.

Collectors' Showcase (MAG), P.O. Box 837, Tulsa, OK 74101.

Collectrix (MAG), 389 New York Avenue, Huntington, NY 11743 (lists books and publications of interest to collectors).

Connecticut Antiquarian (MAG), Antiquarian & Landmarks Society, Inc., 396 Main Street, Hartford, CT 06103.

Connoisseur (MAG), P.O. Box 10173, Des Moines, IA 50350.

E*A*G*L*E*S: An Americana Newsletter (NL), Box 277, New Market, MD 21774.

Early American Life (MAG), P.O. Box 8200, 2245 Kohn Road, Harrisburg, PA 17105-8200.

Flea Marketeer (NP), 21298 Melrose Avenue, Southfield, MI 48076.

Inside Collector (MAG), P.O. Box 98, Elmont Branch, Elmont, NY 11003.

Insight on Collectables (NP), P.O. Box 130, Durham, ON N0G 1R0, Canada.

Joan Walsh Anglund Collectors News (NL), P.O. Box 105, Amherst, NH 03031.

Journal of the Museum of Early Southern Decorative Arts (MAG), P.O. Box 10310 Salem Station, Winston-Salem, NC 27108.

Keystone Country Peddler (NP), P.O. Box 467, Richmond, IL 60071.

Kovels on Antiques and Collectibles (NL), P.O. Box 22200, Beachwood, OH 44122.

Magazine Antiques (MAG), 980 Madison Avenue, New York, NY 10021.

Maine Antique Digest (NP), Box 645, Waldoboro, ME 04572.

MassBay Antiques (NP), 9 Page Street, P.O. Box 293, Danvers, MA 01923.

Mid Atlantic Antiques Magazine (NP), P.O. Box 908, Henderson, NC 27536.

Mountain Heritage & Antiques (NP), Mountain Eagle, Bridge Street, Hunter, NY 12442.

Mountain States Collector (NP), Box 2525, Evergreen, CO 80439.

National Hobby News (NP), P.O. Box 612, New Philadelphia, OH 44663-0612.

New England Antiques Journal (NP), 4 Church Street, P.O. Box 120, Ware, MA 01082.

New York Antique Almanac (NP), P.O. Box 335, Lawrence, NY 11559.

New York-Pennsylvania Collector (NP), Drawer C, Fishers, NY 14453.

Nostalgia Magazine (MAG), 9401 West Beloit Road, Suite 311, Milwaukee, WI 53227.

Old Stuff (NP), P.O. Box 1084, McMinnville, OR 97128.

Renninger's Antique Guide (NP), P.O. Box 495, Lafayette Hill, PA 19444.

Smithsonian (MAG), Smithsonian Institution, P.O. Box 55593, Boulder, CO 80322-5593.

Southern Antiques (NP), P.O. Drawer 1107, Decatur, GA 30031-1107.

Timeline (MAG), 1985 Velma Avenue, Columbus, OH 43211-9990.

Traditional Home (MAG), Locust at 17th, Box 10685, Des Moines, IA 50381-0685.

Treasure Chest (NP), 253 West 72nd Street, Suite 211A, New York, NY 10023.

Upper Canadian (NP), R.R. 1, Smiths Falls, ON K7A 5B8, Canada.

West Coast Peddler (NP), P.O. Box 5134, Whittier, CA 90607.

Western & Eastern Treasures (MAG), P.O. Box 1095, Arcata, CA 95521 (coins, relics, gold, bottles, collectibles).

World of Antiques & Fine Arts (MAG), Conde Nast Publications Ltd., 234 King's Road, London SW3 5UA, England.

World of Interiors (MAG), Conde Nast International, 560 Lexington Avenue, 19th Floor, New York, NY 10022.

Yesteryear (NP), P.O. Box 2, Princeton, WI 54968.

Price Books

Antique Trader Antiques and Collectibles Price Guide, issued annually (Babka).

Blue Book of American Antiques: A Price Guide to Americana Collectibles, Paul Fellows, 1988 (Wynwood Press, 264 Fifth Avenue, New York, NY 10001).

Collector's Guide to Art Deco, Mary Frank Gaston, 1989 (Collector Books).

Emyl Jenkins' Appraisal Book, Emyl Jenkins, 1989 (Crown).

Flea Market Trader, issued annually (Collector Books).

How to Make the Most of Your Investments in Antiques and Collectibles, Harry L. Rinker, 1988 (Arbor House, William Morrow, 105 Madison Avenue, New York, NY 10001).

Kovels' Antiques & Collectibles Price List, issued annually (Crown).

Lyle Official Antiques Review, issued annually (Putnam).

Lyle Price Guide to Collectibles and Memorabilia, issued annually (Putnam).

Miller's International Antiques Price Guide, issued annually (Viking).

Official Identification and Price Guide to Art Deco, Tony Fusco, 1988 (House of Collectibles).

Official Identification and Price Guide to Arts and Crafts, Bruce Johnson, 1988 (House of Collectibles).

Official Identification and Price Guide to Antiques and Collectibles, issued annually (House of Collectibles).

Pictorial Price Guide to American Antiques and Objects Made for the American Market, issued annually (Dutton).

Price Guide to Collectable Antiques, Price Revision List, issued annually (Antique Collectors' Club).

Schroeder's Antiques Price Guide, issued annually (Collector Books).

Sotheby's Art at Auction, issued annually (Harper & Row).

Sotheby's International Price Guide, issued annually (Harper & Row).

Unitt's Canadian Price Guide to Antiques & Collectables, issued annually (Clock House, P.O. Box 103, Peterborough, ON K9J 6Y5, Canada).

Wallace-Homestead Price Guide to American Country Antiques, issued annually (Wallace-Homestead).

Warman's Americana & Collectibles, issued annually (Warman).

Warman's Antiques and Their Prices, issued annually (Warman).

Computer Programs

Antique Connections, P.O. Box 15173, Bradenton, FL 34280 (brings buyers and sellers together, customer lists).

ISA-NET, ISA Computer Networking System, P.O. Box 726, Hoffman Estates, IL 60195 (for appraisers, claim adjusting, etc.).

LEKTRA, 300-1200-2400; Baud 8-N-1; 504-455-1400 (collectibles bulletin board for collectors and clubs.)
SCERA, 2421 W. Pratt Blvd., Suite 1219, Chicago, IL 60645 (Selective Collectors Easy Referral Assistance).

Additional Help

Encyclopedia of Associations, 1990 (Gale Research, Inc.).
Interlibrary Loan (your library searches its computer bank for title and author of book you want and locates it at the nearest library. It is forwarded to your library and you receive a postcard advising the book is available).
U.M.I. Article Clearinghouse (Service), 800-732-0616 (copies of magazine articles available, 10,000 publications on microfilm; fee is $10.75 and credit cards are accepted).

ADVERTISING & COUNTRY STORE COLLECTIBLES

See also the listings in the sections on Labels; Tobacco.

Clubs and Publications

American Pencil Collectors Society, *Pencil Collector* (NL), 307 Lincoln Avenue, Bedford, IN 47421.
Coca-Cola Collectors Club International, *Coca-Cola Collectors News* (NL), P.O. Box 49166, Atlanta, GA 30359-1166.
Dr Pepper Collectors Club, *Lions Roar* (NL), 1614 Ashbury Drive, Austin, TX 78723.
International G.G. Drayton Association, *Kids Illustrated Drayton Supplement (K.I.D.S.)* (NL), 649 Bayview Drive, Akron, OH 44319 (Campbell Kids).
International Society of Antique Scale Collectors, *Equilibrium* (NL), 111 North Canal Street, Chicago, IL 60606.
International Swizzle Stick Collectors Association, *Swizzle Stick News* (NL), P.O. Box 1117, Bellingham, WA 98227-1117.
Museum of Modern Mythology, *Museum of Modern Mythology Newsletter* (NL), 693 Mission Street, #900, San Francisco, CA 94105 (advertising characters and pop culture collectibles).
National Association of Paper and Advertising Collectors, *P.A.C.* (NP), P.O. Box 500, Columbia, PA 17552.
Peanut Pals, *Peanut Papers* (NL), 804 Hickory Grade Road, Bridgeville, PA 15017 (Planters Peanuts).
Pen Fancier's Club, *Pen Fancier's Newsletter* (MAG), 1169 Overcash Drive, Dunedin, FL 34698.

Pepsi-Cola Collectors Club, *Pepsi-Cola Collectors Club Newsletter* (NL), P.O. Box 1275, Covina, CA, 91722.

Tin Container Collectors Association, *Tin Type* (NL), P.O. Box 440101, Aurora, CO 80044.

Box Top Bonanza (MAG), 153½ 15th Avenue, East Moline, IL 61244 (radio & TV premiums; comic, western, adventure & character collectibles).

Flake (NL), P.O. Box 481, Cambridge, MA 02140 (cereal boxes).

For Here Or To Go (NL), P.O. Box 162281, Sacramento, CA 95816 (fast foods).

Hot Boxing: The Quarterly of Lunch Box Collecting (NL), P.O. Box 481, Cambridge, MA 02140.

Ice Screamer (NL), Box 5387, Lancaster, PA 17601-0387 (ice cream and soda fountain collectibles).

Optimistic Pezzimist (NL), P.O. Box 606, Dripping Springs, TX 78620 (Pez containers).

PenFinder (NL), 2240 North Park Drive, P.O. Box 6666, Kingwood, TX 77339 (buy-sell-trade ads).

Pen World Magazine (MAG), P.O. Box 6666, 2240 North Park Drive, Kingwood, TX 77325-6666.

Price Books

Advertising Collectables, Keith & Penny Gretton, 1989 (BBR, 2 Strafford Ave., Elsecar, N. Barnsley, S. Yorks. S74 8AA, England).

Antique Advertising Handbook Price Guide, Ray Klug, 1988 (L-W).

Contemporary Fast-Food and Drinking Glass Collectibles, Mark E. Chase & Michael Kelly, 1988 (Wallace-Homestead).

Food and Drink Containers and Their Prices, Al Bergevin, 1988 (Wallace-Homestead).

Hervey & Bader Collector's Guide to Glass Collecting, Miles Bader, 1988 (P.O. Box 1373, Frisco, TX 75034) (drinking glasses).

Kovels' Bottles Price List, 8th edition, Ralph & Terry Kovel, 1987 (Crown).

Official Price Guide to Lunch Box Collectibles, Scott Bruce, 1989 (House of Collectibles).

Old Advertising Spirits Glasses, Barbara Edmonson, 1988 (701 E. Lassen Ave., #308, Chico, CA 95926).

Pepsi-Cola Collectibles, Revised Prices, Bill Vehling & Michael Hunt, 1988 (L-W).

Petretti's Coca-Cola Collectibles Price Guide, Allan Petretti, 1989 (Nostalgia Publications, 21 South Lake Drive, Hackensack, NJ 07601).

What You Need to Know about Collecting Fountain Pens, Judson Bell, 1989 (World Publications, 2240 North Park Drive, #106, Kingwood, TX 77339).

ARCHITECTURAL ANTIQUES

Club and Publications

Antique Doorknob Collectors of America, *Doorknob Collector* (NL), P.O. Box 126, Eola, IL 60519-0126.

Architectural Digest (MAG), P.O. Box 10040, Des Moines, IA 50340.

Historic Preservation (MAG), National Trust for Historic Preservation, 1785 Massachusetts Avenue NW, Washington, DC 20036.

Old-House Journal (NL), 435 Ninth Street, Brooklyn, NY 11215.

Victorian Homes (MAG), P.O. Box 61, Millers Falls, MA 01349.

Appraiser

Robinson's Antiques, 170 Kent Street, Portland, MI 48875, 517-647-6155 (hardware specialist).

AUTOGRAPHS

Clubs and Publications

Manuscript Society, *Manuscripts* (MAG), 350 North Niagara Street, Burbank, CA 91505.

Universal Autograph Collectors Club, *Pen and Quill* (MAG), 2 Catalpa Road, Providence, RI 02806.

Autograph Collector's Magazine (MAG), P.O. Box 55328, Stockton, CA 95205.

Autograph Review (NL), c/o J.W. Morey, 305 Carlton Road, Syracuse, NY 13207.

Collector (MAG), Walter R. Benjamin Autographs, Inc., P.O. Box 255, Hunter, NY 12442.

Price Book

Price Guide to Autographs, George & Helen Sanders & Ralph Roberts, 1988 (Wallace-Homestead).

BASEBALL CARDS & SPORTS COLLECTIBLES

Clubs and Publications

American Fish Decoy Club, *American Fish Decoy Forum* (NL), 624 Merritt, Fife Lake, MI 49633.

Golf Collectors' Society, *Bulletin* (NL), P.O. Box 491, Shawnee Mission, KS 66201.

National Fishing Lure Collectors Club, *N.F.L.C.C. Gazette* (NL), 2295 Woody Knoll Drive, Portage, MI 49002.

North American Trap Collectors Association, *N.A.T.C.A. Newsletter*

(NL), 21419 NE 212 Avenue, Battle Ground, WA 98604.

Red Reader, *Red Reader Newsletter* (NL), P.O. Box 3404, Trenton, NJ 08619 (Cincinnati Reds).

Sports Schedules Collectors, *Right on Schedules* (NL), Agoura Hills, CA 91301.

Baseball Card News (NP), *Baseball Card Price Guide Monthly* (MAG), *Baseball Cards* (MAG), *Sports Collectors Digest* (MAG), 700 East State Street, Iola, WI 54990.

Baseball Update (MAG), 405 Tarrytown Road, Suite #405, White Plains, NY 10607.

Beckett Baseball Card Monthly (MAG), *Beckett Basketball Card Magazine* (MAG), *Beckett Football Card Magazine* (MAG), 4887 Alpha Road, Suite 200, Dallas, TX 75244.

Beginner's Guide to Baseball Cards (MAG), 700 East State Street, Iola, WI 54990.

Boxing Collector's Newsletter (NL), 59 Bosson Street, Revere, MA 02151.

Card Collectors Bulletin (NL), The Hobby Card Index, 2507 Briarmead Drive, Houston, TX 77057.

Current Card Prices (NL), P.O. Box 480, East Islip, NY 11730.

Football Card News (MAG), 225 Stevens Avenue, #104, Solana Beach, CA 92075.

Legends (MAG), 429-16 Hart Drive, El Cajon, CA 92021.

The Other Newsletter (NL), P.O. Box 41630, Tucson, AZ 85717-1630 (Olympic pins, sports items).

Rookies Ink. (NL), Baseball Card Collectors, P.O. Box 151725, San Diego, CA 92115.

Sporting Classics (MAG), P.O. Box 1017, Camden, SC 29020.

Sports Card Review (MAG), R.F.D. 1, Box 530, Winthrop, ME 04364.

Tackle Trader (NP), P.O. Box 142, Westerville, OH 43081.

Tuff Stuff (NL), P.O. Box 1637, Glen Allen, VA 23060.

Price Books

Bobbin' Head Dolls: Hartland Statues, Patrick Flynn, 1989 (Minnie-Memories, 122 Shadywood Avenue, Mankato, MN 56001).

Official 1988 Price Guide to Football Cards, James Beckett, 1987 (House of Collectibles).

Official 1990 Price Guide to Baseball Cards, 9th edition, James Beckett, 1989 (House of Collectibles).

Sports Collectors Digest Baseball Card Price Guide, Bob Lemke & Dan Albaugh, 1990 (Krause).

Standard Baseball Card Price Guide, 2nd edition, Gene Florence, 1990 (Collector Books).

Computer & Telephone Programs

CARD/FAX, Compu-Quote Software, 2929 Campus Drive, P.O. Box 7600,

San Mateo, CA 94403 (specialized programs for organizing baseball cards, stamps, coins, market-value reports, and inventories).

Sports Collectors Digest, SCD Baseball Card Phone Shoppers Network, 1989 (Krause) (register at 800-245-3830 and receive a special 900 membership telephone number: $2 for first minute, $1 each additional minute.

Appraiser

Sporting Antiquities, Kevin McGrath, 47 Leonard Road, Melrose, MA 02176, 617-662-6588 (golf equipment and collectibles).

BASKETS

Club and Publications

High Country Basketry Guild, *High Country Basketry Guild Newsletter* (NL), P.O. Box 1102, Fairfax, VA, 22030-1102.

Indian Basketry & Other Native Arts Magazine (MAG), P.O. Box 66124, Portland, OR 97266.

Martha Wetherbee Basket Shop News (NL), Star Route HCR 60, Box 116, Sanbornton, NJ 03269.

Price Book

Wallace-Homestead Price to Baskets, Frances Thompson-Johnson, 1987 (Wallace-Homestead).

BEER CANS & BREWERIANA

Clubs and Publications

American Breweriana Association, Inc., *American Breweriana Journal* (MAG), P.O. Box 11157, Pueblo, CO 81001.

Beer Can Collectors of America, *Beer Can Collectors News Report* (NL), 747 Merus Court, Fenton, MO 63026-2092.

National Association of Breweriana Advertising, *Breweriana Collector* (NL), 2343 Met-To-Wee Lane, Wauwatosa, WI 53226.

National Pop Can Collectors, *Can-O-Gram* (NL), 1124 Tyler Street, Fairfield, CA 94533.

Can-O-Rama (MAG), 27 Main Street, Walnut Hill, IL 62893.

Just For Openers (NL), 1478 Albatross Road, Sanibel, FL 33957-3604 (beer advertising openers and corkscrews).

BLACK COLLECTIBLES

Publication

Black Ethnic Collectibles (MAG), 1401 Asbury Court, Hyattsville, MD 20782.

Price Books

Black Americana: A Personal Collection, Darrell A. Smith, 1988 (P.O. Box 24954, Tempe, AZ 85282).

Black Collectables: Mammy and her Friends, Jackie Young, 1988 (Schiffer).

BOOKS

See also the listings in the section on Magazines.

Clubs and Publications

Alice in Wonderland Collector's Network, *Alice in Wonderland Collector's Network Newsletter* (NL), 2486 Brunswick Circle A1, Woodridge, IL 60517.

American Society of Bookplate Collectors & Designers, *Bookplates in the News* (NL), 605 North Stoneman Avenue, #F, Alhambra, CA 91801.

Big Little Book Club of America, *Big Little Times* (NL), P.O. Box 1242, Danville, CA 94526.

Horatio Alger Society, *Newsboy* (NL), 4907 Allison Drive, Lansing, MI 48910.

International Society of Bible Collectors, *Bible Collectors' World* (MAG), Box 311, Oak Creek, WI 53154.

AB Bookman's Weekly (MAG), P.O. Box AB, Clifton, NJ 07015.

American Book Collector (MAG), P.O. Box 1080, Ossining, NY 10562.

Book Source Monthly (MAG), P.O. Box 567, Cazenovia, NY 13035.

Bookmark Collector (NL), 1002 West 25th Street, Erie, PA 16502.

Books Are Everything! (MAG), 302 Martin Drive, Richmond, KY 40475 (paperbacks).

Collector's Price Index (NP), Box 2512-AI, Chattanooga, TN 37409.

Dime Novel Round-Up (MAG), 87 School Street, Fall River, MA 02720.

Echoes (MAG), 504 East Morris Street, Seymour, TX 76380 (dime novels and pulp magazines).

Fine Print, Quarterly Magazine (MAG), P.O. Box 3394, San Francisco, CA 94119.

Martha's KidLit Newsletter (NL), P.O. Box 1488, Ames, IA 50010 (out-of-print and antiquarian children's books).

Modern Library & Viking Portable Collector (NL), c/o A. Oestreich, 340 Warren Avenue, Cincinnati, OH 45220-1135.

Mystery & Adventure Series Review (MAG), P.O. Box 3488, Tucson, AZ 85722.

Paperback Parade (MAG), P.O. Box 209, Brooklyn, NY 11228.

Pulp Collector (MAG), 4704 Col. Ewell Court, Upper Marlboro, MD 20772.

Yellowback Library (MAG), P.O. Box 36172, Des Moines, IA 50315 (for collectors of dime novels and related juvenile series literature).

Price Books

Bookman's Price Index, Daniel F. McGrath, 1988 (Gale, Detroit, MI).
Old Book Value Guide, 1988 (Collector Books).

Reference Books

Antiquarian Book Fairs and Antiquarian Bookseller Associations, Marjorie Parrott Adams (Book Fair Calendar, 18 Otis Street, Watertown, MA 02172) (leaflet).
Bookdealers in North America, 1986 (Europa).
Buy Books Where - Sell Books Where, Ruth E. Robinson and Daryush Farudi, 1988 (Route 7, Box 162A, Morgantown, WV 26505).

Appraisers

Cellar Stories Books, 190 Mathewson Street, Providence, RI 02903, 401-521-2665.
Ingeborg R. Baum, 1733 Sixteenth Street NW, Washington, DC 20009, 202-232-3579 (rare books).
Michael F. Robinson, 1269 First Avenue, #4, New York, NY 10021, 212-517-3819.

BOTTLES & GO-WITHS

Clubs and Publications

American Collectors of Infant Feeders, *Keeping Abreast* (NL), 5161 West 59th Street, Indianapolis, IN 46254.
Avon Times, *Avon Times* (NL), P.O. Box 9868, Kansas City, MO 64134.
Candy Container Collectors of America, *Candy Gram* (NL), P.O. Box 1088, Washington, PA 15301.
Federation of Historical Bottle Clubs, *Federation Glass Works* (NL), Barbara A. Harms, Treasurer, 14521 Atlantic, Riverdale, IL 60627.
Figural Bottle Opener Collectors, *Opener* (NL), 13018 Clarion Road, Fort Washington, MD 20744.
International Association of Jim Beam Bottle and Specialties Clubs, *Beam Around the World* (NL), 5013 Chase Avenue, Downers Grove, IL 60515-4399.
International Chinese Snuff Bottle Society, *Journal of the International Chinese Snuff Bottle Society* (MAG), 2601 North Charles Street, Baltimore, MD 21218.
Jelly Jammers, *Jelly Jammers Journal* (NL), c/o Barbara Bowditch, 1173 Peck Road, Hilton, NY 14468.

Lilliputian Bottle Club, *Gulliver's Gazette* (NL), 5626 Corning Avenue, Los Angeles, CA 90056.

National Privy Diggers Association, *Privy* (NL), 3532 Copley Road, Akron, OH 44321.

National Ski Country Decanter Club, *Ski Country Collector* (NL), 1224 Washington Avenue, Golden, CO 80401.

Perfume and Scent Bottle Collectors, *Perfume and Scent Bottle News* (NP), P.O. Box 6965, Rockford, IL 61125-6965.

Saratoga-type Bottle Collectors Society, *Spouter* (NL), Star Route 1, Box 3A, Sparrow Bush, NY 12780.

Society of Inkwell Collectors, *Stained Finger* (NL), 5136 Thomas Avenue South, Minneapolis, MN 55410.

Tops & Bottoms Club, *Newsletter on Rene Lalique Perfume Bottles* (NL), P.O. Box 15555, Plantation, FL 33317.

Western World Avon Club, *Western World Avon Collectors Newsletter* (NL), P.O. Box 23785, Pleasant Hill, CA 94523.

Antique Bottle & Glass Collector (MAG), P.O. Box 187, 102 Jefferson Street, East Greenville, PA 18041.

Australiana and Collectables (MAG), P.O. Box 245, Deniliquin, NSW 2710, Australia.

Bottles and Extras (MAG), P.O. Box 154, Happy Camp, CA 96039.

British Bottle Review (MAG), 2 Strafford Avenue, Elsecar, Barnsley, S. Yorkshire S74 8AA, England.

Creamers (NL), P.O. Box 11, Lake Villa, IL 60046 (individual glass advertising creamers).

Fruit Jar Newsletter (NL), 364 Gregory Avenue, West Orange, NJ 07052-3743.

Just For Openers (NL), 1478 Albatross Road, Sanibel, FL 33957-3604.

Milk Route (NL), 4 Ox Bow Road, Westport, CT 06880-2602.

Mini Bottle International Auction Magazine (MAG), 25 High Street, Southboro, MA 01772.

Miniature Bottle Collector (MAG), P.O. Box 2161, Palos Verdes Peninsula, CA 90274.

Old Bottle Magazine (MAG), Drawer 5007, Bend, OR 97708.

Price Books

Bud Hastin's Avon Bottle Collector's Encyclopedia, 11th edition, Bud Hastin, 1988 (P.O. Box 43690, Las Vegas, NV 89116).

Collector's Guide to Civil War Period Bottles and Jars (With Prices), 1988 (P.O. Box 5604, Arlington VA 22205).

Fred's Price Guide to Modern Bottles, 1989 (P.O. Box 1423, Cheyenne, WY 82003).

Guide to Jim Beam Bottles, 13th edition, Al Cembura & Constance Avery, 1988 (139 Arlington Avenue, Berkeley, CA 94707).

Kovels' Bottles Price List, 8th edition, Ralph & Terry Kovel, 1987 (Crown).

Perfume Bottles Remembered, Emily Hart Killian, 1989 (1211 East Front Street, Suite 131, Traverse City, MI 49684-2997).
Petretti's Coca-Cola Collectibles Price Guide, Allan Petretti, 1989 (Nostalgia Publications, Inc., 21 South Lake Drive, Hackensack, NJ 07601).
Poison Bottle Workbook, Rudy Kuhn, 1988 (3954 Perie Lane, San Jose, CA 95132).
Red Book No. 5: The Collector's Guide to Old Fruit Jars, Alice M. Creswick, 1986 (0-8525 Kenowa SW, Grand Rapids, MI 49504).
Standard Old Bottle Price Guide, Carlo & Dorothy Sellari, 1989 (Collector Books).
Udderly Delightful, John Tutton, 1989 (Route 4, P.O. Box 929, Front Royal, VA 22630).

BRONZES

Price Books

Animals in Bronze, Price Revision List, Christopher Payne, 1989 (Antique Collectors' Club).
Jacobsen's Tenth Painting and Bronze Price Guide, 1988 (Jacobsen's Publications, Route 2, Box 201, Emmaus, PA 18049).

CAROUSELS & CAROUSEL FIGURES

See also listings in the section on Folk Art.

Clubs and Publications

American Carousel Society, *American Carousel Society Newsletter* (NL), c/o Mary Fritsch, 470 South Pleasant Avenue, Ridgewood, NJ 07450.
National Amusement Park Historical Association, *National Amusement Park Historical News* (NL), P.O. Box 83, Mount Prospect, IL 60056.
National Carousel Association, *Merry-Go-Roundup* (MAG), P.O. Box 8115, Zanesville, OH 43702-8115.
Carousel News & Trader (MAG), 87 Park Avenue West, Suite 206, Mansfield, OH 44902.
Carrousel Art Magazine (MAG), P.O. Box 992, Garden Grove, CA 92642.
HAF Times (NL), Historic Amusement Foundation, 4410 North Keystone Avenue, Indianapolis, IN 46205.

CELEBRITY MEMORABILIA

See also the listings in the sections on Comic Books; Phonographs and Records; Political Memorabilia; Radio and Television Sets.

Clubs and Publications

Back to the Future Fan Club, *Back to the Future Magazine* (MAG), P.O. Box 111000, Aurora, CO 80011.

Beatles Connection, *Beatles Connection* (NL), P.O. Box 1066, Pinellas Park, FL 34665.

C.A.L./N-X-211 Collectors Society, *Spirit of St. Louis* (NL), 727 Younkin Parkway South, Columbus, OH 43207 (Lindbergh memorabilia).

Dionne Quint Collectors, *Quint News* (NL), P.O. Box 2527, Woburn, MA 01888.

Elvis Forever TCB Fan Club, *Elvis Forever TCB Fan Club* (NL), P.O. Box 1066, Pinellas Park, FL 34665.

Galaxy Patrol, *Galaxy Patrol Newsletter* (NL), c/o Dale L. Ames, 22 Colton Street, Worcester, MA 01610 (air and space heroes from radio and TV, Capt. Midnight, etc.).

Hopalong Cassidy Fan Club, *Hopalong Cassidy Newsletter* (NL), P.O. Box 1361, Boyes Hot Springs, CA 95416.

International Al Jolson Society, Inc., *Jolie/The World of Al Jolson* (MAG), 2981 Westmoor Drive, Columbus, OH 43204.

James Bond Fan Club, *Bondage* (MAG), P.O. Box 414, Bronxville, NY 10708.

Lucasfilm Fan Club, *Lucasfilm Magazine* (MAG), P.O. Box 111000, Aurora, CO 80011.

Old Time Western Film Club, *Old Time Western Film Club Newsletter* (NL), Box 142, Siler City, NC 27344.

Shirley Temple Collectors By The Sea, *Lollipop News* (NL), P.O. Box 6203, Oxnard, CA 93031.

Star Trek: The Official Fan Club, *Official Star Trek Magazine* (MAG), P.O. Box 111000, Aurora, CO 80011.

Tara Collectors Club, *Jonesboro Wind* (NL), P.O. Box 1200, Jonesboro, GA 30237 (Gone With the Wind collectibles).

Westerns & Serials Club, *Westerns & Serials* (MAG), Route 1, Box 103, Vernon Center, MN 56090.

Beatlefan (MAG), P.O. Box 33515, Decatur, GA 30033.

Big Reel (NP), Route 3, Box 83, Madison, NC 27025.

Classic Images (NP), P.O. Box 809, Muscatine, IA 52761.

Good Day Sunshine (MAG), 397 Edgewood Avenue, New Haven, CT 06511 (Beatles memorabilia).

Hollywood Movie Archives (NP), P.O. Box 1566, Apple Valley, CA 92307.

Movie Collector's World (NP), P.O. Box 309-K, Fraser, MI 48026.

Silver Bullet (NL), P.O. Box 553, Forks, WA 98331 (Lone Ranger memorabilia).

TV Collector (MAG), P.O. Box 188, Needham, MA 02192 (TV shows and performers).

Price Books

Beatles Memorabilia Price Guide, Marty Eck & Rick Rann, 1988 (Brayan Press, P.O. Box 764, Elburn, IL 60119).
Encyclopedia of Trekkie Memorabilia: Identification and Value Guide, Chris Gentry & Sally Gibson-Downs, 1988 (Books Americana).
Price Guide to: Marilyn Monroe, Denis C. Jackson, 1989 (P.O. Box 1958, Sequim, WA 98382).

CHRISTMAS & HOLIDAY COLLECTIBLES

Club and Publications

National Valentine Collectors Association, *National Valentine Collectors Bulletin* (NL), P.O. Box 1404, Santa Ana, CA 92702.
Deck The Halls (MAG), P.O. Box 476879, Chicago, IL 60647.
Golden Glow of Christmas Past (NL), P.O. Box 14808, Chicago, IL 60614.
Ornament Collector (MAG), R.R. 1K, Canton, IL 61520.
Ornament Trader (MAG), P.O. Box 879, Placentia, CA 92670 (Hallmark ornaments).
Trick or Treat Trader (NL), P.O. Box 499, Winchester, NH 03470.
Twelve Months of Christmas for Hallmark Collectors (NL), P.O. Box 97172, Pittsburgh, PA 15229.

Price Books

Christmas Collectibles, Margaret & Ken Whitmyer, 1987 (Collector Books).
Christmas Ornaments, Lights & Decorations: A Collector's Identification & Value Guide, George Johnson, 1987 (Collector Books).
Hallmark Keepsake Ornaments: A Collector's Guide, Clara Johnson Scroggins, 1987 (Wallace-Homestead).

CIGARETTE LIGHTERS

Publication

On the Lighter Side (NL), Route 3, 136 Circle Drive, Quitman, TX 75783 (lighters).

CLOCKS & WATCHES

Clubs and Publications

Antiquarian Horology Society, *Antiquarian Horology* (MAG), New

House, High Street, Ticehurst, Wadhurst, Sussex TN5 7AL, England.
National Association of Watch and Clock Collectors, Inc., *Bulletin of the National Association of Watch and Clock Collectors, Inc.* (MAG), 514 Poplar Street, Columbia, PA 17512.
Antique Clocks (MAG), Wolsey House, Wolsey Road, Hemel Hempstead HP2 4SS, England.
Collectors Clocks & Jewelry (MAG), 1469 Morstein Road, West Chester, PA 19380.
Comic Watch Times (NL), 106 Woodgate Terrace, Rochester, NY 14625 (comic character timepieces).

Price Books

American Clocks and Clockmakers, Robert W. & Harriett Swedberg, 1989 (Wallace-Homestead).
American Pocket Watches Identification and Price Guide Beginning to End . . . 1830-1980, Roy Ehrhardt & William Meggers, 1982 (Heart of America).
American Wristwatches: Five Decades of Style and Design, Edward Faber & Stewart Unger, 1988 (Schiffer).
Official Price Guide to Watches, Cooksey Shugart & Tom Engle, 1988 (House of Collectibles).
Price Guide to Collectable Clocks 1840-1940, Price Revision List, 1989 (Antique Collectors' Club).
Vintage American & European Character Wrist Watch Price Guide, David A. Mycko & the Ehrhardts, 1989 (Heart of America).
Vintage American & European Wrist Watch Price Guide, Sherry & Roy Ehrhardt & Joe Demesy, 1988 (Heart of America).

Appraisers

Gordon S. Converse & Co., 1029 Lancaster Avenue, Berwyn, PA 19312, 215-296-4938 (antique clocks).
Simonson, East Washington Street, Medina, OH 44256, 216-725-7056 (clocks).

CLOTHING & ACCESSORIES

See also listings in the section on Textiles & Sewing Collectibles.

Clubs and Publications

Association of American Military Uniform Collectors (AAMUC), *Footlocker* (NL), P.O. Box 1876, Elyria, OH 44036.
Costume Society of America, *Dress* (MAG), *Newsletter* (NL), 55 Edgewater Drive, P.O. Box 73, Earleville, MD 21919.

Vintage Clothing Newsletter (NL), P.O. Box 1422, Corvallis, OR 97339.
Vintage Fashions (MAG), 900 Frederick Street, Cumberland, MD 21502.
Vintage Lill's Newsletter (NL), 7501 School Road, Lot 26, Cincinnati, OH 45249.

Price Book

Official Identification and Price Guide to Vintage Clothing, Cynthia Giles, 1989 (House of Collectibles).

COIN-OPERATED MACHINES, JUKEBOXES, SLOT MACHINES

See also the listings in section on Musical Instruments, Player Pianos, Music Boxes.

Publications

Always Jukin Newspaper for Jukebox Enthusiasts (NP), 5136 26th Avenue NE, Seattle, WA 98105.
Chicagoland Antique Advertising, Slot Machine & Jukebox Gazette (NP), 909 26th Street NW, Washington, DC 20037.
Coin Machine Trader (NL), Box 602, 569 Kansas SE, Huron, SD 57350.
Coin Slot (MAG), 4401 Zephyr Street, Wheatridge, CO 80033-3299.
Coin-Op Newsletter (NL), Box 2426, Rockville, MD 20852.
Jukebox Collector Newsletter (NL), 2545 SE 60th Court, Des Moines, IA 50317.
Loose Change (MAG), 1515 South Commerce Street, Las Vegas, NV 89102.
Pinball Trader Newsletter (MAG)(NL), P.O. Box 440922, Brentwood, MO 63144.
Scopitone Newsletter (NL), 810 Courtland Drive, Manchester, MO 63021 (film jukeboxes).

Price Books

Guide to Collectible Jukeboxes, Ben Humphries, 1988 (5136 26th Avenue, Seattle, WA 98105).
Silent Salesmen, Bill Enes, 1989 (8520 Lewis Drive, Lenexa, KS 66227).

Appraiser

Orange Trading Company, 57 South Main Street, Orange, MA 01364, 508-544-6683 (coin-operated machines).

COINS & OTHER NUMISMATIC ITEMS

Clubs and Publications

Active Token Collectors Organization, *ATCO* (MAG), P.O. Box 1573, Sioux Falls, SD 57101.

American Numismatic Association, *Numismatist* (MAG), 818 North Cascade Avenue, Colorado Springs, CO 80903-3279.

American Society of Check Collectors, *Check Collector* (MAG), 2145 Roman Court, Warren, MI 48092.

American Transit Collectors' Association, *Collectors' Item* (NL), c/o B.R. Gilson, 8304 16th Street, #108, Silver Spring, MD 20910.

American Vecturist Association, *Fare Box* (NL), P.O. Box 1204, Boston, MA 02104-1204.

Canadian Numismatic Association, *Canadian Numismatic Journal* (MAG), P.O. Box 226, Barrie, ON L4M 4T2, Canada.

Elongated Collectors, *TEC Elongated Collectors* (NL), P.O. Box 161, Fenton, MI 48430.

International Bank Note Society, *International Bank Note Society Journal* (MAG), P.O. Box 1642, Racine, WI 53401.

International Organization of Wooden Money Collectors, *Bunyan's Chips* (NL), 413 Delaware Avenue, Elkton, MD 21921.

Latin American Paper Money Society, *LANSA* (NL), 3304 Milford Mill Road, Baltimore, MD 21207.

Liberty Seated Collectors Club, *Gobrecht Journal* (MAG), 5718 King Arthur Drive, Kettering, OH 45429 (Liberty Seated coins).

Love Token Society, *Love Letter* (NL), P.O. Box 5465, North Hollywood, CA 91616.

National Scrip Collectors Association, *Scrip Talk* (NL), Box 29, Fayetteville, WV 25840.

Orders & Medals Society of America, *Medal Collector* (MAG), P.O. Box 484, Glassboro, NJ 08028.

Society of Paper Money Collectors, *Paper Money* (MAG), P.O. Box 6011, St. Louis, MO 63139.

Bank Note Reporter (NP), *Coin Prices* (MAG), *Coins Magazine* (MAG), *Numismatic News* (NP), *World Coin News* (MAG), 700 East State Street, Iola, WI 54990.

Canadian Coin News (NP), 103 Lakeshore Road, Suite 202, St. Catharines, ON L2N 2T6, Canada.

Celator (NP), P.O. Box 123, Lodi, WI 53555 (ancient numismatics and antiquities).

Coin Value Research Guide (NP), P.O. Box 3040, Santa Monica, CA 90403.

Coin World (NP), 911 Vandemark Road, Sidney, OH 45365.

Credit Card Collector (NL), c/o Greg Tunks, Hohldale, Houston, TX 77022.

Error Trends Coin Magazine (MAG), P.O. Box 158, Oceanside, NY 11572.

The Restrike (MAG), R.F.D. 1 Box 530, Winthrop, ME 04364.

Price Books

Auction Prices Realized, U. S. Coins, 1990 (Krause).

Discovering America: The Coin Collecting Connection, Russell Rulau, (Krause).

1990 Coin World Guide to U.S. Coins, Prices & Value Trends, William T. Gibbs, 1990 (Coin World, P.O. Box 150, Sidney, OH 45365).

Official Blackbook Price Guide of U.S. Coins, Marc Hudgeons, issued annually (House of Collectibles).

Official Blackbook Price Guide of U.S. Paper Money, Marc Hudgeons, issued annually (House of Collectibles).

Standard Catalog of United States Paper Money, Chester L. Krause & Robert F. Lemke, 1989 (Krause).

Standard Catalog of World Paper Money, 6th edition, Alber Pick, 1990 (Krause).

United States Trade Tokens 1866-1889, Russell Ralau, 1988 (Krause).

Unusual World Coins, Colin R. Bruce, 1988 (Krause).

Computer Program & Additional Help

U.S. COINS-PLUS, Compu-Quote, 6914 Berquist Ave., Canoga Park, CA 91307 (U.S. Coins, Scott's catalog numbers).

Coin Grading done by: *American Numismatic Association*, 818 North Cascade Ave., Colorado Springs, CO 80903 and *Professional Coin Grading Service*, P.O. Box 9458, Newport Beach, CA 92658.

COMIC BOOKS & COMIC STRIPS

Clubs and Publications

Beanie & Cecil Collectors Fan Club, *Beanie & Cecil Collectors Fan Club Newsletter* (NL), 20159 Cohasset Street, #5, Canoga Park, CA 91306.

Collectioneers by the Park, *Mouse Rap Magazine* (MAG), 1900 East Almont, #62, Anaheim, CA 92805.

Mouse Club, *Mouse Club* (NL), 2056 Cirone Way, San Jose, CA 95124 (Disneyana).

Pogo Fan Club, *Fort Mudge Most* (NL), 6908 Wentworth Avenue South, Richfield, MN 55423.

Yellow Kid Society, *Yellow Kid Notes* (NL), 103 Doubloon Drive, Slidell, LA 70461.

Caniffites (NL), 1319 108 Avenue SW, Calgary, AB T2W 0C6, Canada.

Comicist (MAG), P.O. Box 233, Dept. C, Loveland, OH 45140.

Comics Buyer's Guide (NP), 700 East State Street, Iola, WI 54990.

Fawcett Collectors of America and Magazine Enterprise, Too! FCA & ME TOO! (NL), 301 East Buena Vista Avenue, North Augusta, SC 29841.

Nemo: Classic Comics Library (MAG), 7563 Lake City Way, Seattle, WA 98115.

Storyboard (MAG), 2512 Artesia Boulevard, Redondo Beach, CA 90278 (Disneyana).

Price Books

Official Overstreet Comic Book Price Guide Companion, 3rd edition, Robert M. Overstreet 1989 (House of Collectibles).

Stern's Guide to Disney Collectibles, Michael Stern, 1989 (Collector Books).

Tomart's Illustrated Disneyana Catalog and Price Guide, Tom Tumbusch, 1989 (P.O. Box 292102, Dayton, OH 45429).

Walt Kelly Collector's Guide: A Bibliography and Price Guide, Steve Thompson, 1989 (Spring Hollow Books, 6908 Wentworth Avenue South, Richfield, MN 55423).

DECOYS

Publications

Decoy Hunter Magazine (MAG), 901 North 9th Street, Clinton, IN 47842.

Decoy Magazine (MAG), P.O. Box 1900 MBS, Ocean City, MD 21842.

Price Book

Collector's Guide to Decoys, Bob & Sharon Huxford, 1990 (Collector Books).

Additional Help

National Directory of Decoy Collectors, 1990 (Pilgrim Group, P.O. Box 609, Painesville, OH 44077).

FIREARMS & WEAPONS

Clubs and Publications

American Society of Military Insignia Collectors, *Trading Post* (NL), 5443 Fox Road, Cincinnati, OH 45239.

Napoleonic Society of America, *Member's Bulletin* (NL), 1115 Ponce de Leon Boulevard, Clearwater, FL 34616.

National Knife Collectors Association, *National Knife Magazine* (MAG), P.O. Box 21070, Chattanooga, TN 37421.

Sword Society of the United States, *Sword Society of the United States Newsletter/Bulletin* (NL), P.O. Box 4387, Grasso Plaza Branch, St. Louis, MO 63123.

Winchester Arms Collectors Association, Inc., *Winchester Collector* (NL), P.O. Box 6754, Great Falls, MT 59406.

Courier (MAG), P.O. Box 1863, Williamsville, NY 14231-1863 (Civil War memorabilia).

Flag Bulletin (MAG), Flag Research Center, 3 Edgehill Road, Winchester, MA 01890.

Gun List (NP), *Gun Show Calendar* (MAG), 700 East State Street, Iola, WI 54990.

Knife World (NP), P.O. Box 3395, Knoxville, TN 37927.

Man at Arms (MAG), P.O. Box 460, Lincoln, RI 02865.

Military Collector Magazine (MAG), P.O. Box 245, Lyon Station, PA 19536.

Military Collectors' New Press (MAG), P.O. Box 702073, Tulsa, OK 74170.

North South Trader (MAG), 918 Caroline Street, Fredericksburg, VA 22401 (Civil War memorabilia).

Price Books

Field Equipment of the Infantry 1914-1945, Robert Fisch, 1989 (Greenberg).

Manion's Market Report: U.S. Edged Weapons, 1989 (P.O. Box 12214, Kansas City, KS 66112).

Modern Guns: Identification & Values, 7th edition, Russell & Steve Quertermous, 1989 (Collector Books).

Appraiser

Daniel Cullity Restoration, 209 Old County Road, East Sandwich, MA 02537, 508-888-1147.

FOLK ART

See also listings in the section on Carousels & Carousel Figures.

Publications

Clarion (MAG), Museum of American Folk Art, 61 West 62nd Street, New York, NY 10016-7321.

Folk Art Finder (NL), Gallery Press, 117 North Main, Essex, CT 06426.

Price Book

Official Identification and Price Guide to American Folk Art, Henry Niemann & Helaine Fendelman, 1988 (House of Collectibles).

Appraiser

Salt & Chestnut Weathervanes, 651 Route 6A at Maple Street, West Barnstable, MA 02668, 508-362-6085 (weathervanes).

FURNITURE

Club and Publications

Wooton Desk Owners Society, *Wooton Desk Owners Society Newsletter* (NL), Box 128, Bayside, NY 11361.
Minuteman CRIER (NL), 115 North Monroe Street, Waterloo, WI 53594 (furniture restoration supplies, tools, equipment).
Shaker Messenger (MAG), P.O. Box 1645, Holland, MI 49422-1645.
Shaker Spirit (MAG), P.O. Box 1309, Point Pleasant, NJ 08742.

Price Books

American Manufactured Furniture, Don Fredgant, 1988 (Schiffer).
American Oak Furniture Styles and Prices, Book III, Robert W. & Harriett Swedberg, 1988 (Wallace-Homestead).
America's Oak Furniture, Nancy N. Schiffer, 1988 (Schiffer).
Collector's Guide to Country Furniture, Book II, Don & Carol Raycraft, 1988 (Collector Books).
Furniture by Harrods, 1989 (Schiffer).
Furniture Our American Heritage, Kathryn McNerney, 1989 (Collector Books).
Price Guide to Antique Furniture, Price Revision List, 1989 (Antique Collectors Club).
Price Guide to Victorian, Edwardian and 1920s Furniture, Price Revision List, 1989 (Antique Collector's Club).

Library Reference Help

Furniture Library, 1009 North Main Street, High Point, NC 27262 919-883-4011 (research and books on furniture; book list available, 9:00 a.m.-5:00 p.m.).

Appraisers

The Re-Store, Jim Johnson & Teri Browning, Route 25 at 25A, Wentworth, NH 03282, 603-764-9395.

Robinson's Antiques, 170 Kent Street, Portland, MI 48875, 517-647-6155 (including wicker and hardware).

GLASS

Clubs and Publications

American Carnival Glass Association, *American Carnival Glass News* (NL), 4579 Clover Hill Circle, Walnutport, PA 18088.

American Cut Glass Association, *Hobstar* (NL), 1603 SE 19th, Suite 112, Edmond Professional Building, Edmond, OK 73013.

Antique & Art Glass Salt Shaker Collectors Society, *Antique & Art Glass Salt Shaker Collectors Society Newsletter* (NL), 10217 Stickle Road, St. Louisville, OH 43071.

Fenton Art Glass Collectors of America, Inc., *Butterfly Net* (NL), P.O. Box 384, Williamstown, WV 26187.

Fostoria Glass Society of America, Inc., *Facets of Fostoria* (NL), P.O. Box 826, Moundsville, WV 26041.

Glass Art Society, *Glass Art Society Annual Journal* (MAG), P.O. Box 1364, Corning, NY 14830.

Heart of America Carnival Glass Association, *H.O.A.C.G.A. Bulletin* (NL), 3048 Tamarak Drive, Manhattan, KS 66502.

Heisey Collectors of America, *Heisey News* (NL), P.O. Box 4367, Newark, OH 43055.

International Carnival Glass Association, *Carnival Pump* (NL), 1019 South Madison, Sullivan, IL 61951.

Michiana Association of Candlewick Collectors, *MACC Spyglass* (NL), 17370 Battles Road, South Bend, IN 46614.

Monart & Vasart Collectors Club, *Ysartnews* (NL), c/o Peter Pfersick, 869 Cleveland Street, China Hill, Oakland, CA 94606.

National Cambridge Collectors, Inc., *Cambridge Crystal Ball* (NL), P.O. Box 416, Cambridge, OH 43725.

National Candlewick Collectors Club, *Candlewick Collector* (NL), 275 Milledge Terrace, Athens, GA 30606.

National Depression Glass Association, *News & Views* (NL), P.O. Box 69843, Odessa, TX 79769.

National Duncan Glass Society, *National Duncan Glass Journal* (NL), P.O. Box 965, Washington, PA 15301-0965.

National Early American Glass Club, *Glass Club Bulletin* (MAG), *Glass Shards* (NL), Box 8489, Silver Spring, MD 20907.

National Greentown Glass Association, *N.G.G.A. Newsletter* (NL), P.O. Box 1052, Berkley, MI 48072.

National Imperial Glass Collectors Society, *Glasszette* (NL), P.O. Box 534, Bellaire, OH 43906.

National Milk Glass Collectors Society, *Opaque News* (NL), P.O. Box 402, Northfield, MN 55057.

National Toothpick Holder Collectors Society, *Toothpick Bulletin* (NL), Red Arrow Highway, Box 246, Sawyer, MI 49125.

Old Morgantown Glass Collector Guild, *Old Morgantown Glass Collector Guild Newsletter* (NL), P.O. Box 894, Morgantown, WV 26507-0894.

Pairpoint Cup Plate Collectors of America, Inc., *Thistle* (NL), Box 52, East Weymouth, MA 01289.

Stained Glass Association of America, *Stained Glass* (MAG), 1125 Wilmington Avenue, St. Louis, MO 63111.

Tiffin Glass Collectors Club, *Tiffin Glassmasters* (NL), c/o Shirley Baker, P.O. Box 554, Tiffin, OH 44883.

Whimsey Club, *Whimsical Notions* (NL), 22 Meadowbrook Road, Williamsville, NY 14221 (glass whimsies).

American Glass Quarterly (MAG), P.O. Box 1364, Iowa City, IA 52244.

Antique Souvenir Collectors News (NL), P.O. Box 562, Great Barrington, MA 01230 (old "view" souvenir china and glass).

Carnival Glass Encore (NL), P.O. Box 11734, Kansas City, MO 11734.

Collector Glass News (NL), P.O. Box 308, Slippery Rock, PA 16057 (cartoon character, fast-food, and promotional glassware).

Daze (NP), 275 South State Road, Otisville, MI 48463 (Depression glass).

Glass Collector's Digest (MAG), P.O. Box 553, Marietta, OH 45750.

Glass Review, etc. (MAG), P.O. Box 7188, Redlands, CA 92373.

Salty Comments (NL), 401 Nottingham Road, Newark, DE 19711 (open salts).

Tea Room/Pyramid Newsletter (NL), 921 West Lynwood, Phoenix, AZ 85007.

Westmoreland Glass Collector's Newsletter (NL), P.O. Box 143, North Liberty, IA 52317.

Price Books

Auction Comparison Prices, Betty & Burl Whaley, 1988 (300 International Drive, Pataskala, OH 43062).

Bedroom and Bathroom Glassware of the Depression Years, Margaret & Kenn Whitmyer, 1990 (Collector Books).

Collector's Encyclopedia of American Glass, John A. Shuman III, 1988 (Collector Books).

Collector's Encyclopedia of Depression Glass, 9th edition, Gene Florence, 1990 (Collector Books).

Collector's Encyclopedia of Fry Glassware, H. C. Fry Glass Society, 1990 (Collector Books).

Collector's Guide to Black Glass, Marlena Toohey, 1988 (Antique Publications).

Covered Animal Dishes, Everett Grist, 1988 (Collector Books).

Early Duncan Glassware, Neila Bredehoft, George Fogg & Francis Maloney, 1987 (Neila M. Bredehoft, 10217 Stickle Road NE, St. Louisville, OH 43071).

Encyclopedia of Victorian Colored Pattern Glass, Book 9: Cranberry Opalescent from A to Z, 1987 (Antique Publications).

Glass Industry in Sandwich, Volume 2, Raymond E. Barlow & Joan E. Kaiser, 1989 (P.O. Box 265, Windham, NH 03087).

Handbook of Gorham Open Salt Dishes, George & Carolyn Tompkins, 1987 (1180 Narragansett Boulevard, Cranston, RI 02905).

Kitchen Glassware of the Depression Years, 4th edition, Gene Florence, 1990 (Collector Books).

Kovels' Depression Glass & American Dinnerware Price List, 3rd edition, Ralph & Terry Kovel, 1988 (Crown).

Open Salts, A Collector's Guide: Rarity & Price Guide, Patricia Johnson, 1988 (P.O. Box 1221, Torrance, CA 90505).

Pocket Guide to Depression Glass, 6th edition, Gene Florence, 1989 (Collector Books).

Shoes of Glass, Libby Yalom, 1988 (Antique Publications).

Standard Carnival Glass Price Guide, 7th edition, Bill Edwards, 1989 (Collector Books).

Very Rare Glassware of the Depression Years, Gene Florence, 1988 (Collector Books).

Videos

European Glass, National Early American Glass Club (NEAGC), 1222 Pinecrest Circle, Silver Spring, MD 20910 (George Michael interviews Dorothy-Lee Jones, PBS Antiques Series).

Investing in Glass, William Heacock, 1987 (NEAGC) (all glass types, investments, reproductions; advice for beginning collector).

Investing in Glass, Bill Sheriff (NEAGC).

Appraiser

Stained Glass Associates, P.O. Box 1531, Raleigh, NC 27602, 919-266-2493 (stained-glass lampshades and windows).

INDIAN ARTIFACTS

See also the listings in the section on Western Art.

Publications

Daybreak (NP), P.O. Box 98, Highland, MD 20777.

Dig: The Archaeological Newsletter (NL), The Indian Shop, P.O. Box 246, Independence, KY 41051.

Indian Basketry & Other Native Arts Magazine (MAG), P.O. Box 66124, Portland, OR 97266.

Indian Trader (MAG), P.O. Box 1421, Gallup, NM 87301.

Indian-Artifact Magazine (MAG), RD 1, Box 240, Dept. K, Turbotville, PA 17772-9599.

Price Book

Indian Jewelry of the American Southwest, William A. & Sarah Peabody Turnbaugh, 1988 (Schiffer).

Appraisers

White Deer Indian Traders, 1834 Red Pine Lane, Stevens Point, WI 54481.

Warren Anderson, P.O. Box 100, Cedar City, UT 84720, 801-586-9497 (Western Americana, including autographs, books, documents, maps, photos, relics).

IVORY

Club and Publications

Netsuke Kenkyukai Society, *Netsuke Kenkyukai Study Journal* (MAG), P.O. Box 11248, Torrance, CA 90510-1248.

Whalebone (NL), Rappahannock Design, Inc., P.O. Box 2834, Fairfax, VA 22031 (scrimshaw).

JEWELRY

Clubs and Publications

Compact Collectors Club, *Powder Puff* (NL), P.O. Box S, Lynbrook, NY 11563.

International Club for Collectors of Hatpins and Hatpin Holders, *Hatpins and Hatpin Holders Pictorial Journal* (MAG), *Points* (NL), 15237 Chanera Avenue, Gardena, CA 90249.

International Watch Fob Association Inc., *International Watch Fob Association Newsletter* (NL), 6613 Elmer Drive, Toledo, OH 43615.

Collectors Clocks & Jewelry (MAG), 1469 Morstein Road, West Chester, PA 19380.

Margaretologist (NL), Center for Bead Research, 4 Essex Street, Lake Placid, NY 12946.

Ornament (MAG), P.O. Box 35029, Los Angeles, CA 90035-0029.

Price Books

Bakelite Jewelry Book, Corinne Davidov & Ginny Redington Dawes, 1988 (Abbeville).

Collecting Rhinestone Colored Jewelry: An Identification and Value Guide, 2nd edition, Maryanne Dolan, 1989 (Books Americana).

Costume Jewelry: The Fun of Collecting, Nancy Schiffer, 1988 (Schiffer).

Costume Jewelry, The Great Pretenders, Lyngerda Kelley & Nancy Schiffer, 1987 (Schiffer).

Ladies' Compacts of the Nineteenth and Twentieth Centuries, Roselyn Gerson, 1989 (Wallace-Homestead).

Plastic Jewelry, Lyngerda Kelley & Nancy Schiffer, 1987 (Schiffer).

Price Guide to Jewellery, Price Revision List, Michael Poynder, 1989 (Antique Collectors' Club).

KITCHEN PARAPHERNALIA

Clubs and Publications

Antique Stove Association, *Stove Parts Needed* (NL), 417 North Main Street, Monticello, IN 47960.

Cookie Cutter Collectors Club, *Cookie Crumbs* (NL), 1167 Teal Road SW, Dellroy, OH 44620.

Midwest Sad Iron Collectors Club, *Midwest Sad Iron Collectors Club* (NL), 614 SE 12th, Owatonna, MN 55060.

National Graniteware Society, *National Graniteware Society Newsletter* (NL), 4818 Reamer Road, Center Point, IA 52213.

National Reamer Collectors Association, *National Reamer Collectors Association Quarterly Review* (NL), 1265 Mariposa Drive, Brea, CA 92621.

Novelty Salt and Pepper Shakers Club, *Novelty Salt and Pepper Shakers Club Newsletter* (NL), R.D. 2, Box 2131, Stroudsburg, PA 18360.

Table Toppers, *Table Topics* (NL), 1340 West Irving Park Road, P.O. Box 161, Chicago, IL 60613 (everything that goes on the tabletop--pottery, glass, silver, linen, appliances, etc.).

Around Ohio (NL), Milli Simerli, P.O. Box 14, Bloomingburg, OH 43106 (cookie cutters).

Cookies (NL), 5426 27th Street NW, Washington, DC 20015.

Knife Rests (NL), Glassy Mountain Press, Route 1, Box 417-C, Pickens, SC 29671.

Price Books

Collector's Encyclopedia of Granite Ware: Colors, Shapes and Values, Helen Greguire, 1990 (Collector Books).

Collector's Encyclopedia of Salt and Pepper Shakers: Figural and

Novelty, 2nd series, Melva Davern, 1990 (Collector Books).

Hazelcorn's Price Guide to Old Electric Toasters 1908-1940, C. Fisher, 1987 (P.O. Box 1066, Teaneck, NJ 07666).

Salt & Pepper Shakers II: Identification and Values, Helene Guarnaccia, 1989 (Collector Books).

LABELS

See also the listings in the section on Advertising & Country Store Collectibles.

Club and Publications

Citrus Label Society, *Citrus Peal* (NL), P.O. Box 3564, San Clemente, CA 92672.

Antique Label Collecting (NL), P.O. Box 24811, Tampa, FL 33623.

Price Book

Antique Label Collecting, 1990-1991 (Southern Label Collector's Newsletter, P.O. Box 24811, Tampa, FL 33623-4811) (leaflet).

Reference Books

Art Of The Cigar Label, Joe Davidson, 1989 (The Wellfleet Press, 110 Enterprise Avenue, Secaucus, NJ 07094).

California Orange Box Labels: An Illustrated History, Gordon T. McClelland and Jay T. Last, 1985 (Hillcrest Press, Inc., P.O. Box 10636, Beverly Hills, CA 90210).

LAMPS & LIGHTING

Clubs and Publications

Aladdin Knights, *Mystic Light of the Aladdin Knights* (NL), Route 1, Simpson, IL 62985.

Historical Lighting Society of Canada, *Illuminator* (MAG), P.O. Box 561, Station R, Toronto, ON M4G 4E1, Canada.

Old Mine Lamp Collector's Society, *Underground Lamp Post* (NL), 4537 Quitman Street, Denver, CO 80212.

Rushlight Club, *Rushlight* (NL), Old Academy Library, 150 Main Street, Wethersfield, CT 06109.

Coleman Lite (NL), History Department, P.O. Box 1762, Wichita, KS 67201.

Light Revival (NL), 35 West Elm Avenue, Quincy, MA 02170.

Price Books

Aladdin Collectors Manual & Price Guide, No. 12, J. W. Courter, 1988 (Route 1, Simpson, IL 62985).
Aladdin Electric Lamps Price Guide, No. 1, J. W. Courter, 1989 (Route 1, Simpson, IL 62985).
Disposing of an Aladdin Lamp Collection, J. W. Courter, 1989 (Route 1, Simpson, IL 62985) (leaflet).
Electric Lighting of the 20s - 30s, James Edward Black, 1988 (L-W).
"Those Fascinating Little Lamps" Miniature Lamps Value Guide, John F. Solverson, 1988 (Antique Publications).

Appraiser

St. Louis Antique Lighting Company, 801 North Skinker, St. Louis, MO 83130, 314-863-1414; fax, 314-863-6702.

LOCKS & KEYS

Clubs and Publications

American Lock Collectors Association, *American Lock Collectors Association Newsletter* (NL), 36076 Grennada, Livonia, MI 48154.
Key Collectors International, *Key Collectors Journal* (NL), *Padlock Quarterly* (MAG), *Chain Gang* (NL), P.O. Box 9397, Phoenix, AZ 85068 (for key chain and tag collectors).

Price Book

Padlock Collector, 5th edition, 1988 (Collector, P.O. Box 253, Claremont, CA 91711).

MAGAZINES

See also the listings in the section on Books.

Publications

Echoes (MAG), 504 East Morris Street, Seymour, TX 76380 (pulp magazines and dime novels).
Golden Perils (MAG), 5 Milliken Mill Road, Scarboro, ME 04074 (pulps and serials).
Illustrator Collector's News (NL), P.O. Box 1958, Sequim, WA 98382.

MEDICAL ANTIQUES

Clubs and Publications

Medical Collectors Association, *Medical Collectors Association Newsletter* (NL), c/o M. Donald Blaufox, M.D., Ph. D., 1300 Morris Park Avenue, Bronx, NY 10461.
Scientific Instrument Society, *Bulletin of the Scientific Instrument Society* (MAG), P.O. Box 15, Pershore, Worcestershire WR10 2TD, England.
Scientific, Medical & Mechanical Antiques (NL), 11824 Taneytown Pike, Taneytown, MD 21787.

Price Book

Antique Medical Instruments, C. Keith Wilber, 1987 (Schiffer).

MINIATURES & DOLLHOUSES

Club and Publications

National Association of Miniature Enthusiasts, *Miniature Gazette* (MAG), 351 Oak Place, Suite E, Brea, CA 92621.
Miniature Collector (MAG), 12 Queen Anne Place, Marion, OH 43306.
Miniatures Showcase (MAG), 21027 Crossroads Circle, Waukesha, WI 53187.
Nutshell News (MAG), 21027 Crossroads Circle, P.O. Box 1612, Waukesha, WI 53187.

MUSICAL INSTRUMENTS, PLAYER PIANOS, MUSIC BOXES

See also the listings in the section on Coin-operated Machines, Jukeboxes, Slot Machines.

Clubs and Publications

American Musical Instrument Society, *Journal of the American Musical Instrument Society* (MAG), c/o The Shrine to Music Museum, 414 East Clark Street, Vermillion, SD 57069.
Automatic Musical Instrument Collectors Association, *AMICA News Bulletin* (MAG), 191 Riverview Drive, Woodville, OH 43469.
Musical Box Society International, *Mechanical Music* (MAG), *MBS News Bulletin* (MAG), Box 205, Route 3, Morgantown, IN 46160.
Reed Organ Society, Inc., *ROS Bulletin* (MAG), The Musical Museum, Deansboro, NY 13328.

Country Sounds (MAG), 700 East State Street, Iola, WI 54990.
Joslin's Jazz Journal (MAG), Box 213, Parsons, KS 67357.
Music & Automata (MAG), 24 Shepherds Lane, Guildford, Surrey GU2 6SL, England.
Music Mart (MAG), 700 East State Street, Iola, WI 54990.

Price Books

Guide to Old Radios: Pointers, Pictures and Prices, David & Betty Johnson, 1989 (Wallace-Homestead).
Illustrated Radio Premium Catalog and Price Guide, Tom Tumbusch, 1989 (Tomart, P.O. Box 92102, Dayton, OH 45429).

Appraisers

Antique Musical Instruments, Beverly Maher, 45 Grove Street, New York, NY 10014, 212-675-3236 (classical and flamenco guitars, by appointment only).
Horn & Son String Instruments, 2570 Superior Avenue, Cleveland, OH 44114, 216-579-4337 (string and ethnic instruments).
Phoenix Reed Organ Resurrection, Ned Phoenix, Box 3, Jamaica, VT 05343, 802-874-4173; fax, 802-257-5117 (reed organs).
The Pump and Pipe Shop, 7698 Kraft Avenue, Caledonia, MI 49316, 616-891-8743 (pump organs).

PAINTINGS, SCULPTURE & OTHER ORIGINAL ART

See also the listings in the section on Prints, Woodcuts, Poster, Calendar Art.

Publications

American Art Journal (MAG), 40 West 57th Street, 5th Floor, New York, NY 10019.
Fine Art & Auction Review (MAG) (NL), 2245 Granville Street, Vancouver, BC V6H 3G1, Canada.

Price Books

Currier's Price Guide to American Artists 1645-1945 at Auction, William T. Currier, 1989 (P.O. Box 2098S, Brockton, MA 02403).
Currier's Price Guide to European Artists 1545-1945 at Auction, William T. Currier, 1989 (P.O. Box 2098S, Brockton, MA 02403).
Davenport's Art Reference and Price Guide, R. J. Davenport, 1989 (4032 Dean Drive, Ventura, CA 93003).

International Art Auctions, Volume 2, 1989 (Athena Publications, 38 East 57th Street, New York, NY 10126-0830).

Leonard's Annual Price Index of Art Auctions 1988-1989, Volume 8, 1989 (Auction Index, 30 Valentine Park, West Newton, MA 02165).

McKittrick's Art Price Guide, Volume II, Michael & Rosemary McKittrick, 1989 (P.O. Box 461, Sewickley, PA 15143).

Sotheby's Art At Auction 1988-89, 1989 (Harper & Row).

Standard Fine Art Value Guide, 1989 (Collector Books).

Computer Program

ArtFind, P.O. Box 2098, Brockton, MA 02403, 508-588-4509 (matches buyers and sellers of fine paintings and prints)

Additional Help

International Auction Records, Editions Mayer, 1987 (available from Editions Publisol, Box 339, Gracie, NY 10028).

Inventory of American Paintings, Room 351, National Museum of American Art, 8th and G Streets NW, Washington, DC 20560 (reference service).

Inventory of American Sculpture, Room 351, National Museum of American Art, 8th and G Streets NW, Washington, DC 20560 (reference service).

Appraisers

Kramer Gallery, 229 East Sixth Street, St. Paul, MN 55101, 612-228-1301 (19th- and early 20th-century paintings).

Leonard E. Sasso, 23 Krystal Drive, R.D. 1, Somers, NY 10589, 914-248-8289 (paintings).

PAPER COLLECTIBLES & EPHEMERA

Clubs and Publications

American Business Card Collectors Club, *Card Talk* (NL), c/o Karen Proctor, 2001 North Saxon Boulevard, Deltona, FL 32725.

Arcade Collectors International, *Penny Arcade* (NL), 3621 Silver Spur Lane, Acton, CA 93510 (arcade cards).

Association of Map Memorabilia Collectors, *cartomania* (NL), c/o Siegfried Feller, 8 Amherst Road, Pelham, MA 01002.

Ephemera Society of America, Inc., *Ephemera News* (NL), P.O. Box 175, Wynantskill, NY 12198.

International Map Collectors' Society, *International Map Collectors' Society Journal* (MAG), Catherine Batchelor, Membership Secretary,

Pikes, The Ridgeway, Oxshott, Leatherhead, Surrey KT22 0LG, England.

National Association of Paper and Advertising Collectors, *P.A.C.* (NP), P.O. Box 500, Columbia, PA 17552.

Newspaper Collectors Society of America, *Collectible Newspapers* (MAG), P.O. Box 19134, Lansing, MI 48901.

Journal for the Calligraphic Arts (MAG), P.O. Box 8005, Wichita, KS 67208.

Mapline (NL), Hermon Dunlap Smith Center for the History of Cartography, Newberry Library, 60 West Walton Street, Chicago, IL 60610.

Paper Collectors' Marketplace (MAG), P.O. Box 127, Scandinavia, WI 54977.

Paper Pile Quarterly (NL), Box 337, San Anselmo, CA 94960.

Wrapper (NL), 1903 Ronzheimer Avenue, St. Charles, IL 60174 (nonsport cards and wrappers).

Price Books

Antique Maps, Sea Charts, City Views, Celestial Charts & Battle Plans: Price Record & Handbook, Volume 6, David C. Jolly, 1988 (Box 931, Brookline, MA 02146).

Illustrated Price Guide to Scandal Magazines 1952-'66, Alan Betrock, 1988 (Shake Books, 449 Twelfth Street, #2-R, Brooklyn, NY 11215).

Maxfield Parrish 1988 Price & Identification Guide, 6th edition, Denis C. Jackson, 1988 (P.O. Box 1958, Sequim, WA 98382).

Military Postcards 1870-1945, Jack H. Smith, 1988 (Wallace-Homestead).

Official Overstreet Comic Book Price Guide, 3rd edition, Robert M. Overstreet, 1989 (House of Collectibles).

Official Price Guide to Science Fiction and Fantasy Collectibles, 3rd edition, Don & Maggie Thompson, 1989 (House of Collectibles).

100 Greatest Cult Exploitation Magazines 1950-'65, Alan Betrock, 1988 (Shake Books, 449 Twelfth Street, #2-R, Brooklyn, NY 11215).

Postcard Companion: The Collector's Reference, Jack H. Smith, 1989 (Wallace-Homestead).

Price & Identification Guide to: Rose O'Neill, Denis C. Jackson, 1988 (P.O. Box 1958, Sequim, WA 98382).

Rock 'N' Roll Magazines, Alan Betrock, 1988 (Shake Books, 449 Twelfth Street, #2-R, Brooklyn, NY 11215).

Appraiser

W. Graham Arader III, 1000 Boxwood Court, King of Prussia, PA 19406, 215-825-6570 (rare maps, books, and prints).

PAPERWEIGHTS

Clubs and Publications

Friends of Degenhart, *Heartbeat* (NL), P.O. Box 186, Cambridge, OH 43725.

Paperweight Collectors Association, *Paperweight Collectors Association Newsletter* (NL), *Bulletin of the Paperweight Collectors Association* (MAG), P.O. Box 468, New Hyde Park, NY 11040.

Caithness Collectors Newsletter (NL), *Reflections* (MAG), Caithness Glass, Inc., 141 Lanza Avenue, Building 12, Garfield, NJ 07026.

Gatherer (NL), Arthur Gorham Paperweight Shop, Wheaton Village, Millville, NJ 08332.

Paperweight News (NL), L. H. Selman, Ltd., 761 Chestnut Street, Santa Cruz, CA 95060.

Appraiser

George N. Kulles, Route 2, 115 Little Creek Drive, Lockport, IL 60441, 312-301-0996.

PEWTER, COPPER, CHROME & OTHER METALS

Clubs and Publications

Cloisonne Collectors Club, *Cloison* (NL), 1631 Mimulus Way, La Jolla, CA 92037.

Enamelist Society, *Glass on Metal* (MAG), P.O. Box 310, Newport, KY 41072.

Pewter Collectors Club of America, *Pewter Bulletin* (NL), *PCCA Newsletter* (NL), B. B. Hillmann, Treasurer, 740 Highview Drive, Wyckoff, NJ 07481.

Aluminist (NL), P.O. Box 1346, Weatherford, TX 76086 (hand-hammered aluminum).

Repairing Metalwork (NL), Institute of Metal Repair, 1558 South Redwood, Escondido, CA 92025.

Price Books

Art Deco Chrome, The Chase Era, Richard J. Kilbride, 1988 (Jo-D Books, 81 Willard Terrace, Stamford, CT 06903).

Farber Brothers Krome Kraft, A Guide for Collectors, Julie Sferrazza, 1988 (Antique Publications).

Hazelcorn's Price Guide to Tin Vienna Art Plates: Dresden, Royal Saxony, Kaufmann & Strauss & Bachrach, Jane & Howard Hazelcorn, 1987 (P.O. Box 1066, Teaneck, NJ 07666).

Price Guide to Antique Silver, Price Revision List, Peter Waldron, 1989 (Antique Collectors' Club).

Appraiser

Peninsula Plating Works, 232 Homer Avenue, Palo Alto, CA 94301, 415-326-7825, 415-322-8806; fax, 415-322-7392.

PHONOGRAPHS & RECORDS

Club and Publications

International Association of Jazz Record Collectors, *IAJRC Journal* (MAG), 127 Briarcliff Lane, Bel Air, MO 21014.
Antique Phonograph Monthly (MAG), 502 East 17th Street, Brooklyn, NY 11226.
DISCoveries (NP), Box 255, Port Townsend, WA 98368 (records).
Record Collector's Journal (NP), P.O. Box 1200, Covina, CA 91722.
Record Collector's Monthly (NP), P.O. Box 75, Mendham, NJ 07945.
Record Finder (NP), Memory Lane Records, 8047 West Broad Street, Richmond, VA 23229.
Record Research (MAG), 65 Grand Avenue, Brooklyn, NY 11205.

Price Book

Goldmine's Price Guide to Collectible Record Albums, Neal Umphred, 1989 (Krause).

Computer Program

Cotton Software, Inc., 2325 Anderson Road, #364, Covington, KY 41017 (roster program to keep inventory of records).

PHOTOGRAPHY

Clubs and Publications

American Photographic Historical Society, *Photographica* (MAG), 520 West 44th Street, New York, NY 10036.
Magic Lantern Society of U.S. & Canada, *Magic Lantern Bulletin* (MAG), 445 Burr Road, San Antonio, TX 78209.
National Stereoscopic Association, Inc., *Stereo World* (MAG), P.O. Box 14801, Columbus, OH 43214 (stereoscopes, Viewmasters and anything 3-D).

Nikon Historical Society, *Nikon Journal* (MAG), P.O. Box 3213, Munster, IN 46321.

Photographic Historical Society, *Photographic Historical Society Newsletter* (NL), P.O. Box 9563, Rochester, NY 14604.

Photographic Historical Society of New England, Inc., *New England Journal of Photographic History* (MAG), P.O. Box 189, West Newton Station, Boston, MA 02165 (cameras and images).

Wallace Nutting Collectors Club, *Wallace Nutting Collectors Club Newsletter (NL),* George Monro, Jr., 186 Mountain Avenue, North Caldwell, NJ 07006.

Western Photographic Collectors Association, *Photographist* (MAG), P.O. Box 4294, Whittier, CA 90607.

Military Images (MAG), R.D. 2, Box 2542, East Stroudsburg, PA 18301 (military photographs, 1839-1900).

Photique (MAG), One Magnolia Hill, West Hartford, CT 06117 (buy-sell-trade magazine for antique, classic, and used photographic equipment and images).

Price Books

Photographic Art Market: Auction Prices, Robert S. Persky, editor, issued annually (Photographic Art Center, Ltd., 163 Amsterdam Avenue, New York, NY 10023.

Price Guide to Antique & Classic Cameras, 6th edition, James & Joan McKeown, 1987 (Centennial Photo Service, Grantsburg, WI 54840).

POLITICAL MEMORABILIA

Clubs and Publications

American Political Items Collectors, *Keynoter* (MAG), *Political Bandwagon* (NP), Box 340339, San Antonio, TX 78234.

Bush Political Items Collectors, *Bush Bandwagon* (NL), c/o Ronald Wade, 229 Cambridge, Longview, TX 75601.

Kennedy Political Items Collectors, *Hyannisporter* (NL), P.O. Box 922, Clark, NJ 07066.

Nixon Political Items Collectors, *Checkers* (NL), P.O. Box 2354, Mission Viejo, CA 92690.

Reagan Political Items Collectors, *Reagan Review* (NL), 101 Paris Street, Lafayette, LA 70506.

Political Collector (NP), 420 Madison Avenue, York, PA 17404.

Price Books

Official Price Guide to Political Memorabilia, Richard Friz, 1988 (House of Collectibles).

Presidential and Campaign Memorabilia with Prices, 2nd edition, Stan Gores, 1988 (Wallace-Homestead).

POSTCARDS

Clubs and Publications

Deltiologists of America, *Postcard Classics* (MAG), P.O. Box 8, Norwood, PA 19074.

Monumental Postcard Club of Baltimore, Maryland, *Bulletin* (MAG), *Newsletter* (NL), P.O. Box 20899, Baltimore, MD 21209.

Postcard History Society, *Postcard History Society Bulletin* (NL), P.O. Box 1765, Manassas, VA 22110.

Barr's Postcard News (NP), 70 South Sixth Street, Lansing, IA 52151.

Gloria's Corner (NL), 908 West Heron, Denison, TX 75020.

Picture Postcard Monthly (MAG), 15 Debdale Lane, Keyworth, Nottinghamshire NG12 5HT, England.

Postcard Collector (MAG), P.O. Box 337, Iola, WI 54945.

Postcard Journal (MAG), Lakewood Forest Preserve, Wauconda, IL 60084.

POTTERY & PORCELAIN

Clubs and Publications

Abingdon Pottery Collectors, *Abingdon Pottery Collectors Newsletter* (NL), c/o Dianne L. Beetler, R.R. 1, Box 29-A, Altona, IL 61414.

American Art Pottery Association, *Journal of the American Art Pottery Association* (MAG), Tom Layman, 9825 Upton Circle, Bloomington, MN 55431.

American Ceramic Circle, *American Ceramic Circle Journal and Newsletter* (NL), P.O. Box 1495, Grand Central Station, New York, NY 10163.

Belleek Collectors Society, *Belleek Collector* (NL), P.O. Box 675, 1 Chapin Road, Pine Brook, NJ 07058.

Blue & White Pottery Club, *Blue & White Pottery Club* (NL), 224 12th Street NW, Center Point, IA 52405.

Collectors of Illinois Pottery and Stoneware, *Collectors of Illinois Pottery and Stoneware Newsletter* (NL), 704 East Twelfth Street, Streator, IL 61364.

ENESCO Precious Moments Collectors' Club, P.O. Box 1466, Elk Grove Village, IL 60009-1466.

Flow Blue International Collectors' Club, *Blue-Berry Notes* (NL), 1328 Camp Avenue, Rockford, IL 61103.

Goss Collectors' Club, *Goss Collectors' Club* (MAG), 3 Carr Hall Gardens, Barrowford, Nelson, Lancs. BB9 6PU, England.

Handle on the Teapot Enthusiast Association, *Hot Tea* (NL), 882 South Mollison Avenue, El Cajon, CA 92020.

Honiton Pottery Collectors Society, *Honiton Pottery Collectors Newsletter* (NL), Honiton and Crown Dorset Pottery, 112 Sylvan Avenue, London N22, England.

International Association of R.S. Prussia Collectors, Inc., *International Association of R.S. Prussia Collectors* (NL), 22 Canterbury Drive, Danville, IN 46122.

International Bossons Collectors Society, *Bossons Briefs* (NL), 21 John Maddox Drive, Rome, GA 30161 (collectors of Bossons artware - plaster wall masks and figures).

International Nippon Collectors Club, *INCC Newsletter* (NL), P.O. Box 230, Peotone, IL 60468.

International Willow Collectors, *American Willow Report* (NL), 1733 Chase Street, Cincinnati, OH 45223.

Lithophane Collectors' Club, *Lithophane Collectors' Club Bulletin* (NL), P.O. Box 4557, 2032 Robinwood Avenue, Toledo, OH 43620.

Lladro Collectors Society, *Expressions* (MAG), 43 West 57th Street, New York, NY 10019.

Lowell Davis Farm Club, *Lowell Davis Farm Club Gazette* (NL), Schmid Bros. Inc., 55 Pacella Park Drive, Randolph, MA 02368.

M.I. Hummel Club, *Insights* (NL), P.O. Box 11, Pennington, NJ 08534-0011.

Majolica Collectors Association, P.O. Box 332, Wolcottville, IN 46795.

Majolica International Society, *Newsletter of M.I.S.* (NL), 1275 First Avenue, Suite 103, New York, NY 10021.

National Shaving Mug Collectors Association, *Barber Shop Collectibles Newsletter* (NL), 818 South Knight Avenue, Park Ridge, IL 60068.

O.J. Club, *Upside Down World of an O.J. Collector* (NL), 29 Freeborn Street, Newport, RI 02840 (Occupied Japan).

Occupied Japan Collectors Club, *Occupied Japan Collectors Club Newsletter* (NL), 18309 Faysmith Avenue, Torrance, CA 90504.

Old Sleepy Eye Collectors Club of America, Inc., *Sleepy Eye Newsletter* (NL), P.O. Box 12, Monmouth, IL 61462.

Phoenix-Bird Collectors of America, *Phoenix-Bird Discoveries* (NL), 5912 Kingsfield Drive, West Bloomfield, MI 48322.

Red Wing Collectors Society, *Red Wing Collectors Newsletter* (NL), Route 3, Box 174, Monticello, MN 55362.

Rogers Group, *Newsletter of The Rogers Group* (NL), 4932 Prince George Avenue, Beltsville, MD 20705.

Royal Doulton International Collectors Club, *Royal Doulton International Collectors Club Newsletter* (NL), 700 Cottontail Lane, Somerset, NJ 08873.

Sebastian Miniatures Collectors Society, *Sebastian Miniatures Collectors Society News* (NL), c/o Mrs. Judy Wilson, 321 Central Street, Hudson, MA 01749.

Shelley Group, *Shelley Group Newsletter* (NL), 228 Croyland Road, Lower Edmonton, London N9 7BG, England.

Souvenir China Collectors Society, *Souvenir China Collectors News* (NL), Box 562, Great Barrington, MA 01230.

Stein Collectors International, *Prosit* (MAG), P.O. Box 661125, Los Angeles, CA 90066.

Tea Leaf Club International, *Tea Leaf Readings* (NL), P.O. Box 904, Mount Prospect, IL 60056.

Tiles & Architectural Ceramics Society, *Glazed Expressions* (NL), c/o Miss Kathryn Huggins, Reabrook Lodge, 8 Sutton Road, Shrewsbury, Shropshire SY2 6DD, England.

Torquay Pottery Collectors' Society, *Torquay Pottery Collectors' Society Newsletter* (NL), c/o Mrs. Barbara Treat, 479 Burley, Colliersville, TN 43537.

Uhl Collectors' Society, *Uhl Family Happenings* (NL), 800 West Maumee Street, #13, Angola, IN 46703.

Wedgwood Collectors Society, *Wedgwood Collectors Society Newsletter* (NL), 41 Madison Avenue, New York, NY 10010.

Antique Souvenir Collectors News (NL), P.O. Box 562, Great Barrington, MA 01230.

Collecting Doulton (MAG), B.B.R. Publishing, 2 Strafford Avenue, Elsecar, Barnsley, South Yorkshire S74 8AA, England.

Egg Cup Collectors' Corner (NL), 67 Stevens Avenue, Old Bridge, NJ 08857.

Flash Point (MAG), Tile Heritage Foundation, P.O. Box 1850, Healdsburg, CA 95448.

Geisha Girl Porcelain Newsletter (NL), P.O. Box 394, Morris Plains, NJ 07950.

Goebel Miniatures Newsletter (NL), Country Cousin Inc., P.O. Box 522, Occoquan, VA 22125-0522.

National Blue Ridge Newsletter (NL), c/o Norma Lilly, Highland Drive, Route 5, Box 62, Blountville, TN 37617.

New Glaze (NL), P.O. Box 4782, Birmingham, AL 35206.

Noritake News (NL), 1237 Federal Avenue East, Seattle, WA 98102.

Orientalia Journal (NL), P.O. Box 94, Little Neck, NY 11363.

"Our McCoy Matters" (NL), 12704 Lockleven Lane, Woodbridge, VA 22191.

Plate World (MAG), 9200 North Maryland Avenue, Niles, IL 60648.

Precious Collectibles (MAG), R.R. 1K, Canton, IL 61520 (Precious Moments collectibles).

Sebastian Exchange Quarterly (NL), P.O. Box 4905, Lancaster, PA 17604.

Studio Potter (NL), Box 70, Goffstown, NJ 03045.

Vernon Views (NL), P.O. Box 945, Scottsdale, AZ 85252.

Price Books

Antique Steins: A Collectors' Guide, 2nd edition, James Stevenson, 1989 (Cornwall Books, Cranbury, NJ).

Blue Willow: An Identification and Value Guide, 2nd edition, Mary Frank Gaston, 1990 (Collector Books).

Book of Buffalo Pottery, Seymour & Violet Altman, 1987 (Schiffer).

Bradford Book of Collector's Plates, issued annually (Bradford Exchange, 9333 North Milwaukee Avenue, Chicago, IL 60648).

Character Jug Collectors Handbook, 4th edition, Kevin Pearson, 1988 (Kevin Francis, 13540 North Florida Avenue, Tampa, FL 33613).

Collectibles Market Guide & Price Index to Limited Edition Plates, Figurines, Bells, Graphics, Ornaments and Dolls, 7th edition, Diane Carnevale, 1989 (Collectors' Information Bureau, 2059 Edgewood SE, Grand Rapids, MI 49506).

Collecting Clarice Cliff, Howard Watson, 1988 (Kevin Francis, 13540 North Florida Avenue, Tampa, FL 33613).

Collecting Hull Pottery's "Little Red Riding Hood," Mark E. Supnick, 1989 (L-W).

Collecting Royal Haeger, Lee Garmon & Doris Frizzell, 1989 (Collector Books).

Collecting Shawnee Pottery: A Pictorial Reference and Price Guide, Mark E. Supnick, 1989 (L-W).

Collecting Victorian Tiles, Price Revision List, Terrence A. Locket, 1989 (Antique Collectors' Club).

Collector's Encyclopedia of Geisha Girl Porcelain, Elyce Litts, 1988 (Collector Books).

Collector's Encyclopedia of Weller Pottery, Price Guide No. 4, 1989 (Collector Books).

Collector's Guide and History of Uhl Pottery, F. Earl & Jane A. McCurdy, 1988 (Ohio Valley Books, P.O. Box 4753, Evansville, IN 47724).

Concise Encyclopaedia and Price Guide to Goss China, 5th edition, Nicholas Pine, 1988 (Milestone).

Doulton Figure Collectors Handbook, 2nd edition, Kevin Pearson, 1988 (Seven Hills Books, 49 Central Avenue, Cincinnati, OH 45202).

Encyclopedia of Hall China, 2nd edition, Margaret & Kenn Whitmyer, 1989 (Collector Books).

Face to Vase with Glamour Gals, Polly Gipson, 1988 (P.O. Box 405, Weston, OR 97886) (head vases).

German Military Steins 1914 to 1945, Gary Kirsner, 1989 (P.O. Box 8807, Coral Springs, FL 33075).

Head Vases: Identification & Values, Kathleen Cole, 1989 (Collector Books).

Hummel Copycats with Values, Lawrence L. Wonsch, 1987 (Wallace-Homestead).

Kovels' Depression Glass & American Dinnerware Price List, 3rd edition, Ralph & Terry Kovel, 1988 (Crown).

Lady Head Vases, Mary Zavada, 1988 (Schiffer).

Limited Edition Collectibles: Everything You May Ever Need to Know, Paul Stark, 1988 (New Gallery Press, P.O. Box 981, Wilkes Barre, PA 18703).

Majolica Pottery, 1989 Values, Mariann K. Marks, 1989 (Collector Books).

McCoy Cookie Jars From the First to the Latest, Harold Nichols, 1987 (P.O. Box 1125, Ames, IA 50010).

Mettlach Book, 2nd edition, Gary Kirsner, 1987 (P.O. Box 8807, Coral Springs, FL 33075).

1988-1989 Sebastian Exchange Value Register for Sebastian Miniatures, Paul J. Sebastian, 1988 (P.O. Box 4905, Lancaster, PA 17604).

1989 Price Guide to Crested China, Nicholas Pine, 1988 (Milestone).

No. 1 Price Guide to M. I. Hummel Figurines, Plates, More..., Robert L. Miller, 1989 (112 Woodland Drive, Eaton, OH 45320).

Official Price Guide to Collector Plates, 5th edition, Gene Ehlert, 1988 (House of Collectibles).

Official Price Guide to Royal Doulton, 6th edition, Ruth M. Pollard, 1988 (House of Collectibles).

Original Price Guide to Royal Doulton Discontinued Character Jugs, 6th edition, Princess & Barry Weiss, 1987 (P.O. Box 296, New City, NY 10956).

Phillips Collectors Guides: Royal Doulton, Catherine Braithwaite, 1989 (Boxtree Ltd., 36 Tavistock Street, London WC2 7PB, England).

Price Guide to 18th Century English Porcelain, Price Revision List, 1988 (Antique Collectors' Club).

Price Guide to 19th and 20th Century British Pottery, Price Revision List, David Battie & Michael Turner, 1989 (Antique Collectors' Club).

Price Guide to 19th and 20th Century Porcelain, Price Revision List, 1989 (Antique Collectors' Club).

Price Guide to Pot-Lids and Other Underglaze Multicolour Prints on Ware, Price Revision List, 1989 (Antique Collectors' Club).

Price Guide to the Models of W. H. Goss, Price Revision List, Nicholas Pine, 1989 (Antique Collectors' Club).

Red Wing Collectibles, Values Updated, Dan & Gail DePasquale & Larry Peterson, 1988 (Collector Books).

Redware: America's Folk Art, Kevin McConnel, 1988 (Schiffer).

Southern Potteries Inc. Blue Ridge Dinnerware, 3rd edition, Betty & Bill Newbound, 1989 (Collector Books).

United States Decorated Stoneware, Carmen A. Guappone, 1988 (R.D. No. 1, Box 10, McClellandtown, PA 15458).

Watt Pottery Company, Crooksville, Ohio: Collectibles, William Iliff Watt, 1988 (Box 5, Roseville, OH 43777).

World of Wade: Collectable Porcelain and Pottery, Ian Warner, 1988 (Antique Publications).

Video

The Magic of a Name, Quill Productions, 166 Elmdon Lane, Marston Green, Birmingham B377EB, England (2 volumes on Royal Doulton, £55 for both).

Appraisers

Connecticut Notary Services, 128 Hall Avenue, Wallingford, CT 06492 (collector plates and figurines).

F.T.S., Inc., 416 Throop Street, North Babylon, NY 11704, 516-669-7232 (steins, European glass, drinking vessels).

Donna M. Towle-Rupprecht, 129 Dexter Avenue, Watertown, MA 02172, 617-924-8408 (Hummels).

PRINTS, WOODCUTS, POSTERS, CALENDAR ART

See also the listings in the section on Paintings, Sculpture & Other Original Art.

Clubs and Publications

American Historical Print Collectors Society, *Imprint* (MAG & NL), P.O. Box 1352, Fairfield, CT 06430.

Gutmann Collectors Club, Inc., *Gutmann Collectors Club Newsletter* (NL), 10502 Product Drive, Rockford, IL 61111.

Harrison Fisher Society, *Exchange Newsletter* (NL), c/o The Rocking Chair Emporium, 123 North Glassell, Orange, CA 92666.

Poster Society, Inc., *P.S.* (MAG), 138 West 18th Street, New York, NY 10011.

Fox Hunt (NL), c/o Rita Mortenson, 727 North Spring, Independence, MO 64050 (prints of R. Atkinson Fox).

Price Books

Currier and Ives in 20th Century America, Robert L. Searjeant, 1989 (P.O. Box 23942, Rochester, NY 14692).

Currier's Price Guide to American and European Prints at Auction, William P. Carl & William T. Currier, 1989 (P.O. Box 2098, Brockton, MA 02403).

Currier's Price Guide to Currier & Ives Prints. Robert Kipp & William T. Currier, 1989 (P.O. Box 2098, Brockton, MA 02403).

Gordon's Print Price Annual, 1989 (Martin Gordon, Inc., 1000 Park Avenue, New York, NY 10028).

Price Guide to Baxter Prints, Price Revision List, A. Ball & M. Martin, 1988 (Antique Collectors' Club).

Price Guide to Wallace Nutting Pictures, 3rd Edition, Michael Ivan-kovich, (P.O. Box 2458, Doylestown, PA 18901).
Printworld Directory of Contemporary Prints and Prices, 1988 (Print-world, P.O. Box 785, Bala Cynwyd, PA 19004).
Those Wonderful Yard-Long Prints and More: An Illustrated Value Guide, W. D. & M. J. Keagy & C. G. & J. M. Rhoden, 1989 (P.O. Box 106, Bloomfield, IN 47424).

Computer Program

ArtFind, P.O. Box 2098, Brockton, MA 02403, 508-588-4509 (matches buyers and sellers of fine paintings and prints).

Appraisers

American Antique Prints, Robert Wieland, 33 South St. Andrews Drive, Ormond Beach, FL 32174, 904-672-9972 (prints).
Lyons Ltd., Charles R. Lyons, 2700 Hyde, San Francisco, CA 94109, 415-441-2202 (antique prints).
Robert L. Searjeant, P.O. Box 23942, Rochester, NY 14692, 716-424-2489 (Currier & Ives prints).

RADIO & TELEVISION SETS

Clubs and Publications

Antique Radio Club of America, *Antique Radio Gazette* (MAG), 81 Steeplechase Road, Devon, PA 19333.
Antique Wireless Association, Inc., *Old Timer's Bulletin* (MAG), Main Street, R.D. 3, Holcomb, NY 14469.
Dark Shadows Fan Club, *Dark Shadows Announcement* (MAG), P.O. Box 90A04, West Hollywood, CA 90069.
Girl Groups Fan Club, *Girl Groups Gazette* (MAG), P.O. Box 69A04, West Hollywood, CA 90069.
Munsters & The Addams Family Fan Club, *Munsters & The Addams Family Reunion* (MAG), P.O. Box 69A04, West Hollywood, CA 90069.
Southern California Antique Radio Society, *California Antique Radio Gazette* (MAG), 1545 Raymond, Glendale, CA 91201.
TV Western Collectors Fan Club, *Television Western Collectors News-letter* (NL), P.O. Box 1361, Boyes Hot Springs, CA 95416.
Vintage Radio & Phonograph Society, *Reproducer* (NL), *Soundwaves* (NL), P.O. Box 165345, Irving, TX 75016.
Antique Radio Classified (MAG), P.O. Box 2, Carlisle, MA 01741.
Antique Radio Topics (NL), Box 28572, Dallas, TX 75228.

Bandstand Boogie (MAG), P.O. Box 131-A, Adamstown, PA 19501 (1950s/1960s American Bandstand).
Goldmine (MAG), 700 East State Street, Iola, WI 54990 (records).
Horn Speaker (NP), Box 1193, Mabank, TX 75147 (radios).
New Amberola Graphic (MAG), 37 Caledonia Street, St. Johnsbury, VT 05819.
Radio Age (MAG), 636 Cambridge Road, Augusta, GA 30909.
Sight Sound Style (NL), P.O. Box 2224, South Hackensack, NJ 07606 (vintage radios and TVs).
Straight Arrow POW-WOW (NL), 301 East Buena Vista Avenue, North Augusta, SC 29841 (radio heroes).
VideoMania, The Newspaper for Video Nuts (NP), P.O. Box 47-KV, Princeton, WI 54968.

Price Book

1990 Price Guide to Vintage TV's and Collectable Radios, Harry Poster & John Sakas, 1989 (P.O. Box 2224, South Hackensack, NJ 07606).

Appraiser

Puett Electronics, Box 28572, Dallas, TX 75228, 214-321-0927, 214-321-8721 (antique radios).

RUGS

Publications

Decorative Rug (MAG), P.O. Box 709, Meredith, NH 03253 (oriental rugs).
Oriental Rug Review (NP), P.O. Box 709, Meredith, NH 03253.

Computer Program

RUGNET, 601 West 54th Street, Suite 827, New York, NY 10019 (oriental rugs inventory and directory).

Appraisers

Aladdin Company, Oriental Rug Specialists, 221 South Elm Street, Greensboro, NC 27401, 919-275-6351 (oriental rugs).
Koko Boodakian & Sons, 1026 Main Street, Winchester, MA 01890, 617-729-2213 (oriental, antique hooked, and Navajo rugs).

SHEET MUSIC

Clubs and Publications

National Sheet Music Society, Song Sheet (NL), 1597 Fair Park Avenue, Los Angeles, CA 90041.
New York Sheet Music Society, *New York Sheet Music Society Newsletter* (NL), P.O. Box 1214, Great Neck, NY 11023.
"Remember That Song" (NL), 5821 North 67th Avenue, Suite 103-306, Glendale, AZ 85301.
Sheet Music Exchange (NL), P.O. Box 69, Quicksburg, VA 22847.

SILVER

Clubs and Publications

American Spoon Collectors, *Spooners Forum* (NP), 4922 State Line, Westwood Hills, KS 66205.
Northeastern Spoon Collectors Guild, 756 East River Road, Rochester, NY 14623.
Silver (MAG), P.O. Box 1243, Whittier, CA 90609.
Spoony Scoop (NL), 84 Oak Avenue, Shelton, CT 06484.

Price Book

Official Identification and Price Guide to Silver and Silver Plate, 6th edition, Jeri Schwartz, 1989 (House of Collectibles).

Appraisers

Peninsula Plating Works, 232 Homer Avenue, Palo Alto, CA 94301, 415-326-7825, 415-322-8806; fax, 415-322-7392 (sterling and silver plate).
Venette's Table, Box 6113, Santa Barbara, CA 93111, 805-965-9584.

STAMPS

Clubs and Publications

Aerophilatelic Federation of the Americas, *AFA News* (MAG), P.O. Box 1239, Elgin, IL 60120.
American Philatelic Society, *American Philatelist* (MAG), P.O. Box 8000, State College, PA 16803.
American Topical Association, *Topical Time* (MAG), P.O. Box 630, Johnstown, PA 15907.

Bureau Issues Association, *United States Specialist* (MAG), P.O. Box 3467, Crofton, MD 21114.

Carto-Philatelists, *Carto-Philatelist* (MAG), 303 South Memorial Drive, Appleton, WI 54911 (maps on stamps).

Christmas Philatelic Club, *Yule Log* (NL), P.O. Box 77, Scottsbluff, NE 69361.

Chistmas Seal and Charity Stamp Society, *Seal News* (NL), 3833 16th Avenue South, Minneapolis, MN 55407.

Collectors of Religion on Stamps, *COROS Chronicle* (MAG), 208 East Circle Street, Appleton, WI 54911.

Confederate Stamp Alliance, *Confederate Philatelist* (MAG), P.O. Box 14, Manitowoc, WI 54220.

Dogs on Stamps Study Unit, *DOSSU Journal* (NL), 3208 Hana Road, Edison, NJ 08817.

Errors, Freaks, Oddities Collectors Club, *EFO Journal* (NL), 1903 Village Road West, Norwood, MA 02062-2524.

International Philatelic Golf Society, *Tee Time* (NL), P.O. Box 2183, Norfolk, VA 23501.

Junior Philatelists of America, *Philatelic Observer* (NL), P.O. Box 527, Mansfield, PA 16933-0527.

Korea Stamp Society, Inc., *Korean Philately* (NL), P.O. Box 1057, Grand Junction, CO 81502.

Liechtenstudy USA, Liechtenstudy (NL) 100 Elizabeth Street, #112, Duluth, MN 55803.

Post Mark Collectors Club, *PMCC Bulletin* (NL), 7629 Homestead Drive, Baldwinsville, NY 13027.

Tonga/Tin Can Mail Study Circle, *Tin Canner* (NL), 36975 South Highway 213, Mount Angel, OR 97362.

Universal Ship Cancellation Society, *USCS Log* (MAG), 35 Montague Circle, East Hartford, CT 06118.

Canadian Stamp News (NP), 103 Lakeshore Road, Suite 202, St. Catharines, ON L2N 2T6, Canada.

Linn's Stamp News (NP), P.O. Box 29, Sidney, OH 45365.

Mekeel's Weekly Stamp News (NP), Box 5050, White Plains, NY 10602.

Scott Stamp Monthly (MAG), P.O. Box 828, 911 Vandemark Road, Sidney, OH 45365.

Stamp Collector (NP), Box 10, Albany, OR 97321-0006.

Price Books

Harris Postage Stamp Catalog, issued annually (H. E. Harris and Co., Inc., 645 Summer Street, Boston, MA 02210) (U.S., Canadian, and U.N. stamps).

Official 1988 Blackbook Price Guide of U.S. Postage Stamps, 10th edition, Marc Hudgeons, 1987 (House of Collectibles).

Scott Standard Postage Stamp Catalogue, issued annually (Scott Publishing Co., 604 Fifth Avenue, New York, NY 10020).

A series of price books is available from the Christmas Seal & Charity Stamp Society, 3833 16th Avenue South, Minneapolis, MN 55407.

Computer Programs

Stamp Collectors Data Base Advanced Edition, Roger Edelman, 3001 Veazey Terrace NW, Suite 1507, Washington DC 10008 (2,900 U.S. Scott Stamps).

U.S. STAMPS; STAMPS DATA DISKS, Compu-Quote, 6914 Berquist Avenue, Canoga Park, CA 91307 (U.S., Great Britain, Canada, Germany, and United Nations valuation disks).

STOCKS & BONDS

Club and Publications

Bond & Share Society, *Bond & Share Society Newsletter* (NL), c/o R. M. Smythe & Co., Inc., 26 Broadway, New York, NY 10004.

Friends of Financial History (MAG), R. M. Smythe & Co., Inc., 24 Broadway, New York, NY 10004 (stocks and bonds).

TELEPHONE COLLECTIBLES

Clubs and Publications

Antique Telephone Collectors Association, *Antique Telephone Collectors Association Newsletter* (NL), Box 94, Abilene, KS 67410.

National Insulator Association, Drip Point (NL), 5 Brownstone Road, East Granby, CT 06026.

Telephone Collectors International, *TCI Newsletter* (NL), 4716 North Britton Drive, Stillwater, OK 74075.

Crown Jewels of the Wire (MAG), P.O. Box 1003, St. Charles, IL 60174.

TEXTILES & SEWING COLLECTIBLES

See also listings in the section on Clothing & Accessories.

Clubs and Publications

Dorset Thimble Society, *"At Your Fingertips"* (NL/MAG), Pinecroft, 28 Avon Road, Westmoors, Wimborne, Dorset BH22 0EG, England.

Stevengraph Collectors' Association, *Stevengraph Collectors' Association Newsletter* (NL), 2103-2829 Arbutus Road, Victoria, BC V8N 5X5, Canada.

Thimble Collectors International, *TCI Bulletin* (NL), 6411 Montego Bay Road, Louisville, KY 40228.

Quilter's Newsletter Magazine (MAG), *Quiltmaker* (MAG), Box 394, 6700 West 44th Avenue, Wheat Ridge, CO 80033.

Textile Museum Newsletter (NL), Textile Museum, 2320 "S" Street NW, Washington, DC 20008.

Thimbletter (NL), 93 Walnut Hill Road, Newton Highlands, MA 02161.

Vintage Quilt Newsletter (NL), 311 West 6th, Alice, TX 78332.

Price Books

Gallery of American Quilts, 1849-1988, 1988 (American Quilter's Society, P.O. Box 3290, Paducah, KY 42002).

Official Price Guide to Sewing Collectibles, Joyce Clement, 1987 (House of Collectibles).

Old Lace & Linens, Including Crochet: Identification and Value Guide, Maryanne Dolan, 1989 (Books Americana).

Zalkin's Handbook of Thimbles & Sewing Implements, Estelle Zalkin, 1988 (Warman).

Videos

How To Buy Antique Quilts, Hilltop Productions, Dept. B, P.O. Box 853, Warwick, NY 10990, 1989 (60 minutes of evaluating and dating quilts; $34.95 plus $2 for postage and handling).

Appraisers

American Quilter's Society, P.O. Box 3290, Paducah, KY 42002, 502-898-7903.

Margaret Cavigga, 8648 Melrose Avenue, Los Angeles, CA 90069, 213-659-3020 (quilts, linens, lace, American folk art, woven coverlets).

Stephen & Carol Huber, 82 Plants Dam Road, East Lyme, CT 06333, 203-739-0772 (antique needlework).

TOBACCO

See also the listings in the section on Advertising & Country Store Collectibles.

Clubs and Publications

American Matchcover Association, *Front Striker* (NL), 3417 Clayborne Avenue, Alexandria, VA 22306-1410.

Cigarette Pack Collectors Association, *Brandstand* (NL), 61 Searle Street, Georgetown, MA 01833.

International Seal, Label & Cigar Band Society, *International Seal, Label & Cigar Band Society News Bulletin* (NL), 8915 East Bellevue Street, Tucson, AZ 85715.

New Moon Matchbox & Label Club, *New Moon News* (NL), 2501 West Sunflower, H-5, Santa Ana, CA 92704.

Pipe Collector Club of America/Pipe Collectors International, *Smoker's Pipeline* (NP), P.O. Box 2089, Merrifield, VA 22116-2089.

Rathkamp Matchcover Society, *Voice of the Hobby* (NL), 1359 Surrey Road, Dept. KA, Vandalia, OH 45377-1646.

United States Cartophilic Society, *Tobacco Card Quarterly* (NL), P.O. Box 2259, Leesburg, FL 32749.

Universal Coterie of Pipe Smokers, *Pipe Smokers Ephemeris* (NL), 20-37 120th Street, College Point, NY 11356.

Windy City Matchcover Club, *Windy City Matchcover News* (NL), 3104 West Fargo Avenue, Chicago, IL 60645.

Cigarette Card Monthly (MAG), 15 Debdale Lane, Keyworth, Nottingham NG12 5HT, England.

Match Hunter (NL), 740 Poplar, Boulder, CO 80304.

Price Books

Matchcover Collectors Book and Price Guide, 1989 (*Front Striker* (NL), 3417 Clayborne Avenue, Alexandria, VA 22306-1410).

Price List '88: Handbook of Cigar Boxes, Tony Hyman, 1987 (Box 699, Claremont, CA 91711).

Tobacco Pocket Tin Guide (Flats & Uprights), Franklyn Kircher, 1988 (636 Hillcrest Avenue, East Lansing, MI 48823).

TOOLS

Clubs and Publications

American Precision Museum Association, Inc., *Tools & Technology* (NL), P.O. Box 679, 196 Main Street, Windsor, VT 05089.

Early American Industries Association, Inc., *Chronicle* (MAG), *Shavings* (NL), c/o John J. Watson, Treasurer; Cultural Education Center, P.O. Box 2128 Empire State Plaza Station, Albany, NY 12220-0128.

Mid-West Tool Collectors Association, *Gristmill* (MAG), P.O. Box 105, Austerlitz, NY 12017-0105.

Ohio Tool Collectors Association, *Ohio Tool Box* (NL), Box 261, London, OH 43140.

Tool and Trades History Society, *Tools and Trades* (NL), 60 Swanley Lane, Swanley, Kent BR8 7JG, England.

Tool Group of Canada, *Newsletter* (NL), 112 Holmcrest Trail, Scarboro, ON M1C 1V5, Canada

Fine Tool Journal (NL), c/o Iron Horse Antiques, Inc., R.D. 2, Box 245B, Pittsford, VT 05763.

Plane Talk (NL), P.O. Box 338, Morristown, NJ 07963-0338.

Tool Ads (NP), Box 33, Hamilton, MT 59840.

Price Books

Antique & Collectable Keen Kutter Hand Tools 1989 Price Guide, John Walter, 1989 (P.O. Box 6471, Akron, OH 44312).

Antique & Collectable Stanley Carpenters Hand Tools 1989 Price Guide, John Walter, 1989 (P.O. Box 6471, Akron, OH 44312).

Antique & Collectable Stanley Planes 1989 Price Guide, 5th edition, John Walter, 1989 (P.O. Box 6471, Akron, OH 44312).

Antique & Collectable Winchester Hand Tools 1989 Price Guide, John Walter, 1989 (P.O. Box 6471, Akron, OH 44312).

Antique Tool Collector's Guide to Value, Ronald S. Barlow (Windmill Publishing, 2147 Windmill View Road, Dept. AT, El Cajon, CA 92020).

Boxwood & Ivory Stanley Rules, 1989 Price Guide, John Walter, 1989 (P.O. Box 6471, Akron, OH 44312).

Keen Kutter Collectibles: An Illustrated Price Guide, 2nd edition, Jerry & Elaine Heuring, 1990 (Collector Books).

TOYS

Clubs and Publications

American Game Collectors Association, *Game Researchers' Notes* (NL), *Game Times* (NL), 4628 Barlow Drive, Bartlesville, OK 74006.

American-International-Matchbox, *A.I.M.* (NL), 522 Chestnut Street, Lynn, MA 01904.

Anchor Block Foundation, *Anchor House News* (MAG), c/o George Hardy, 980 Plymouth Street, Pelham Manor, NY 10803.

Automotive Modelers Society, *Scale Wheels* (MAG), 8125 Concho Road, Richmond, VA 23237.

Chess Collector's Association, *Checkmate* (NL), P.O. Box 99444, Louisville, KY 40299.

Chicago Playing Card Collectors Inc., Chicago Playing Card Collectors Inc. (NL), 1559 West Pratt Boulevard, Chicago, IL 60626.

CTM Farm Toy & Collectors Club, *Canadian Toy Menia* (MAG), Box 489, Rocanville, SK S0A 3L0, Canada.

Diecast Exchange Club, *Diecast Exchange Club* (NL), P.O. Box 1066, Pinellas Park, FL 34665.

Doll Artisan Guild, *Doll Artisan* (MAG), P.O. Box 1113, Oneonta, NY 13820-5113 (reproduction dolls).

English Playing Card Society, *English Playing Card Society Newsletter* (NL), 11 Pierrepont Street, Bath, Avon BA1 1LA, England.

Ertl Collector's Club, *Ertl Replica* (NL), Highways 136 & 20, Dyersville, IA 52040.

52 Plus Joker - The American Antique Deck Collectors Club, *Clear the Decks* (MAG), c/o Roy Harte, P.O. Box 1002, 749 Linncrest Drive, Westerville, OH 43081 (playing card decks).

Good Bears of the World, *Bear Tracks* (MAG), P.O. Box 8236, Honolulu, HI 96815 (provide bears to people in hospitals and institutions).

International Doll Restoration Artists Association, *IDRAA Workshop* (MAG), Route 2, Box 7, Worthington, MN 56187.

International Rose O'Neill Club, *Kewpiesta Kourier* (NP), P.O. Box 668, Bronson, MO 65616.

Lionel Collectors Club of America, *Lion Roars* (NL), Southeastern Louisiana University, P.O. Box 877, Hammond, LA 70402.

Madame Alexander Doll Club, *Madame Alexander Doll Club Newsletter* (NL), P.O. Box 330, Naperville, IL 60060.

Marble Collectors Society of America, *Marble Mania* (NL), P.O. Box 222, Trumbull, CT 06611.

Marble Collectors Unlimited, *Marble Mart/Newsletter* (NL), P.O. Box 206, Northboro, MA 01532.

Marklin Club, *Marklin Club Newsletter* (NL), P.O. Box 795, Elm Grove, WI 53122.

Matchbox Collectors Club, *Matchbox Collectors Club Official Quarterly Newsletter* (NL), P.O. Box 278, Durham, CT 06422.

Matchbox International Collectors Association, *MICA* (MAG), 574 Canewood Crescent, Waterloo, ON N2L 5P6, Canada.

Mechanical Bank Collectors of America, *Banker* (NL), P.O. Box 128, Allegan, MI 49010.

Modern Doll Club, *Modern Doll Club News* (NL), 305 West Beacon Road, Lakeland, FL 33803.

National Marble Club of America, *National Marble Club of America Newsletter* (NL), 440 Eaton Road, Drexel Hill, PA 19026.

Pennsylvania "Matchbox" Collector's Club, *Pennsylvania "Matchbox" Collector's Club Newsletter* (NL), 1515 North 12th Street, Reading, PA 19604.

Society for the Preservation and Encouragement of Scale Model Kit Collecting, *Kit Collectors Clearinghouse* (MAG), 3213 Hardy Drive, Edmond, OK 73013.

Southern California Marble Collectors Society, *Southern California Marble Collectors Society Bulletin* (NL), P.O. Box 84179, Los Angeles, CA 90073.

Still Bank Collectors Club of America, *Penny Bank Post* (NL), Carl White, Apt. 5-A, 401 East 84th Street, New York, NY 10028-6205.

Toy Gun Collectors of America, *Toy Gun Collectors of America News-*

letter (NL), 312 Starling Way, Anaheim, CA 92807.

Toy Gun Purveyors, *Toy Gun Newsletter* (NL), Box 243-K, Burke, VA 22015.

Toy Train Operating Society, *Toy Train Operating Society (T.T.O.S.) Bulletin* (MAG), *TTOS Order Board* (MAG), 25 West Walnut Street, Suite 408, Pasadena, CA 91103.

Train Collectors Association, *Train Collectors Quarterly* (MAG), P.O. Box 248, Strasburg, PA 17579.

United Federation of Doll Clubs, *Doll News* (NL), 8B East Street, P.O. Box 14146, Parkville, MO 64152.

Xavier Roberts Collectors Club, *Xavier Roberts Limited Edition* (NL), P.O. Box 714, 19 Underwood Street, Cleveland, GA 30528.

American Toy Trucker (NL), 1143 46th Street, Des Moines, IA 50311.

Antique Toy World (MAG), P.O. Box 34509, Chicago, IL 60634.

Barbie Bazaar (MAG), 2526 80th Place, Kenosha, WI 53140.

Barbie Talks Some More! (NL), 7501 School Road, Lot 26, Cincinnati, OH 45249.

Celebrity Doll Journal (MAG), 5 Court Place, Puyallup, WA 98372.

Classic Toy Trains (MAG), 21027 Crossroads Circle, Waukesha, WI 53187.

Collectors' Gazette (NP), 92 Kirkby Road, Sutton-in-Ashfield, Nottinghamshire NG17 1GH, England.

Collectors United: A Master Key to the World of Dolls (NP), P.O. Box 1160, Chatsworth, GA 30705.

Costume Quarterly for Doll Collectors (NL), c/o May Wenzel, 38 Middlesex Drive, St. Louis, MO 63144.

Doll Castle News (MAG), P.O. Box 247, Washington, NJ 07882.

Doll Designs (MAG), *National Doll World* (MAG), 306 East Parr Road, Berne, IN 46711.

Doll Reader (MAG), 900 Frederick Street, Cumberland, MD 21502.

Doll Times (NP), 218 West Woodin, Dallas, TX 75224.

Dolls - The Collector's Magazine (MAG), 1910 Bisque Lane, P.O. Box 1972, Marion, OH 43305.

Gameroom Magazine (MAG), 1014 Mount Tabor Road, New Albany, IN 47150.

International Dolls' House News (MAG), P.O. Box 79, Southampton SO9 7EZ, England.

Lledo U.S.A. (NL), RR #3, Box 216, Saw Mill Road, Durham, CT 06422.

"Loretta's Place" Paperdoll Booklet (NL), 808 Lee Avenue, Tifton, GA 31794.

Matchbox U.S.A. (NL), R.R. 3, Box 216, Saw Mill Road, Durham, CT 06422.

McElwee's Small Motor News (NL), 40 Fornof Lane, Pittsburgh, PA 15212 (toys, cars, trucks, etc.).

Midwest Paper Dolls & Toys Quarterly (NL), Box 131, Galesburg, KS 66740.

Miniature Tractor & Implement (NL), 1881 Eagley Road, East Springfield, PA 16411.

Model & Toy Collector (NL), 15354 Seville Road, Seville, OH 44273.

Model Auto Review (MAG), P.O. Box 589, Fort Belvoir, VA 22060.

National Doll & Teddy Bear Collector (NP), 215 Greenridge Drive, #126, Lake Oswego, OR 97035.

Old Toy Soldier Newsletter (MAG), 209 North Lombard, Oak Park, IL 60302.

Our Paper Playhouse (MAG), P.O. Box 456, Rocklin, CA 95677 (paper dolls).

Paper Doll News (NL), P.O. Box 807, Vivian, LA 71082.

Plastic Fanatic (MAG), 19088 Santa Maria Avenue, Castro Valley, CA 94546 (model cars).

Plastic Figure & Playset Collector (MAG), P.O. Box 1355, LaCrosse, WI 54602-1355.

Playing Card (MAG), *Playing Card World* (NL), 188 Sheen Lane, East Sheen, London SW14 8LF, England.

Poker Chip Newsletter (NL), P.O. Box 3491, Westlake Village, CA 91362.

Schoenhut Newsletter (NL), 45 Louis Avenue, West Seneca, NY 14224.

Spin-offs (NL), Toy Museum, 380 North Pine, Burlington, WI 53105.

Steiff Life (NL), Hobby Center Toys, 7956 Hill Avenue, Holland, OH 43528.

Teddy Bear and Friends (MAG), 900 Frederick Street, Cumberland, MD 21502.

Teddy Bear Review (MAG), 170 Fifth Avenue, New York, NY 10010.

Teddy Bear, Toy & Doll Finder (NP), 3211 Crow Canyon Place, A-206, San Ramon, CA 94583.

Teddy Tribune (NL), 254 West Sidney Street, St. Paul, MN 55107.

Toy Collector News (MAG), P.O. Box 451, River Forest, IL 60305.

Toy Farmer (MAG), Route 2, Box 5, LaMoure, ND 58458.

Toy Shop (NP), 700 East State Street, Iola, WI 54990.

Toy Soldier Review (MAG),127 74th Street, North Bergen, NJ 07047.

Toy Tractor Times (MAG), P.O. Box 156, Osage, IA 50461.

Traders Horn (NL), 1903 Schoettler Valley Drive, St. Louis, MO 63017 (miniature vehicles).

Train Collectors Letter (NL), P.O. Box 80167, Canton, OH 44708.

Trainmaster (NL), Joe Jones Publications, P.O. Box 337, Iola, WI 54945.

U.S. Toy Collector (MAG), P.O. Box 4244, Missoula, MT 59806.

Wheel Goods Trader (NL), P.O. Box 435, Fraser, MI 48026.

YesterDaze Toys (MAG), 275 South State Road, Otisville, MI 48463.

Price Books

American Rag Dolls, Straight from the Heart, Estelle Patino, 1988 (Collector Books).

Antique & Collectible Marbles, 2nd edition, Everett Grist, 1988 (Collector Books).

Collectible Male Action Figures, Paris & Susan Manos, 1990 (Collector Books).

Collecting Toy Soldiers: An Identification and Value Guide, Richard O'Brien, 1988 (Books Americana).

Collecting Toys, 5th edition, Richard O'Brien, 1990 (Books Americana).

Collector's Guide to Nesting Dolls, Histories, Identification, Values, Michele Lyons Lefkovitz, 1989 (Books Americana).

Evolution of the Pedal Car and Other Riding Toys with Prices 1884-1970's, Neil S. Wood, 1989 (L-W).

Farm Toy Price Guide, 1989 edition, Dave L. Nolt, 1988 (P.O. Box 422, New Holland, PA 17557).

Fashionable Terri Lee Dolls, Peggy Wiedman Casper, 1988 (Hobby House).

Fisher-Price, 1931-1963: Historical, Rarity, Value Guide, John J. Murray & Bruce R. Fox, 1987 (Books Americana).

French Dolls in Color, Third Series, Patricia R. Smith, 1989 (Collector Books).

G.I. Joe Value Guide: 1964-1978 Dolls, Gear & Equipment, Carol Moody, 1989 (Hobby House).

Glamour Dolls of the 1959s & 1960s: Identification & Values, Polly & Pam Judd, 1988 (Hobby House).

Greenberg's Chaptered Pocket Price Guide and Inventory Checklist to: American Flyer S Gauge, 7th edition, Jack Fazenbaker, 1990 (Greenberg).

Greenberg's Guide to American Flyer Prewar O Gauge, Steve H. Kimball, 1987 (Greenberg).

Greenberg's Guide to American Flyer S Gauge, 3rd edition, James Patterson & Bruce Greenberg, 1988 (Greenberg).

Greenberg's Guide to American Flyer Wide Gauge, Alan R. Schuweiler, 1989 (Greenberg).

Greenberg's Guide to Kusan Trains, John O. Bradshaw, *Matchcover Collectors Resource Book and Price Guide*, 1987 (Greenberg).

Greenberg's Guide to LGB Trains, 2nd edition, John R. Ottley, 1989 (Greenberg).

Greenberg's Guide to Lionel Trains 1901-1942, Volumes I and II, Bruce Greenberg, 1988 (Greenberg).

Greenberg's Guide to Lionel Trains 1945-1969, Volumes I and II, Bruce Greenberg, 1989 (Greenberg).

Greenberg's Guide to Lionel Trains 1970-1988, 2nd edition, Roland LaVoie, 1989 (Greenberg).

Greenberg's Guide to Marbles, Mark E. Randall & Dennis Webb, 1988 (Greenberg).

Greenberg's Guide to Marklin OO/HO, Robert P. Monaghan, 1989 (Greenberg).

Greenberg's Guide to Marx Toys, Volume I, Maxine A. Pinsky, 1988 (Greenberg).

Greenberg's Guide To Marx Trains, Volume I, 3rd Edition, Eric J. Matzke, 1989 (Greenberg).

Greenberg's Guide to Super Hero Toys, Volume I, Steven H. Kimball, 1988 (Greenberg).

Greenberg's Numerical Pocket Price Guide and Inventory Checklist to American Flyer S Gauge, 7th edition, Jack Fazenbaker, 1990 (Greenberg).

Greenberg's Pocket Price Guide and Inventory Checklist To: Lionel Trains 1901-1942 & 1945-1988, 10th edition, Bruce Greenberg, 1988 (Greenberg).

Greenberg's Pocket Price Guide and Inventory Checklist to Marx Trains, James Flynn, 1989 (Greenberg).

Hard Plastic Dolls, II: Identification and Price Guide, Polly & Pam Judd, 1989 (Hobby House).

Ives Toys, 1989 (L-W).

Liddle Kiddles Dolls & Accessories, Tamela Storm & Debra van Dyke, 1986 (Collector Books).

Lionel Price & Rarity Guide 1970-1989, Tom McComas & James Tuohy, 1988 (TM Books, Box 279, New Buffalo, MI 49117).

Madame Alexander Collector's Dolls Price Guide #15, Patricia R. Smith, 1990 (Collector Books).

Matchbox and Lledo Toys, Edward Force, 1988 (Schiffer).

McElwee's Collectors Guide #3: Tonka Toys 1947-1961, Neil & Lois McElwee, 1987 (40 Fornof Lane, Pittsburgh, PA 15212).

McElwee's Collectors Guide #4: Doepke Model Toys, Neil & Lois McElwee, 1989 (40 Fornof Lane, Pittsburgh, PA 15212).

McElwee's Collectors Guide #5: Postwar Buddy 'L' 1945-1970, Neil & Lois McElwee, 1987 (40 Fornof Lane, Pittsburgh, PA 15212).

Modern Collector's Dolls: Identification and Value Guide, 5th series, Patricia R. Smith, 1989 (Collector Books).

1989 Value Guide to the Original 1933 Tootsietoy Catalog Reproduction, Carol & Jerry, 1989 (Noble House, P.O. Box 964, Mundelein, IL 60060).

1987-1988 Collectors Value Guide for Scale Model Plastic Kits, John W. Burns, 1987 (3213 Hardy Drive, Edmond, OK 73013).

9th Blue Book Dolls & Values, Jan Foulke, 1989 (Hobby House).

Official Price Guide to Toys, 5th edition, Richard Friz, 1988 (House of Collectibles).

Patricia Smith's Doll Values Antique to Modern, 6th series, 1990 (Collector Books).

Plasticville: An Illustrated Price Guide "O" and "S" Scale Plus Littletown, Marx, Skyline and Storyline, Frank C. Hare, 1989 (P.O. Box 218, Bethel Park, PA 15102).

Price Guide 1989, 1989 (Marble Collectors Society, P.O. Box 222, Trumbull, CT 06611).

Price Guide to Dolls, Price Revision List, Constance Eileen King, 1988 (Antique Collectors' Club).

Price Guide to Metal Toys, Price Revision List, 1988 (Antique Collectors' Club).

Story of Williams Electric Trains, John Hubbard, 1987 (Greenberg).

Theriault's Doll Registry Price Guide, Volume III, Florence Theriault, 1988 (Theriault's, P.O. Box 151, Annapolis, MD 21404).

Toy Parade: A Pictorial Price Guide To "Squeek" Toys, Tiffee Jasso, 1988 (P.O. Box 85, Likely, CA 96116).

Toys: Antique and Collectible, David Longest, 1990 (Collector Books).

View-Master Single Reels, Volume 1, Roger Nazeley, 1987 (Reel Collector, 4921 Castor Avenue, Philadelphia, PA 19124).

World of Barbie Dolls: An Illustrated Value Guide, Paris & Susan Manos, 1988 (Collector Books).

Computer Programs

Train Board, Decker Doggett, Blue Caboose (train store), Cincinnati, OH, 531-398-0928.

Train Collector's Friend, Lawrence E. Fisher, P.O. Box 80167, Canton, OH 44708-0167.

Appraisers

Bertoia's Sales & Appraisals, Bill Bertoia, 1217 Glenwood Drive, Vineland, NJ 18630, 609-692-4092 (antique toys and related collectibles).

Chili Doll Hospital & Victorian Doll Museum, Linda Greenfield, 4332 Buffalo Road, North Chili, NY 14514, 716-247-0130 (dolls).

Continental Hobby, P.O. Box 193, Sheboygan, WI 53082, 414-693-3371; fax, 414-693-8211 (trains, steam-related toys, other toys).

Doll Connection, 117 Market Street, Portsmouth, NH 03801, 603-431-5030 (dolls).

Dr. Re's Doll Clinic, Main Street, Elm City, NC 27822-0846, 919-236-3144 (dolls).

Kandyland Dolls, 7600 Birch Avenue, P.O. Box 146, Grand Ronde, OR 97347, 503-879-5153 (dolls).

New York Doll Hospital, 787 Lexington Avenue, New York, NY 10021, 212-838-7527 (dolls).

Theriault's, P.O. Box 151, Annapolis, MD 21404, 301-224-3655, fax 301-224-2515 (dolls).

Yesteryears Museum, P.O. Box 609, Sandwich, MA 02563, 508-888-2788 winter, 508-888-1711 summer (dolls, toys, miniatures).

Bernard L. Scott, 117 Highview Drive, Cocoa, FL 32922, 407-632-0665 (farm toys).

Jim Smith, P.O. Box 472113, Garland, TX 75047, 214-271-8917 (battery-operated, windup, and friction toys).

TRANSPORTATION, AUTOMOBILES, PLANES, TRAINS

Clubs and Publications

American Aviation Historical Society, *AAHS Journal* (MAG), *Newsletter* (NL), 2333 Otis Street, Santa Ana, CA 92704.

American Driving Society, *Whip* (NL), P.O. Box 160, Metamora, MI 48455.

Antique Airplane Association, Inc., *Antique Airplane News & Digest* (MAG), Route 2, Box 172, Ottumwa, IA 52501.

Antique & Classic Boat Society, Inc., *Rusty Rudder* (NL), P.O. Box 831, Lake George, NY 12845.

Antique Automobile Club of America, Inc., *Antique Automobile* (MAG), 501 West Governor Road, Hershey, PA 17033.

Antique Motorcycle Club of America, *Antique Motorcycle* (MAG), 14943 York Road, Sparks, MD 21152.

Antique Outboard Motor Club Inc., *Antique Outboarder* (MAG), P.O. Box 09293, Milwaukee, WI 53209.

Antique Truck Club of America, Inc., *Double Clutch* (MAG), P.O. Box 291, Hershey, PA 17033.

Automobile License Plate Collectors Association, Inc., *ALPCA Newsletter* (NL), Box 712, Weston, WV 26452.

Carriage Association of America Inc., *Carriage Journal* (MAG), R.D. 1, Box 115, Salem, NJ 08079.

Chesapeake & Ohio Historical Society, Inc., *Chesapeake & Ohio Historical Magazine* (MAG), P.O. Box 146, Alderson, VA 24910 (railroad collectibles).

Chris Craft Antique Boat Club, Inc., *Brass Bell* (NL), 217 South Adams Street, Tallahassee, FL 32301.

Contemporary Historical Vehicle Association Inc., *Action Era Vehicle* (MAG), R. Lehew, 4619 Sprucewood Drive, Macon, GA 31210.

Cushman Club of America, *Cushman Club of America Magazine* (MAG), P.O. Box 661, Union Springs, AL, 36089 (motor scooters).

F-4 Phantom Society, *Smoke Trails* (MAG), 3381 Apple Tree Lane, Erlanger, KY 41018 (McDonnell Douglas F-4 Phantom II jet memorabilia).

Historical Construction Equipment Association, *Equipment Echoes* (NL), 485 South Hillside Drive, Canfield, OH 44406.

International Antique Power Association, *Antique Power* (MAG), P.O. Box 838, Yellow Springs, OH 45387 (articles on full-size and toy tractors).

International Petroliana Collectors Association, *Check The Oil!* (NL), P.O. Box 1000-K, Westerville, OH 43081.

Milestone Car Society, Mile Post (MAG), P.O. Box 50850, Indianapolis, IN 46250 (postwar cars, 1945-1970).

Model "A" Restorers Club, *Model "A" News* (MAG), 24822 Michigan Avenue, Dearborn, MI 48124.

Mustang Club of America, Inc., *Mustang Times* (MAG), P.O. Box 447, Lithonia, GA 30058-0447.

Nautical Research Guild, *Nautical Research Journal* (MAG), 12919 Moray Road, Silver Spring, MD 20906.

Oceanic Navigation Research Society, Inc., *Ship to Shore* (MAG), P.O. Box 8005, Studio City, CA 91608-0005.

Railroadiana Collectors Association, Inc., *Railroadiana Express* (MAG), 795 Aspen Drive, Buffalo Grove, IL 60089.

Sea Heritage Foundation, *Sea Heritage News* (NP), 254-26 75th Avenue, Glen Oaks, NY 11004.

Spark Plug Collectors of America, *Ignitor* (NL), *Hot Sheet* (NL), 3816 NE Riverside, Pendleton, OR 97801.

Steamship Historical Society of America, Inc., *Steamboat Bill* (MAG), 345 Blackstone Boulevard, Hall Bldg., Providence, RI 02906.

Threaded Hubcap Collectors Club International, *Hubcapper* (NL), 220 North 5th, Box 54, Buckley, MI 49620.

Titanic Historical Society, Inc., *Titanic Commutator* (MAG), P.O. Box 51053, Indian Orchard, MA 01151-0053.

Titanic International, Inc., *Voyage* (MAG), Regency Building, 31 Schanck Road, Suite D, Freehold, NJ 07728.

Two-Cylinder Tractor Club, *Two-Cylinder Tractor Club* (MAG), P.O. Box 2275, Waterloo, IA 50704.

Veteran Motor Car Club of America, *Bulb Horn* (MAG), P.O. Box 360788, Strongsville, OH 44136.

Wheelmen, *Wheelmen* (MAG), 55 Bucknell Avenue, Trenton, NJ 08619.

World Airline Historical Society, *Captain's Log* (MAG), 3381 Apple Tree, Erlanger, KY 41018.

Zeppelin Collectors Club, *Zeppelin Collector* (NL), c/o C. Ganz, P.O. Box A3843, Chicago, IL 60690.

American Neptune (MAG), Journal of Maritime History, Peabody Museum of Salem, East India Square, Salem, MA 01970.

Antique & Classic Bicycle News (MAG), P.O. Box 1049, Ann Arbor, MI 48106.

Automobile Quarterly (MAG), 420 North Park Road, Wyomissing, PA 19610.

Bicycle Trader (NL), P.O. Box 5600, Pittsburgh, PA 15207.

Car Collector & Car Classics (MAG), 8601 Dunwoody Place, Suite 144, Atlanta, GA 30350.

Car Corral (MAG), *Car Show and Auction* (MAG), *Old Car Price Guide* (MAG), *Old Cars Weekly* (NP) (cars/parts for sale), 700 East State Street, Iola, WI 54990.

Cars & Parts (MAG), P.O. Box 482, Sidney, OH 45365.

Classic Bicycle & Whizzer News (NL), P.O. Box 765, Huntington Beach, CA 92648.

Classic Boating (MAG), P.O. Box 1634K, Colton, CA 92324.

Collectible Automobile (MAG), 7373 North Cicero, Lincolnwood, IL

60646 (includes a section on scale models).
du Pont Registry (MAG), 2502 Rocky Point Drive, Suite 1095, Tampa, FL 33607 (cars).
Hemmings Motor News (MAG), Box 100, Bennington, VT 05201.
Key, Lock and Lantern (MAG), Box 65, Demarest, NJ 07627.
Live Steam Magazine (MAG), P.O. Box 629, Traverse City, MI 49685.
Muscle Cars of the 60s/70s (MAG), P.O. Box 4251, Sidney, OH 45365.
Nautical Brass (NL), P.O. Box 744, Montrose, CA 91020.
Old Bike Journal (MAG), 6 Prowitt Street, Norwalk, CT 06855 (motorcycle ads).
Oliver Collector's News (NL), Turtle River Toy Co., R.R. 1, Box 44, Manvel, ND 58256 (tractors).
Signpost (NL), P.O. Box 41381, St. Petersburg, FL 33743 (highway signs and markers).
Skinned Knuckles: A Journal of Car Restoration (MAG), 175 May Avenue, Monrovia, CA 91016.
Travel Collector (NP), P.O. Box 40, Manawa, WI 54949-0040.
Truck Prices (MAG), 700 East State Street, Iola, WI 54990.

Price Books

Classic Old Car Value Guide, Quentin Craft, 1987 (Wallace-Homestead).
Railroad Collectibles: An Illustrated Value Guide, 4th edition, Stanley Baker, 1990 (Collector Books).
Truck Prices, John Gunnell, editor, 1989-90 (Old Cars Weekly, Division of Krause Publications).

Appraiser

The Warehouse, 251 Orchard Street, Fairport Harbor, OH 44077, 216-352-7120 (motorcycles).

WESTERN ART

Club and Publications

National Bit-Spur & Saddle Collectors Association, *National Bit-Spur & Saddle Collectors Association Newsletter* (NL), P.O. Box 3098, Colorado Springs, CO 80934.
Southwest Art (MAG), P.O. Box 460535, Houston, TX 77256-0535.
Spur Collectors' Quarterly (MAG), Box 882, Canyon, TX 79015.

AND ALL THE REST

Clubs and Publications

Air Horn & Steam Whistle Enthusiasts, *Horn & Whistle* (NL), 2655

North Friendship, Lot 18, Paducah, KY 42001.

American Bell Association, *Bell Tower* (NL), Box 286, R.D. 1, Natrona Heights, PA 15065.

American Fan Collector Association, *Fan Collector Newsletter* (NL), 15633 Cold Spring Court, Granger, IN 46530 (electric fans).

American Printing History Association, *APHA Newsletter* (NL), P.O. Box 4922, Grand Central Station, New York, NY 10163 (antique printing equipment, type, and presses).

Angel Collectors' Club of America, *Halo Everybody!* (NL), 4319 Mount Vernon Road, Louisville, KY 40220.

Antique Comb Collectors Club, *Antique Comb Collectors Club Newsletter* (NL), 237 Society Drive, Holiday, FL 34691.

Buttonhook Society, *Boutonneur* (NL), 222 Bishopsgate, London EC2M 4JS, England.

Cast Iron Seat Collectors Association, *Newsletter of the Cast Iron Seat Collectors Association* (NL), Box 14, Ionia, MO 65335.

Cat Collectors, *Cat Talk* (NL), 31311 Blair Drive, Warren, MI 48092.

Circus Fans Association of America, *White Tops* (MAG), 315 Second Street, Rochelle, IL 61068.

Club ANRI, *Club ANRI* (NL), 55 Pacella Park Drive, Randolph, MA 02368.

Early Typewriter Collectors Association, ETCetera (MAG), P.O. Box 150, Arcadia, CA 91006.

Fan Association of North America, *Quarterly of the Fan Association of North America* (MAG), 505 Peachtree Road, Orlando, FL 32804.

Fan Circle International, *Fans* (NL), c/o The Hon. Sec., 24 Asmuns Hill, Hampstead Garden Suburb, London NW11 6ET, England.

Firemark Circle of the Americas, *FMCA Journal* (NL), *FMCA Newsletter* (NL), 2859 Marlin Drive, Chamblee, GA 30341-5119.

Great American Candy Bar Club, *Candy Bar Gazebo* (NL), Six Edge Street, Ipswich, MA 01938.

International Barb Wire Collectors Historical Society, c/o Jack Glover, Sunset, TX 76270.

International Brick Collectors Association, *Journal of the International Brick Collectors Association* (MAG), 90 Elizabeth Street, Lake Orion, MI 48036.

International Pin Collectors Club, *IPCC News* (NL), P.O. Box 430, Marcy, NY 13403 (Olympic pins).

International Society of Animal License Collectors, *Paw Prints* (NL), 4420 Wisconsin Avenue, Tampa, FL 33616-1031.

International Wood Collectors Society, *World of Wood* (MAG), P.O. Box 1102, Chautauqua, NY 14722.

Key Chain Tag & Mini License Plate Collectors Club, *Key Chain Tag & Mini License Plate Collectors Newsletter* (NL), 888 Eighth Avenue, New York, NY 10019.

Lottery Collector's Club, *Lottery Collector's Newsletter* (NL), 1824 Lyndon Avenue, Lancaster. PA 17602.

Nailer News (NL), *Texas Date Nail Collectors Association*, 501 West Horton, Brenham, TX 77833

National Button Society, *National Button Bulletin* (NL), 2733 Juno Place, Akron, OH 44313.

National Elephant Collectors Society, *Jumbo Jargon* (NL), Box 7, 89 Massachusetts Avenue, Boston, MA 02115-1813.

National Toothpick Holder Collectors Society, *Toothpick Bulletin* (NL), Red Arrow Highway, Box 246, Sawyer, MI 49125.

New Mexico Barbed Wire Collectors Association, *Wire Barb & Nail* (NL), Box 102, Stanley, NM 87056.

Police Insignia Collectors Association, Inc., *Police Insignia Collectors Association Newsletter* (NL), 35 Pierson Street, Bloomfield, NJ 07003.

Queens Museum New York World's Fair Association, *N.Y. World's Fair Newsletter* (NL), New York City Boulevard, Flushing Meadow Park, Flushing, NY 11368 (1939 and 1964 World's Fairs).

Russell's Owl Collector's Club, *Russell's Owl Collector's Club Membership Letter* (NL), P.O. Box 1292, Bandon, OR 97411.

Safecrackers International Inc./National Antique Safe Association, *Safe World* (MAG), P.O. Box 110099, Aurora, CO 80011.

Smurf Collectors Club, *Smurf Collectors Club Newsletter* (NL), 24 Cabot Road West, Dept. K, Massapequa, NY 11758.

Society for Decorative Plastics, *Collectible Plastics* (NL), P.O. Box 1099, Forestville, CA 95436.

Stamp-Box Collectors Society, *Journal of the Stamp-Box Collectors Society* (NL), P.O. Box 54, Stanmore, Middlesex HA7 4ED, England.

Sugar Packet Collectors Club, *Sugar Packet* (NL), 15601 Burkhart Boulevard, Orrville, OH 44667.

Thermometers Collectors Club of America, *Temps* (NL), 4555 Auburn Boulevard, Suite E, Sacramento, CA 95841.

World's Fair Collectors' Society, Inc., *Fair News* (NL), P.O. Box 20806, Sarasota, FL 33583.

Basically Buckles (MAG), P.O. Box 215, La Moure, ND, 58458.

Bill Nelson Newsletter (NL) (Olympic pins), *The Other Newsletter* (NL) (trivia and treasures), P.O. Box 41630, Tucson, AZ 85717-1630.

Buy-Sell-Trade (NL), R.R. 1, Canton, IL 61520 (Precious Moments, Hallmark, and other collectibles).

Canine Collector's Companion (MAG), P.O. Box 2948, Portland, OR 97208-2948.

Circus Report (MAG), 525 Oak Street, El Cerrito, CA 94530-3699.

Crown Point (NL), 525 East Illinois Street, Wheaton, IL 60187 (lightning rods).

Hendersons Clown Collectors Newsletter (NL), Box 5125, Garden Grove, CA 92645.

Horsin' Around (NL), Box 4764 New River Stage 2, Phoenix, AZ 85027.

"On the Move" (NL), The Manor House, Westhay, Glastonbury, Somerset,

England (ads for collectors of luggage, picnic paraphernalia, sporting and campaign equipment).

Owl's Nest (NL), P.O. Box 5491, Fresno, CA 93755 (owl collectibles).

Scottie Sampler (NP), P.O. Box 1512, Columbus, IN 47202-1512 (Scottie dog collectibles).

Scout Memorabilia (MAG), Lawrence L. Lee Scouting Museum, P.O. Box 1121, Manchester, NH 03105-1121.

Typewriter Exchange (NL), P.O. Box 150, Arcadia, CA 91006.

Typewriter Trader (NL), P.O. Box 150, Arcadia, CA 91006 (buy-sell ads).

Will's Safety-Razor & Safety-Razor-Blade Newsletter (NL), P.O. Box 522, Crescent City, CA 95531.

Windmillers' Gazette (MAG), P.O. Box 507, Rio Vista, TX 76093.

World's Fair (NL), P.O. Box 339-ABK, Corte Madera, CA 94925.

Price Books

Collectibles Market Guide and Price Index to Limited Edition Plates, Figurines, Bells, Graphics, Ornaments and Dolls, 7th edition, Diane Carnevale & Susan K. Jones, 1990 (Collectors' Information Bureau, 2420 Burton SE, Grand Rapids, MI 49546).

Date Nails Complete, Glen Wiswell & John Evans, 1988 (Date Nails East, P.O. Box 463, Colmar, PA 18915) (photos of individual date nails, also prices).

Wallace-Homestead Price Guide to Plastic Collectibles, Lyndi Stewart McNulty, 1987 (Wallace-Homestead).

Appraisers

American Marine Model Gallery, 12 Derby Square, Salem, MA 01970, 508-745-5777 (antique ship models).

Oriental Corner, 2805 Main Street, Los Altos, CA 94022, 415-941-3207 (oriental antiques).

Jonathan Thomas, 74 Wright Street, Westport, CT 06880, 203-227-2622 (scientific and surveying instruments).

SELLING THROUGH AUCTION HOUSES

Most antiques can be sold through an auction gallery. It is best to show the actual antique to the gallery, but if distance makes that impossible, the mail will help. Write a letter about the antique, giving its size and a description of all its flaws. Copy any markings as closely as possible. It is necessary to send a clear photograph for most items. Black-and-white pictures show the details best when you are selling paintings. Some things like plates, fabrics, books, and other flat objects can be placed on the glass of a photocopy machine and pictured in this way. Be sure to describe the colors. Include a stamped self-addressed envelope and a letter explaining where you live, how many items you wish to sell, and any history of the antique.

Ask for a contract from the gallery outlining their sales policies and charges. Reread the advice in the Introduction of this book before you sign a contract. Never ship merchandise without a contract. All items should be sent by mail or parcel delivery with insurance and a return receipt request. If you are shipping a large piece of furniture by truck, be sure you have insurance and a receipt stating the value with a full description including condition. Remember, the antique is yours until you have proof it has been received by the auction house. If it is lost or damaged on the way to the sale, your insurance is expected to pay the claim. We once shipped a large sideboard with gilt-bronze ormolu and a porcelain plaque on the front cabinet door. The porcelain was removed by the movers and packed separately. When the piece arrived, the two small gold-headed screws that held the plaque in place were missing. The movers paid the claim of over $100 for these small items because we could prove that the replacements had to be exact or the value of the sideboard would be lowered.

There are many regional auction houses. Those listed here advertise nationally and offer catalogs and sale results through the mail. We have seen the advertising and catalogs from these auction galleries and have attended many of their sales. Do not take inclusion in this list as any form of endorsement. To those who may have been omitted, we apologize. The lack of listing is an oversight and is not a lack of endorsement.

Most of these auction houses sell all types of antiques and collectibles during the year. A few sell just specialty items such as coins or dolls. We have indicated some of these in parentheses.

Auction Houses

A-1 Auction Service, P.O. Box 540672, Orlando, FL 32854, 407-841-6681 (American art pottery).

Alderfer Auction Company, 501 Fairgrounds Road, Hatfield, PA 19440, 215-368-5477, 215-723-1171, fax 215-368-9055.

Neal Alford Company, 4139 Magazine Street, New Orleans, LA 70115, 504-899-5329.

Col. Doug Allard, P.O. Box 460, St. Ignatius, MT 59865, 406-745-2951 (American Indian art and artifacts).

American West Archives, P.O. Box 100, Cedar City, UT 84720, 801-586-9497 (early Western ephemera).

Apple Tree Auction Center, 1616 West Church Street, Newark, OH 43055, 614-344-9449 (Heisey glass).

Arman's - Newport, P.O. Box 3239, Newport, RI 02840, 401-683-6000, fax 401-683-4044 (early American glass, historical Staffordshire, general antiques).

The Auction Gallery of Paul J. Dias, Inc., 30 East Washington Street, Route 58, Hanson, MA 02341, 617-447-9057 (antique and modern guns; antique, classic, and specialty cars).

Noel Barrett Antiques & Auctions Ltd., Carversville Road, Carversville, PA 18913, 215-297-5109 (toys and advertising).

Barridoff Galleries, 26 Free Street, Portland, ME 04101, 207-772-5011.

Frank H. Boos Gallery, 420 Enterprise Court, Bloomfield Hills, MI 48013, 313-332-1500, fax 313-332-6370.

Richard A. Bourne Company, Inc., P.O. Box 141, Hyannis Port, MA 02647, 508-775-0797 (decoys, marine, general antiques; street address: Corporation St., Hyannis, MA).

Bowers and Merena Galleries, Inc., Box 1224, Wolfeboro, NH 03894, 603-569-5095, fax 603-569-5319 (coins and paper money).

Butterfield & Butterfield, 220 San Bruno Avenue at 15th Street, San Francisco, CA 94103, 415-861-7500; in Los Angeles, 213-850-7500, 415-861-8951.

Cards from Grandma's Trunk, Box 404, Northport, MI 49670, 616-386-5351 (mail auction: paper ephemera).

Sally S. Carver Postcard Mail Auctions, 179 South Street, Chestnut Hill, MA 02167, 617-469-9175 (mail auction: pre-1920 quality postcards).

Christie's, 502 Park Avenue, New York, NY 10022, 212-546-1120, fax 212-752-3956.

Christie's East, 219 East 67th Street, New York, NY 10021, 212-606-0400.

Clearing House Auction Galleries, Inc., 207 Church Street, Wethersfield, CT 06109, 203-529-3344.

Cobb's Doll Auctions, 803 Franklin Avenue, Columbus, OH 43205, 614-252-8844 (dolls).

Russ Cochran's Comic Art Auction, 202 Aid Avenue, P.O. Box 469, West Plains, MO 65775, 417-256-2224, fax 417-256-4545 (Disneyana, comic strip art, drawings and paintings done for youth groups).

Marvin Cohen Auctions, Box 425, Routes 20 and 22, New Lebanon, NY 12125, 518-794-9333 (antique dolls).

Bob & Sallie Connelly, 205 State Street, Binghamton, NY 13901, 607-722-9593 (clocks).

Cottone Auctions & Appraisals, 15 Genesee, Mount Morris, NY 14510, 716-658-3180 (early Americana, decorated stoneware).

Coyle's Auction Gallery, 21 Westminster Avenue, Bellingham, MA 02019, 508-883-1659.

J. C. Devine, Inc., P.O. Box 413, Savage Road, Milford, NH 03055, 603-673-4967 (traps).

Douglas Auctioneers, Routes 5 and 10, South Deerfield, MA 01373, 413-665-2877.

Doyle Auctioneers & Appraisers, R.D. #3, Box 137, Osborne Hill Road, Fishkill, NY 12524, 914-896-9492, fax 914-896-5874.

William Doyle Galleries, Inc., 175 East 87th Street, New York, NY 10128, 212-427-2730, fax 212-369-0892 (decoys, general antiques, estate property).

DuMouchelle Art Galleries Co., 409 East Jefferson Avenue, Detroit, MI 48226, 313-963-6255, fax 313-963-8199 (estate auctions).

Dunning's Auction Service, Inc., 755 Church Road, Elgin, IL 60123, 708-741-3483.

Early's Antiques & Auction Company, 123 Main Street, Milford, OH 45150, 513-831-4833 (art glass, art pottery, general antiques).

Robert C. Eldred Company, Inc., Route 6A, East Dennis, MA 02641-0796, 617-385-3116.

Ferrel Gallery, 7111 Truman Road, Kansas City, MO 64126, 816-231-2839, fax 816-241-9769.

Frank's Antiques, Box 516, Hilliard, FL 32046, 904-845-2870 (live and mail auctions: advertising, tobacco collectibles).

Frasher's Doll Auction, Inc., Route 1, Box 142, Oak Grove, MO 64075, 816-625-3786 (dolls and doll-related items).

Freeman/Fine Arts, 1808 Chestnut Street, Philadelphia, PA 19103, 215-563-9275.

David J. Frent, P.O. Box 455, Oakhurst, NJ 07755, 201-922-0768 (mail auction: presidential political campaign memorabilia).

F.T.S., Inc., 415 Throop Street, North Babylon, NY 11704, 516-669-7232 (steins and European glass).

Garth's Auctions, Inc., 2690 Stratford Road, P.O. Box 369, Delaware, OH 43015, 614-362-4771.

Lynn Geyer's Advertising Auctions, 329 West Butler Drive, Phoenix, AZ 85021, 602-943-2283 (mail auction: antique advertising, breweriana).

Glass-Works Auctions, P.O. Box 187, East Greenville, PA 18041, 215-679-5849 (glass, bottles, and bottle-related items).

Morton M. Goldberg Auction Galleries, Inc., 547 Baronne Street, New Orleans, LA 70113.

Greenberg Auctions, 7566 Main Street, Sykesville, MD 21784, 301-795-7447 (toy trains).

Greenwich Auction Room, 110 East 13th Street, New York, NY 10003, 212-533-5550.

C. E. Guarino, Box 49, Berry Road, Denmark, ME 04022, 207-452-2123.

Guernsey's, 108 East 73rd Street, New York, NY 10021, 212-794-2280, fax 212-744-3638.

Hake's Americana, P.O. Box 1444, York, PA 17405, 717-848-1333, fax 717-848-4977 (mail auction: toys, political, comic, advertising, other small collectibles).

Hanzel Galleries, Inc., 1120 South Michigan Avenue, Chicago, IL 60605, 312-922-6234.

Harmer Rooke Galleries, 3 East 57th Street, New York, NY 10022, 800-221-7276, 212-751-1900, fax 212-758-1713.

Gene Harris Antique Auction Center, 203 South 18th Avenue, P.O. Box 476, Marshalltown, IA 50158, 515-752-0600 (carnival glass, R.S. Prussia, general antiques).

Harris Auction Galleries, Inc., 873-875 North Howard Street, Baltimore, MD 21201, 301-728-7040.

Hays Auction Center, 4740 Bardstown Road, Louisville, KY 40218, 502-499-8942 (dolls, clocks, general antiques).

Norman C. Heckler & Company, Bradford Corner Road, Woodstock Valley, CT 06282, 203-974-1634 (early glass, bottles, and flasks).

Willis Henry Auctions, 22 Main Street, Marshfield, MA 02050, 617-834-7774 (Shaker, American Indian and tribal art, Americana, Victorian, general antiques).

Hesse Galleries, 53 Main Street, Otego, NY 13825, 607-988-6322, 607-988-2523 (American antiques, American Indian artifacts, estates).

Leslie Hindman Auctioneers, 225 West Ohio Street, Chicago, IL 60610, 312-670-0010, fax 312-670-4248 (books, autographs, general antiques).

Historicana, P.O. Box 348, Leola, PA 17540, 717-656-7780 (mail auction: political memorabilia; nostalgia).

T. Glenn Horst & Son, Inc., 12 Fairview Drive, Akron, PA 17501, 717-859-1331.

Tony Hyman, Treasure Hunt Publications, P.O. Box 699, Claremont, CA 91711, 714-621-5952, fax 714-621-7525 (cigar and tobacco items).

Iroquois Auctions, Box 66 or Box 736, Brewerton, NY 13029, 315-668-2346.

Michael Ivankovich, 272 East Court Street, P.O. Box 2458, Doylestown, PA 18901, 215-345-6094, fax 215-340-1564 (Wallace Nutting prints, books, furniture, plus other colored pictures and photographs).

James D. Julia & Gary Guyette Inc., Route 201, Skowhegan Road, R.F.D. 1, Box 91, Fairfield, ME 04937, 207-453-7904, fax 207-453-2502 (decoys, general antiques).

John Kaduck, P.O. Box 02152, Cleveland, OH 44102, 216-333-2958 (mail auction: watch fobs, postcards, paper, military and political items, and other collectibles).

Donn Kinzle Company, 579 Hillside Drive, State College, PA 16803, 800-228-7161, 814-238-7161.

Kruse International, Kruse Building, P.O. Box 190, Auburn, IN 46706, 219-925-5600, fax 219-925-5467 (automobiles, general antiques).

Litchfield Auction Gallery, 425 Bantam Road, P.O. Box 1337, Litchfield, CT 06759, 203-567-3126, fax 203-567-3266.

The Manion's International Auction House, Box 12214, Kansas City, KS 66112, 913-299-6692, fax 913-299-6792 (mail auction: military, scouting, general antiques).

Mapes Auctioneers & Appraisers, 1600 Vestal Parkway West, Vestal, NY

13850, 607-754-9193 (antiques, oriental rugs, decorative arts, Arts & Crafts era).

Maritime Auctions, 935 U.S. Route 1, P.O. Box 322, York, ME 03909, 207-363-4247 (nautical and firehouse antiques).

Martin Auctioneers, P.O. Box 477, Intercourse, PA 17534 (carriage auctions).

M-C Associates, 11910 Lafayette Drive, Silver Spring, MD 20902, 301-949-4029 (printed ephemera).

Paul McInnis Inc., 356 Exeter Road, Hampton Falls, NH 03844, 603-778-8989.

Mid-Hudson Galleries, 1 Idlewild Avenue, Cornwall-on-Hudson, NY 12520, 914-534-7828, 914-534-4802.

Mini Bottle International Auction Magazine, P.O. Box 777, Brewster, MA 02631, 508-896-6491.

NASCA (Numismatic & Antiquarian Service Corporation of America), a division of R. M. Smythe & Co., Inc., 24 Broadway, New York, NY 10004, 800-622-1880, 212-943-1880, fax 212-908-4047 (coins, paper currency, stocks).

New England Auction Gallery, Box 2273, West Peabody, MA 01960-7273, 508-535-3140 (antique and collectible toys, cartoon-related items, antique games, sports items).

Northeast Auctions, P.O. Box 363, Hampton, NH 03842, 603-926-9800, fax 603-926-3545.

Nostalgia Galleries, 657 Meacham Avenue, Elmont, NY 11003, 516-326-9595 (advertising, toys, baseball memorabilia, banks).

Nostalgia Publications, Inc., 21 South Lake Drive, Hackensack, NJ 07601, 201-448-4536 evenings (mail auction: Coca-Cola items).

Richard W. Oliver Auction Gallery, Route 1, Plaza One, P.O. Box 337, Kennebunk, ME 04043, 800-992-0047, 207-985-3600, fax 207-985-7734 (decoys, general antiques).

The Opener, 20 Fairway Drive, Stamford, CT 06903 (mail auction: bottle openers).

Richard Opfer Auctioneering, Inc., 1919 Greenspring Drive, Timonium, MD 21093, 301-252-5035 (advertising and black collectibles, general antiques).

Pennypacker-Andrews Auction Centre, Inc., 1540 New Holland Road, Kenhorst, Reading, PA 19607, 215-777-6121, 215-777-5890.

Phillips, 406 East 79th Street, New York, NY 10021, 212-570-4830.

David Rago Arts & Crafts, P.O. Box 3592, Station E, Trenton, NJ 08629, 609-585-2546, fax 609-396-2468 (Arts & Crafts art pottery, decorative ceramics).

Lloyd Ralston Gallery, 173 Post Road, Fairfield, CT 06430, 203-255-1233 (antique toys and collectibles).

Remember When - Barbie & Friends Auctions, S.R. Box 11, Oak Hill, VA 23416, 804-824-5524 (mail auctions throughout year; annual live auction).

R. Neil Reynolds Poster Mail Auction, 2 Patrick Street, P.O. Box 133,

Waterford, VA 22190, 703-882-3574 (mail auction: posters).

Riba Auctions, Inc., 894 Main Street, P.O. Box 53, South Glastonbury, CT 06073, 203-633-3076 (historical ephemera, photographs, general antiques).

Roan Inc., R.D. 3, Box 118, Cogan Station, PA 17728, 717-494-0170 (American antiques).

Selkirk's, 4166 Olive Street, St. Louis, MO 63108, 314-533-1700.

The Sheet Music Center, Box 367, Port Washington, NY 11050, 516-938-4905 (mail auction: piano rolls, sheet music).

Shute Auction Galleries, 50 Turnpike Street, West Bridgewater, MA 02379, 508-588-0022, 508-588-7833.

Skinner Inc., 357 Main Street, Bolton, MA 01740, 508-779-6241, fax 508-779-5144.

Smith House Toy Auctions, P.O. Box 336-C, Eliot, ME 03903, 207-439-4614 (mail and phone bid catalog auctions).

Sotheby's, 1334 York Avenue, New York, NY 10021, 212-606-7000.

Sporting Antiquities, 47 Leonard Road, Melrose, MA 02176, 617-662-6588 (golf equipment and collectibles).

Rex Stark - Americana, 49 Wethersfield Road, Bellingham, MA 02019, 508-966-0994 (mail auction: historical Americana).

Swann Galleries, Inc., 104 East 25th Street, New York, NY 10010, 212-254-4710, fax 212-979-1017.

Theriault's, P.O. Box 151, Annapolis, MD 21404, 301-224-DOLL, fax 301-224-2515 (dolls and toys).

Three Behrs, R.D. 1, Horsepound Road, Carmel, NY 10512 (stoneware).

Don Treadway, 2128 Madison Road, Cincinnati, OH 45208, 513-321-6742, fax 513-871-7722 (furniture and decorative arts of the American Arts & Crafts era, American art pottery, American and European art glass, Tiffany and Handel lamps).

Christopher L. Wallenstein Auctionworld Inc., 5 South State Street, Concord, NH 03301, 603-225-8808.

Adam A. Weschler & Son, 909 E Street NW, Washington, DC 20004, 800-331-1430, 202-628-1281 (fine arts).

Willowcreek Auction Service, 5377 Ridge Road West, Route 104, Spencerport, NY 14559, 716-352-1760 (furniture, tools, general antiques).

Winter Associates Inc., Auctioneers & Appraisers, 21 Cooke Street, Box 823, Plainville, CT 06062-0823, 203-793-0288, 203-525-6116 (general antiques, fine arts).

Richard W. Withington, Inc., R.R. 2, Box 440, Hillsboro, NH 03244, 603-464-3232 (dolls, toys, general antiques).

Wolf's Auctioneers & Appraisers, 1239 West 6th Street, Cleveland, OH 44113, 800-526-1991, 216-575-9653, fax 216-621-8011.

Woody Auction Company, P.O. Box 618, Douglass, KS 67039, 316-746-2694 (mail auction: carnival glass, R.S. Prussia, general antiques).

Your Country Auctioneer, Center Road, Hillsboro, NH 03244, 603-478-5723, 603-456-3705 (antique tools).

APPRAISAL GROUPS

These are the major antiques appraisal associations. Most have lists of members and will send you a complete list or the names of local appraisers. Many appraisers include their membership information in their advertising in the Yellow Pages of the telephone book.

American Society of Appraisers, P.O. Box 17265, Washington, DC 20041, 703-478-2228, fax 703-742-8471.
Antique Appraisal Association of America, 11361 Garden Grove Boulevard, Garden Grove, CA 92643, 714-530-7090.
Appraisers Association of America, 60 East 42nd Street, New York, NY 10165, 212-867-9775.
International Society of Appraisers, P.O. Box 726, Hoffman Estates, IL 60195, 312-882-0706.
International Society of Fine Arts Appraisers Ltd., P.O. Box 280, River Forest, IL 60305, 312-848-3340.
Mid-Am Antique Appraisers Association, P.O. Box 981 C.S.S., Springfield, MO 65803.
New England Appraisers Association, 104 Charles Street, Boston, MA 02114, 617-523-6272 (also at 5 Gill Terrace, Ludlow, VT 05149).
United States Appraisers Association, Inc., 1041 Tower Road, Winnetka, IL 60093, 708-446-3434.

COMPUTER PROGRAMS

Data Base Management Program, Michael Rulison, Data-Nomix, 3256 Lewis Farm Road, Raleigh, NC 27607-6723 (appraisal inventory).
ISA-NET, International Electronic Appraisal Networking and Bulletin Board Service (BBS), International Society of Appraisers, P.O. Box 726, Hoffman Estates, IL 60195 (conferencing, electronic mail, and data retrieval).

MATCHING SERVICES

This is a list of matching services for china, silver, and crystal patterns. When writing, include the name of your pattern and a clear photograph, photocopy, or sketch showing the design and any markings. It is important to include the manufacturer's name if it appears. You can just put a plate or spoon on a photocopy machine to get a usable photocopy. List the pieces you want, and be sure to include a stamped, self-addressed envelope for a reply. These dealers have a general replacement line unless a specialty is indicated. This list is not an endorsement of any kind. It includes those services that sent us the requested information. There are probably many others we have not yet discovered. If you can suggest any additions, please let us know.

CHINA MATCHING SERVICES

A & A Locators of Austin, P.O. Box 50222, Austin, TX 78763, 512-472-1548 (Castleton, Denby, Franciscan, Lenox, Mikasa, Noritake, Royal Doulton, Spode, Syracuse, Wedgwood, and other major manufacturers).

Abby's Attic, P.O. Box 1041, Picayune, MS 39466, 601-799-1758, 601-798-5309.

Aberdeen Crockery Co., 511 South Main Street, Aberdeen, SD 57401 (Noritake).

Abrahante's Tableware Matching Service, 7175 SW 47th Street, #209, Miami, FL 33155, 305-661-1456.

Ackerman Antiques, Box 2310, Athens, OH 45701, 614-593-7681 (Warwick).

The Antique Place, 1524 South Glenstone, Springfield, MO 65804, 417-887-3800.

Dick and Adele Armbruster, Dorian House, P.O. Box 2430, Dearborn, MI 48123 (embossed white ironstone, flow blue, mulberry, tea leaf).

Richard Blair, Box 325 Cathedral Station, New York, NY 10025, 212-222-3494 (Noritake, and American, English, and European china).

Mildred G. Brumback, Route 2, Box 21, Middletown, VA 22645, 703-869-1261 (Castleton, Haviland, Lenox, Minton, Royal Doulton, Royal Worcester, Syracuse).

Bygone China Match, 1225 West 34th North, Wichita, KS 67204, 316-838-6010 (Castleton, Dansk, Denby, Fitz & Floyd, Franciscan, Gorham, Haviland, Lenox, Metlox, Noritake, Royal Doulton, Sango, Syracuse, Wedgwood).

Cee Cee China, P.O. Box 15520, Chevy Chase, MD 20815, 301-654-7308 (Lenox, Oxford, Syracuse, Wedgwood).

China & Crystal Marketing Group, P.O. Box 24602, Philadelphia, PA 19111, 215-342-7919, 8:00 a.m.-10:00 p.m.

China & Crystal Matching, 141 Sedgwick Road, Dept. RTK, Syracuse, NY 13203, 315-472-6834.

China & Crystal Replacements, 5613 Manitou Road, P.O. Box 187, Excelsior, MN 55331, 612-474-2144 (Adams, Aynsley, Castelton, Coalport, Cuthbertson, Denby, Fostoria, Franciscan, Gorham, Lenox, Oxford, Minton, Mikasa, Noritake, Oxford, Picard, Royal Crown Derby, Royal Worcester, Royal Doulton, Spode, Syracuse, Wedgwood).

China Chasers, Inc., 3280 Peachtree Corners Circle, Norcross, GA 30092, 404-441-9146 (Castleton, Franciscan, Franconia, Gorham, Heinrich, Hutschenreuther, Johnson Bros., Lenox, Metlox, Minton, Noritake, Oxford, Pickard, Royal Copenhagen, Royal Doulton, Royal

Worcester, Spode, Syracuse, Villeroy & Boch, Wedgwood).

The China Connection, Box 972, 329 Main Street, Pineville, NC 28134, 704-889-8198, 800-421-9719 (Noritake, Haviland, Lenox, Spode; appraisals).

The China Hutch, 6453 Shoreline Drive, Charlotte, NC 28214, 704-398-1141 (discontinued patterns).

China Match, 9 Elmford Road, Rochester, NY 14606, 716-426-2783. (Minton, Syracuse, Royal Doulton, Royal Worcester).

China Matching Service, 56 Meadowbrook, Ballwin, MO 63011, 314-227-3444 (American, Austrian, English, Bavarian, German, and Czechoslovakian china; also early 1900s patterns).

China Replacements, 2263 Williams Creek Road, High Ridge, MO 63049, 314-677-5577 (discontinued patterns).

China Teacup, 1018 Glen Haven Court, Irving, TX 75061, 214-438-8074.

China Trade Ltd., 2133 Birchwood Avenue, Wilmette, IL 60091, 708-256-7414 (discontinued patterns).

China Unlimited, P.O. Box 1032, Lithia Springs, GA 30057, 404-948-5441 (discontinued patterns).

CK's China Trace, Box A-5297, Ocala, FL 32678, 904-622-4077 (Mikasa, Royal Jackson).

Millie Conner, 1060 Crestline Drive, Crete, NE 68333, 402-826-2622 (French and American Haviland).

Crystal Corner, 317 Dyar Boulevard, P.O. Box 756, Boaz, AL 35957, 205-593-6169, 205-593-2102.

Irene DeLengyel, 215 Federal Road, Englishtown, NJ 07726, 201-462-6390 (Stangl).

Dick's Haviland China, 6210 Fawnwood, Spring, TX 77389, 713-376-7987, Mon.-Fri. after 7:00 p.m. and weekends (French and American Haviland).

Dining Elegance, Ltd., P.O. Box 4203, St. Louis, MO 63163 (Haviland, Lenox, Oxford, Raynaud-Ceralene, English and Bavarian manufacturers).

Dunbar Antiques, R.D. 2, Box 231, Owego, NY 13827, 607-687-2998, 607-687-2556 (Noritake).

Eileen's Elite Haviland China Service, 2300 Van Dorn, Lincoln, NE 68502, 402-475-6868 (Haviland).

Ettelman's Discontinued China & Crystal, P.O. Box 6491 Kov, Corpus Christi, TX 78466, 512-888-8391 (Castleton, Flintridge, Franciscan, Haviland, Lenox, Oxford, Syracuse).

5th Generation Antiques, 124 West 8th Avenue, Chico, CA 95926, 916-895-0813 (Haviland, Noritake).

Finders Keepers, China Lady, 3943 Magazine Street, New Orleans, LA 70115, 504-895-2702, 504-455-1530 (Noritake).

Franciscan Dinnerware Matching Service, Delleen Enge, 912 North Signal Street, Ojai, CA 93023, 805-646-2549 (Franciscan).

Galerie de Porcelaine - The Little Shops, 526 Crescent, Glen Ellyn,

IL 60137, 708-858-9494 (old French and American Haviland).

Gallen's Antiques, 1682 Virginia Avenue, College Park, GA 30337, 404-761-5166 (Johnson Brothers only).

Garbo, P.O. Box 41197, Los Angeles, CA 90041 (Franciscan, Metlox Poppytrail, Mikasa, Noritake, Vernonware, Winfield).

Judy Giangiuli, R.D. 6, Box 292, New Castle, PA 16101, 412-652-5806 (Castleton).

Gibson Ace Hardware, 114 North Madison Street, Clinton, IL 61727 (Noritake).

Glass Lady, Kaleidoscope, 7501 Iron Bridge Road, Richmond, VA 23237, 804-743-9846.

Grace Graves - Haviland Matching Service, Ltd., 3959 North Harcourt Place, Milwaukee, WI 53211, 414-964-9180 (French and American Haviland).

H. L. Art Jewelers, 20 North Park Place, Newark, OH 43055, 614-345-9791 (Lenox, Noritake).

Jacquelyn B. Hall, 10629 Baxter Avenue, Suite K, Los Altos, CA 94024, 408-739-4876 (Lenox only).

Larry Hamm, 2265 Hamilton-Middletown Road, Hamilton, OH 45011, 513-892-0803 (French and American Haviland).

Harners Gift Shop Inc., 218 North Main Street, Pontiac, IL 61764, 815-844-7333 (Fostoria, Mikasa, Pfalzgraff, Pickard).

Heirloom Completions Division, Don's Antiques & Gifts, 1620 Venice Street, Granite City, IL 62040, 618-931-4333.

Heritage Antiques, P.O. Box 49, Palo, IA 52324 (Noritake, Sango).

House of Serendipity, 13 South Main, Montevallo, AL 35115, 205-665-7996 (American dinnerware and china).

International Association of Dinnerware Matchers, P.O. Box 50125, Austin, TX 78763, 515-263-1836 (list of dinnerware matchers).

J & M Wright Co., 709 Everist Drive, Aberdeen, MD 21001, 301-272-2918 (flow blue).

Jacquelynn's China Matching Service, 219 North Milwaukee Street, Milwaukee, WI 53202, 414-272-8880 (Castleton, Coalport, Flint-ridge, Franciscan, Gorham, Lenox, Minton, Pickard, Royal Doulton, Royal Worcester, Spode, Wedgwood).

Johnson's Matching Service, P.O. Box 304, Des Moines, IA 50302, 515-263-1836 (discontinued patterns).

Judy's House of Hope, 1400 Third Avenue, West Point, GA 31833, 404-643-7181 (Wedgwood and others).

Kims Kollector's Korner, 555 NE 34th Street, Apartment 2401, Miami, FL 33137 (American dinnerware of the thirties through the fifties).

Laura's China & Crystal, 2625 West Britton Road, Oklahoma City, OK 73120, 405-755-0582 (Lenox, Oxford, Royal Doulton, Spode, Syracuse, and Wedgwood).

Lillian Johnson Antiques, 405 Third Street, San Juan Bautista, CA 95045, 408-623-4381 (Haviland).

Locator's Inc., 908 Rock Street, Little Rock, AR 72202, 800-367-9690,

501-371-0858 (American and English china).

Lois's China Replacement, 102 Front Street, Cramerton, NC 28032.

Louise's Old Things, 163 West Main Street, Kutztown, PA 19530, 215-683-8370, 215-683-6388 (flow blue and willow, including blue willow).

Marjann's Tabletops, P.O. Box 06255, Columbus, OH 43206, 614-444-1694, 614-878-4792 (Franciscan, Lenox, Royal Doulton, Spode, Syracuse).

Marv's Memories, 1914 West Carriage Drive, Santa Ana, CA 92704, 714-751-2463 (Franciscan).

The Matchers, 181 Belle Meade, Memphis, TN 38117, 901-683-1337. (Noritake and other name brand china).

Matchmakers, 1718 Airport Court, Placerville, CA 95667, 916-626-5672 (Haviland, Noritake).

Louise Donoghue McKay, P.O. Box 8561, Mobile, AL 36689, 205-344-8124 (Haviland).

Dirck & Sjoeke Meengs, P.O. Box 6066, Thousand Oaks, CA 91359, 805-495-4378 (Castleton, Flintridge, Franciscan, Lenox, Minton, Spode).

Midwest Coin Exchange - Silverware Division, 4311 NE Vivion Road, Kansas City, MO 64119, 816-454-1990.

Milbra's Crystal Matching, P.O. Box 363, Rio Vista, TX 76093, 817-645-6066, 817-373-2468 (Cambridge, Fostoria, Heisey, Imperial, Lenox, Tiffin).

Old China Patterns Limited, 1560 Brimley Road, Dept. NB, Scarborough, Ontario, Canada M1P 3G9, 416-299-8880 (discontinued china patterns).

The Old Toll Gate Antiques, 600 North Avenue, Milan, IL 61264, 309-787-2392 (French Haviland).

Past & Presents, Alice Korman, 65-07 Fitchett Street, Rego Park, NY 11374, 718-897-5515 (Adams, Aynsley, Coalport, Denby, Franciscan, Gorham, Johnson Brothers, Lenox, Mikasa, Minton, Noritake, Oxford, Royal Doulton, Royal Worcester, Spode, Wedgwood, and others).

Pattern Finders, P.O. Box 206, Port Jefferson Station, NY 11776, 516-928-5158 (Denby, Lenox, Noritake, Oxford, Rosenthal, Royal Doulton, Royal Worcester, Spode, Wedgwood, and others).

Peggy's Matching Service, P.O. Box 476, Ocala, FL 32678, 904-629-3954 (Noritake).

Vera L. Phillips, 6427 South Prince Street, Littleton, CO 80120, 303-794-4135 (French and American Haviland).

Pope-Pourri Antiques - Martin A. Pope, Box 1496, Platte City, MO 64079 (Haviland).

Popkorn, P.O. Box 1057, Flemington, NJ 08822, 201-782-9631. (Fiesta, Hall, Russel Wright, Stangl, blue willow)

Presence of the Past, 488 Main Street, Old Saybrook, CT 06475, 203-388-9021 (Haviland and Theodore Haviland, Noritake).

Proper Setting Discontinued Patterns, P.O. Box 3093, Covina, CA 91722.

David N. Reichard, Haviland Matching Service, 150 South Glenoaks Boulevard, Suite 9245, Burbank, CA 91510, 818-848-5087, evenings preferred (Haviland).

Replacements, Ltd., 302 Gallimore Dairy Road, Greensboro, NC 27409, 919-668-2064.

Roseville Pottery Mart, P.O. Box 6382, Ventura, CA 93006, 805-659-4733 (Roseville).

Roundhill's Patterns Unlimited International, P.O. Box 15238, Dept. KOOH, Seattle, WA 98115-0238, 206-523-9710 (English, French, German, and American china).

Side Door, 103 Main Street, Box 573, Dennisport, MA 02639, 508-394-7715 (flow blue, mulberryware).

Silver & China Exchange, P.O. Box 4601, Springdale, CT 06907, 203-322-5963 (discontinued Lenox and Oxford patterns).

Silver Lane Antiques, P.O. Box 322, San Leandro, CA 94577, 415-483-0632 (Castleton, Flintridge, Franciscan, Lenox, Minton, Royal Doulton, Royal Worcester, Spode, Syracuse, Wedgwood).

Linda Skuba, Box 7400, Edmonton, AB, Canada T5E 6C8 (British patterns).

Ferne & David Stephenson, 730 North 5th Street, Hamburg, PA 19526, 215-562-4967 (Noritake Azalea).

Straw Flowers, Inc., 801 West Eldorado, Decatur, IL 62522, 217-428-7212, 217-423-8303, or 217-864-2938 (French and American Haviland).

Table Treasures, P.O. Box 4265, Dept. KG, Stockton, CA 95204, 209-463-3607 or 209-463-3877 (most manufactuers of china and earthenware).

Tabletop Matching Service and Collectors Items, Mrs. Betty H. Allen, P.O. Box 205, Cookeville, TN 38501, 615-526-4303 (Coalport, Oxford, Syracuse, Stangl dinnerware, and German china).

Nora Travis, 13337 East South Street, Suite 161, P.O. Box 6008, Cerritos, CA 90701, 714-521-9283 (French and American Haviland).

Treasure Hunt, 792 Nadeau Road, Monroe, MI 48161, 313-241-4840; 800-634-6920 out of state (Castleton, French and American Haviland, Lenox, Noritake, and others).

Unique Antiques, P.O. Box 15815, San Diego, CA 92115, 619-281-8650 (Lenox).

Van Ness China Company, 1124 Fairway Drive, Waynesboro, VA 22980, 703-942-2827 (Aynsley, Coalport, Minton, Oxford, Royal Doulton, Royal Worcester, Spode, Wedgwood).

Varner's Matching Service, 1439 NE 13th Avenue, Rochester, MN 55904, 507-289-2938 (French and American Haviland).

Vintage Patterns Unlimited, 3571 Crestnoll Drive, Cincinnati, OH 45211, 513-662-2543 (Rosenthal and others).

Vintage Wedgwood Patterns, Rosemary Evans, 9303 McKinney Road,

Loveland, OH 45140, 513-489-6247 (Adams, Coalport, Wedgwood).

Walker's Haviland China, P.O. Box 357, Athens, OH 45701, 614-593-5631 (French and American Haviland).

Walter Drake Silver & China Exchange, Drake Building, Colorado Springs, CO 80940, 719-596-3140 (Aynsley, Castleton, Franciscan, Haviland, Lenox, Minton, Noritake, Royal Doulton, Spode, Syracuse, Wedgwood).

Warwick China Matching Service, P.O. Box 2310, Athens, OH 45701, 614-593-7681 (Warwick).

Wedgewood China Cupboard, 740 North Honey Creek Parkway, Milwaukee, WI 53213, 414-259-1025 (Adams, Coalport, Midwinter, Wedgwood).

Westerling, 5311 St. Charles Road, Berkeley, IL 60163, 312-547-8488.

White's Collectibles & Fine China, 616 East First, P.O. Box 680, Newberg, OR 97132, 503-538-7421 (Castleton, Denby, Franciscan, Lenox, Minton, Oxford, Royal Doulton, Royal Worcester, Spode, Syracuse, Wedgwood).

Willow Wood Antiques, Box 380, Valentine, NE 69201, 402-376-2622. (French Haviland).

CRYSTAL MATCHING SERVICES

A & A Locators of Austin, P.O. Box 50222, Austin, TX 78763, 512-472-1548.

Abby's Attic, P.O. Box 1041, Picayune, MS 39466.

Abrahante's Tableware Matching Service, 7175 SW 47th Street, #209, Miami, FL 33155, 305-661-1456.

Ackerman Antiques, Box 2310, Athens, OH 45701, 614-593-7681. (Candlewick)

The Antique Place, Eleanor Hunter, 1524 South Glenstone, Springfield, MO 65804, 417-887-3800 (stemware).

Mildred G. Brumback, Route 2, Box 21, Middletown, VA 22645, 703-869-1261 (Fostoria and Lenox).

Bygone China Match, 1225 West 34th North, Wichita, KS 67204, 316-838-6010 (Cambridge, Fostoria, Gorham, Imperial, Lenox, Noritake, Tiffin).

Candlewick (by Imperial) Matching Service, P.O. Box 2310, Athens, OH 45701, 614-593-7681 (Candlewick).

China & Crystal Marketing Group, P.O. Box 24602, Philadelphia, PA 19111, 215-342-7919, 8:00 a.m.-10:00 p.m.

China & Crystal Matching, 141 Sedgwick Road, Dept. RTK, Syracuse, NY 13203, 315-472-6834.

China & Crystal Replacements, 5613 Manitou Road, P.O. Box 187, Excelsior, MN 55331, 612-474-2144 (Fostoria, Mikasa, Waterford, Wedgwood).

China Replacements, 2263 Williams Creek Road, High Ridge, MO 63049, 314-677-5577 (discontinued crystal).

Millie Conner - Fostoria Registry, 1060 Crestline Drive, Crete, NE 68333, 402-826-2622 (Fostoria).

Diana Cramer, P.O. Box 1243, Whittier, CA 90609, 213-696-6738 afternoons (cut glass).

Crystal Connection, Nancy A. Skaja, 8661 West Midland Drive, Greendale, WI 53129, 414-425-1321 (discontinued patterns of Lenox and Fostoria crystal).

Crystal Corner, 317 Dyar Boulevard, P.O. Box 756, Boaz, AL 35957, 205-593-6169, 205-593-2102.

Dining Elegance, Ltd., P.O. Box 4203, St. Louis, MO 63163 (Franciscan, Gorham, Josair, Lenox, Lotus, St. Louis, Seneca, Stuart, Tiffin, Val St. Lambert).

Elizabeth's, Box 347, Mount Holly, NC 28120, 704-827-0555.

Ettelman's Discontinued China & Crystal, P.O. Box 6491 Kov, Corpus, Christi, TX 78466, 512-888-8391 (Cambridge, Duncan, Fostoria, Heisey, Lenox, Tiffin).

5th Generation Antiques, 124 West 8th Avenue, Chico, CA 95926, 916-895-0813 (stemware).

Finders Keepers, China Lady, 3943 Magazine Street, New Orleans, LA 70115, 504-895-2702, 504-455-1530 (Noritake).

Judy Giangiuli, R.D. No. 6, Box 292, New Castle, PA 16101, 412-652-5806 (Fostoria).

Glass Lady, Kaleidoscope, 7501 Iron Bridge Road, Richmond, VA 23237, 804-743-9846.

Jacquelyn B. Hall, 10629 Baxter Avenue, Suite K, Los Altos, CA 94024, 408-739-4876 (Lenox crystal only).

Hawkes Hunter, 5384 Pennock Point Road, Jupiter, FL 33458, 407-746-6382 (Hawkes).

Heirloom Completions Division, Don's Antiques & Gifts, 1620 Venice Street, Granite City, IL 62040, 618-931-4333.

House of Serendipity, 13 South Main, Montevallo, AL 35115, 205-665-7996 (American crystal).

Fran Jay, 10 Church Street, Lambertville, NJ 08530, 609-397-1571 (Cambridge, Fostoria, Heisey, Tiffin, and Depression glass).

Judy's House of Hope, 1400 Third Avenue, West Point, GA 31833, 404-643-7181 (Wedgwood).

Laura's China & Crystal, 2625 West Britton Road, Oklahoma City, OK 73120, 405-755-0582 (Cambridge, Duncan, Fostoria, Lenox, Rock Sharpe, Tiffin).

Lil-Bud Antiques, 142 Main, Yarmouthport, MA 02675 (Early American pattern glass).

Locator's Inc., 908 Rock Street, Little Rock, AR 72202, 800-367-9690, 501-371-0858 (American and English crystal).

Margaret Lane Antiques, 2 East Main Street, New Concord, OH 43762, 614-826-7414 (Cambridge, Fostoria, Heisey).

The Matchers, 181 Belle Meade, Memphis, TN 38117, 901-683-1337 (Fostoria, Lenox, and Noritake stemware).

Miki's Crystal Registry, P.O. Box 22506, Minneapolis, MN 55422, 612-522-5856 (Fostoria and Depression glass).

Milbra's Crystal Registry, P.O. Box 363, Rio Vista, TX 76093, 817-645-6066, 817-373-2468 (Cambridge, Fostoria, Heisey, Imperial, Lenox, Tiffin).

Nadine Pankow, 207 South Oakwood, Willow Springs, IL 60480, 708-839-5231 (Cambridge, Depression glass, Duncan Miller, Fostoria, Heisey).

Popkorn, P.O. Box 1057, Flemington, NJ 08822, 201-782-9631 (Cambridge, Fostoria, Imperial, Depression glass, and kitchen glassware).

Hazel Rawls, 2117 Monterrey, Orange, TX 77630 (pattern glass).

Red Horse Inn, Jerry Gallagher, 420 1st Avenue NW, Plainview, MN 55964, 507-534-3511 (Cambridge, Duncan, Fostoria, Heisey, Old Morgantown, Tiffin, and other American glass).

Replacements, Ltd., 302 Gallimore Dairy Road, Greensboro, NC 27409, 919-668-2064.

Saints' House of Crystal, 314 Buckingham Place, Prescott, AZ 86303, 602-445-2282.

Table Treasures, P.O. Box 4265, Dept. KG, Stockton, CA 95204, 209-463-3607 or 209-463-3877.

Tabletop Matching Service and Collectors Items, Mrs. Betty H. Allen, P.O. Box 205, Cookeville, TN 38501, 615-526-4303 (Duncan, Fostoria, Heisey, Tiffin).

Unique Antiques, P.O. Box 15815, San Diego, CA 92115, 619-281-8650 (French and American Haviland, Lenox, Oxford).

Varner's Matching Service, 1439 NE 13th Avenue, Rochester, MN 55904, 507-289-2938 (Heisey).

Vintage Patterns Unlimited, 3571 Crestnoll Drive, Cincinnati, OH 45211, 513-662-2543 (Rosenthal).

Westerling, 5311 St. Charles Road, Berkeley, IL 60163, 312-547-8488 (Dansk, Denby, Lenox, Tiffin, and others).

SILVER MATCHING SERVICES

Aaron's Antiques, 1050 Second Avenue, New York, NY 10022, 212-644-5868; fax: 212-935-5969 (sterling flatware, including Tiffany and Georg Jensen).

Abrahante's Tableware Matching Service, 7175 SW 47th Street, #209, Miami, FL 33155, 305-661-1456.

Mrs. Frances T. Andrews, 1105 South Delaware Avenue, Bartlesville, OK 74003 (silver plate).

Robert L. Anstey Antique Garden, P.O. Box 6095, East Lansing, MI 48826 (silver-plated flatware, hollowware).

The Antique Place, 1524 South Glenstone, Springfield, MO 65804, 417-887-3800 (sterling, silver plate).

Antiques Olde and Nue, 6960 North Interstate, Portland, OR 97217, 503-289-2922 (silver plate).

Apple Tree Antiques, 301 North Harrison Street, Bldg. B, #375, Princeton, NJ 08540 (sterling and silver-plated flatware).

Arlene's Silverplate Matching Service, N 109 W 15426 Lyle Lane, Germantown, WI 53022, 414-255-3889 (silver plate).

As You Like It Silver Shop, 3025 Magazine Street, New Orleans, LA 70115, 504-897-6915, 800-828-2311 (sterling flatware: active, inactive, obsolete; hollowware).

As You Like It Silver Shop, 410 North Commerce Street, Natchez, MS 39120, 601-422-0933, 800-848-2311 (sterling flatware: active, inactive, obsolete; hollowware).

Beverly Bremer Silver Shop, 3164 Peachtree Road NE, Atlanta, GA 30305, 404-261-4009 (sterling flatware, hollowware).

Robert D. Biggs, 1155 East 58, Chicago, IL 60637, 312-702-9540. (sterling and silver-plated flatware).

Mary S. Butler, 2518 Taylor, Dept. RTK, Commerce, TX 75428, 214-886-7289 (silver plate).

Carman's Collectables, P.O. Box 258, Levittown, PA 19059, 215-946-9315 (silver plate).

Cherishables, Sally A. Peelen, 1214 Matanzas Way, Santa Rosa, CA 95405, 707-579-2475, evenings and weekends (silver plate and stainless).

China & Crystal Matching, 141 Sedgwick Road, Dept. RTK, Syracuse, NY 13203, 315-472-6834.

Coinways, 136 Cedarhurst Avenue, Cedarhurst, NY 11516, 516-374-1970, 800-645-2102 (sterling).

Colonial Silver Shoppe, 20-D Gaylan Court, Montgomery, AL 36109, 205-272-7282 (sterling: active, inactive, obsolete).

Joan Cookson, 1111 Union Street, Alameda, CA 94501, 415-523-4106; message only 415-523-1993 (silver plate).

Coronado Coins, P.O. Box 181440, 942 Orange Avenue, Coronado, CA 92118-1440, 619-437-1435 (sterling).

Diana Cramer, P.O. Box 1243, Whittier, CA 90609, 213-696-6738, afternoons (sterling flatware, novelties, hollowware).

Fisher Silver Exchange, P.O. Box 680042, Houston, TX 77268-0042, 713-353-4167 (sterling and silver plate: specializing in "grape" patterns, 1847 Rogers, and Community).

Martin M. Fleisher, Silversmith, 143 North Park Avenue, Rockville Centre, NY 11570 (sterling and silver plate: active, inactive, obsolete; silver plating).

Gebelein Silversmiths Inc., P.O. Box 157, East Arlington, VT 05252, 802-375-6307 (19th- and 20th-century sterling, coin silver).

R.S. Goldberg, 67 Beverly Road, Hawthorne, NJ 07506, 201-427-6555 (sterling).

Graham Silver, P.O. Box 6021, Omaha, NE 68106, 800-228-2294, 402-556-0516 (sterling: active, inactive, and obsolete American patterns).

Tere Hagan, P.O. Box 25487, Tempe, AZ 85285, 800-528-7425; in Arizona 602-966-8838 (sterling, silver plate, stainless, dirilyte flatware).

Heirloom Completions Division, Don's Antiques & Gifts, 1620 Venice Street, Granite City, IL 62040, 618-931-4333 (American sterling and silver plate, stainless, dirilyte).

Heritage Gallery of Antiques, P.O. Box 3474, Champaign, IL 61821.

Johnson's Matching Service, P.O. Box 304, Des Moines, IA 50302, 515-263-1836 (discontinued patterns).

Kendall's Antiques, RR 1, Box 337, Dodge Center, MN 55927, 507-374-6515 (silver plate, sterling souvenir spoons).

John F. Kingston, Silver Merchant, P.O. Box 6037, Syracuse, NY 13217, 315-446-0630 (silver plate, sterling, hollowware).

Kinzie's, P.O. Box 522, Turlock, CA 95380, 209-634-4880 (silver plate).

Lampost Silver Co., 8312 East 11th Street, Tulsa, OK 74112 (sterling and silver plate, old and new).

Helen Lawler's Silverplate Matching Service, Route 1, Box 334, Blytheville, AR 72315, 314-720-8502 (silver-plated flatware).

Lee and Helen Dunkel Collectibles, 222 Belle Avenue, Boalsburg, PA 16827, 814-466-6494 (silver plate).

Leopard's Head, 1750 Union Street, San Francisco, CA 94123-4407, 415-673-7509 (antique English sterling flatware, Shreve & Co., San Francisco patented flatware patterns).

Littman's, 151 Granby Street, Norfolk, VA 23510, 804-622-6989 (sterling).

Locator's Inc., 908 Rock Street, Little Rock, AR 72202, 800-367-9690, 501-371-0858 (sterling).

Margaret Lane Antiques, 2 East Main Street, New Concord, OH 43762, 614-826-7414 (silver plate).

Marjann's Tabletops, P.O. Box 06255, Columbus, OH 43206, 614-444-1694, 614-878-4792 (sterling, silver plate).

Margaret & Joseph Martines, Martines' Antiques, 516 East Washington, Chagrin Falls, OH 44022, 216-247-6421.

Matchmaker of Iowa, P.O. Box 43, Waterloo, IA 50704, 319-233-0578 (silver-plated, pewter, stainless steel, and gold electroplated flatware).

C. H. McCarthy, P.O. Box 11278, Oakland, CA 94611-0278, 415-530-3216 (sterling flatware and hollowware).

Midwest Coin Exchange - Silverware Division, 4311 NE Vivion Road, Kansas City, MO 64119, 816-454-1990 (sterling, silver plate, stainless: matching, repair, and polishing).

Mrs. Kay's Stainless, Sterling & Silverplate, P.O. Box 291245-G,

Los Angeles, CA 90029-9245, 213-661-6279 (sterling, silver plate, stainless).

Nelwyn's Antiques, Box 375, McLean, VA 22101 (antique and Victorian English and American silver).

Overtons Sterling Matching, 200 Avenida Santa Margarita, San Clemente, CA 92672, 714-498-5330 (sterling, specializing in discontinued and obsolete patterns).

Patricia Ann's Sterling, P.O. Box 33099, Decatur, GA 30033, 404-451-6045.

Replacements, Ltd., 302 Gallimore Dairy Road, Greensboro, NC 27409, 919-668-2064.

Jane Rosenow, Route 1, Box 177-AA, Galva, IL 61434, 309-932-3953 (sterling, silver plate).

Wilma Saxton, Inc., P.O. Box 395, Berlin, NJ 08009, 609-767-8640 (sterling, silver plate, stainless, dirilyte, pewter: active, inactive, obsolete patterns).

Silver & China Exchange, P.O. Box 4601, Springdale, CT 06907, 203-322-5963 (discontinued sterling flatware replacements).

Silver Antiquities, P.O. Box 6137, Leawood, KS 66206, 816-753-5589. (Not a matching service, but they stock some popular patterns, specializing in ornate sterling, 1840-1910, by Durgin, Gorham, Kirk, Stieff, Tiffany, and others.)

Silver Chest, 941 Mandalay Avenue, Clearwater Beach, FL 34630, 813-441-4606, 9:00 a.m.-10:00 p.m. (silver plate, resilvering, restoration, and removal of monograms on sterling flatware).

Silver Chest, P.O. Box 12108, Atlanta, GA 30355-2108, 404-364-0555, 404-3610-0465 (sterling flatware and hollowware; "want list" published monthly).

Silver Lady, P.O. Box 792, Friday Harbor, WA 98250, 206-378-5512 (silver plate).

Silver Lane Antiques, P.O. Box 322, San Leandro, CA 94577, 415-483-0632 (sterling: active, inactive, obsolete).

Silver Match, Marge Mathis, HCR63 Box 4, Snyder, TX 79549, 915-573-8044 (silver plate).

Silver Queen Inc., 730 North Indian Rocks Road, Belleair Bluffs, FL 34640, 813-581-6827, 800-262-3134 (sterling).

Silver Sails, 8 Manor Oak Drive, Tonawanda, NY 14150, 716-691-8802 (silver-plated flatware).

Silver Season, P.O. Box 1136, Norwalk, CT 06850, 203-847-8217. (American silver plate)

Silver Shop, 2288 West Holcombe Boulevard, Houston, TX 77030, 713-661-2051 (sterling flatware, hollowware).

Silver Smiths, P.O. Box 5118, Fresno, CA 93755, 209-431-1611 (sterling).

The Silver Talent, Donna Young, P.O. Box 9182, Norfolk, VA 23505, 804-587-9016 (sterling, silver plate, coin silver; active, inactive, obsolete).

Cecil F. Skillin, 111 Caribbean Road, Naples, FL 33963-2795, 813-597-3676 (silver plate, stainless, sterling II, pewter, dirilyte, dirigold).

Sterling & Collectables Ltd., 248 Park Avenue West, P.O. Box 1665, Mansfield, OH 44901, 800-537-5783; in Ohio 419-522-1561 (new and restored sterling, new silver plate, stainless).

Sterling Shop, P.O. Box 595, Silverton, OR 97381, 503-873-6315. (sterling, silver plate, hollowware)

Table Treasures, P.O. Box 4265, Dept. KG, Stockton, CA 95204, 209-463-3607 or 209-463-3877.

Tabletop Matching Service & Collectors Items, Mrs. Betty H. Allen, P.O. Box 205, Cookeville, TN 38501, 615-526-4303 (silver plate, specializing in 1847 Rogers).

Venette's Table, Box 6113, Santa Barbara, CA 93111, 805-965-9584 (sterling silver flatware and hollowware).

Vintage Silver, 33 LeMay Court, Williamsville, NY 14221, 716-631-0419 (silver-plated flatware, all patterns active, inactive, obsolete, and individual items).

Vi Walker, P.O. Box 88377, Indianapolis, IN 46208, 317-283-3753 (sterling and silver plate, specializing in American silver and rare serving pieces).

Walter Drake Silver and China Exchange, Drake Building, Colorado Springs, CO 80940, 719-596-3140 (sterling and silver plate: active, inactive, obsolete American patterns).

Westerling, 5311 St. Charles Road, Berkeley, IL 60163, 312-547-8488 (silver, goldware, stainless, pewter).

Edward G. Wilson Antiques, 1802 Chestnut Street, Philadelphia, PA 19103, 215-563-7369 (sterling and coin silver: active, inactive, obsolete).

Woodland Antiques, P.O. Box 3793, Mansfield, OH 44907-3793, 419-756-7831 (sterling and silver plated flatware).

Your Majesty's Service, 4849 Oakton Street, Skokie, IL 60077, 708-982-0103.

Index